PENGUIN

THE HISTORY OF THE KINGS OF BRITAIN

ADVISORY EDITOR: BETTY RADICE

A tentative outline of the life of GEOFFREY OF MONMOUTH can be made from evidence in his text and from various other sources. He calls himself *Gaufridus Monemutensis*, which suggests he was born and brought up in Monmouthshire, most likely not far from Caerleon-on-Usk, which he often mentions and which is only some twenty miles from Monmouth. From 1129 to 1151 he seems to have lived in Oxford and was probably a canon of the secular college of St George's. During this time he wrote his *History of the Kings of Britain*, the 'Prophecies of Merlin', originally conceived as a separate volume, and the *Life of Merlin*. In 1151 Geoffrey became Bishop Elect of St Asaph, North Wales. He was ordained priest at Westminster in February 1152 and consecrated a week later at Lambeth by Archbishop Theobald. According to the Welsh chronicles he died in 1155.

•

LEWIS THORPE, Ph.D., D. de l'U., LL.D., was professor of French at the University of Nottingham from 1958. He joined the staff of that University in 1946 after distinguished war service. He was International President of the Arthurian Society, and a member of the Calvin Publications Committee of the World Alliance of Reformed and Protestant Churches. His books include *La France Guerriére* (1945), *Le roman de Laurin, fils de Marques le Sénéchal* (1950), *Le roman de Laurin, text of MS. B.N. f. fr. 22548* (1960). *Guido Farina, painter of Verona, 1896–1957* (1967) with Barbara Reynolds, *Einhard the Frank: The Life of Charlemagne* (1970), *Le roman de Silence, by Heldris de Cornuälle* (1972), and *The Bayeux Tapestry and the Norman Invasion* (1973). He also translated *The Two Lives of Charlemagne*, *Gregory of Tours: The History of the Franks* and *Gerald of Wales: The Journey Through Wales and The Description of Wales* for the Penguin Classics. Lewis Thorpe was a member of the M.C.C. He died in 1977.

GEOFFREY OF MONMOUTH

THE HISTORY OF THE
KINGS OF BRITAIN

TRANSLATED
WITH AN INTRODUCTION
BY LEWIS THORPE

PENGUIN BOOKS

Penguin Books Ltd, Harmondsworth, Middlesex, England
Viking Penguin Inc., 40 West 23rd Street, New York, New York 10010, U.S.A.
Penguin Books Australia Ltd, Ringwood, Victoria, Australia
Penguin Books Canada Limited, 2801 John Street, Markham, Ontario, Canada L3R 1B
Penguin Books (N.Z.) Ltd, 182–190 Wairau Road, Auckland 10, New Zealand

—

This translation first published 1966
Reprinted 1968, 1973, 1976, 1978, 1979, 1980, 1982,
1983, 1984, 1986

—

Copyright © the Estate of Lewis Thorpe, 1966
All rights reserved

—

Set, printed and bound in Great Britain by
Cox & Wyman Ltd, Reading
Set in Monotype Bembo

For
KERSTIN THORPE

Contents

CONTENTS

Introduction

I. GEOFFREY'S PURPOSE

IN some ways the *History of the Kings of Britain*, this strange, uneven and yet extraordinarily influential book written in Latin by Geoffrey of Monmouth and finished c. 1136,[1] may be said to bear the same relationship to the story of the early British inhabitants of our own island as do the seventeen historical books in the Old Testament, from Genesis to Esther, to the early history of the Israelites in Palestine.

As he explains to us in his preface, Geoffrey's purpose in writing the book was to trace the history of the Britons through a long sweep of nineteen hundred years, stretching from the mythical Brutus, great-grandson of the Trojan Aeneas, whom he supposed to have given his name to the island after he had landed there in the twelfth century before Christ, down to his last British King, Cadwallader, who, harassed by plague, famine, civil dissension and never-ending invasion from the continent, finally abandoned Britain to the Saxons in the seventh century of our era. Between these two extreme limits in time, he planned to relate for us the history of the British people, sometimes as a mere genealogy of royal primogeniture, sometimes in succinct chronicle form, more often as a dynastic sequence told with considerable detail, reign by reign, and occasionally even, when he considered this to be worthy of our close attention, by permitting an individual incident or anecdote to swell out of proportion and to become a narrative in its own right. For Geoffrey, his history was a pageant of striking personalities, moving forward to the greatest personality of them all, Arthur, son of Utherpendragon and Ygerna. With the passing of Arthur his interest gradually died away, and so indeed, does that of the modern reader.

Geoffrey's essential inspiration was a patriotic one. At the point where the story ends, that is, with the death of Cadwallader in

Rome, 'in the six hundred and eighty-ninth year after our Lord's Incarnation', Britain is still the best of all lands, providing in unfailing plenty everything that is suited to the use of human beings; but the British people, who once ruled the country from sea to sea, have now allowed themselves to be divided into two separate nations: those who crossed back over the Channel and settled in the Armorican peninsula and those who stayed on in the island. The vengeance of God and the domination of the Saxons have overtaken these last, who are now called the Welsh, and they live precariously and in greatly reduced numbers in the remote recesses of the western forests.[2] Let these Welshmen remember their glorious past, cries Geoffrey towards the end of his story, their descent from the Kings of Troy and the various moments in their history when they dominated Europe. Above all let them remember the prophecies of Merlin, made to King Vortigern and set out in full in this book, which tell of the triumphs of the British people yet to come, when the mountains of Armorica shall erupt, Kambria shall be filled again with joy and the Cornish oaks shall once more flourish.

As J. S. B. Tatlock pointed out, in Geoffrey's time 'the lack of accounts of British history was notorious' (*Tatlock*, p. 430). Geoffrey had several clear-cut political reasons for what he wrote, his desire to give 'a precedent for the dominions and ambitions of the Norman kings' (ibid., p. 426) and his wish to ingratiate himself with his various dedicatees. To some degree the book pretends to be an ecclesiastical history as well as a political one. Through it runs a deep-felt and often bitter desire to denigrate the Romans and to put the Britons in their place in the forefront of history.

2. WHO WAS GEOFFREY OF MONMOUTH?

Who then was this Geoffrey of Monmouth who wrote the *History of the Kings of Britain* more than eight hundred years ago? We can learn a number of things about him from a careful reading of his book. On three occasions he refers to himself by name, each time adding the information that he has some connexion with Monmouth. In vii. 2 he calls himself *Gaufridus Monemutensis*, this being a repetition of the genitive form *Galfridi Monemutensis* given in i.1; and in xi.1 the name comes a third time and is spelt *Galfridus Monumotensis*.

In his later chapters Geoffrey occasionally mentions other monastic and ecclesiastical centres in Wales: Llandaff, ix.15, for example, Bangor Iscoed, xi.3, xi.12–13, and Llanbadarn xi.3. Much more striking than this, however, are the many references to Caerleon-on-Usk, thirteen in all,[3] working up to the long chapter ix.12, which describes in full detail a plenary court which Arthur held in that city after he had conquered the whole of Gaul, this with a wealth of topographical and architectural information.

Where Geoffrey found his material will be discussed later, but for the moment we can observe his clear-cut statement, made in i.1, that he was translating directly into Latin from 'a certain very ancient book written in the British language', that is, presumably, from early Welsh.[4] Three times he names an acquaintance of his, Walter, Archdeacon of Oxford, the man who, so he maintains, gave him the ancient book in Welsh.[5] The 'Prophecies of Merlin', printed on pp. 170–85, were originally conceived as a separate volume;[6] and they have a short preface of their own, in which Geoffrey praises Alexander, Bishop of Lincoln, the churchman who had asked him to make this part of his translation and from whom he obviously expected some reward for his pains. Finally, there is in this text the double dedication of the work as a whole, which is here presented jointly to Robert, Earl of Gloucester, the natural son of Henry I, and to Waleran, Count of Mellent, son of Robert de Beaumont.[7]

Considerable external evidence can be added to these few facts culled from the text itself.

Geoffrey's signature appears in the list of witnesses appended to six different twelfth-century charters which have been dated between 1129 and 1151, all of them connected with religious foundations in or near Oxford.[8] In two of these charters Walter, Archdeacon of Oxford, appears as co-signatory; in three others the statement witnessed is a grant or an agreement made by Walter himself; and the sixth charter was signed towards the end of 1151, a few months after Walter's death. Twice Geoffrey signed himself *magister*. The island of Oseney, in Oxford, with which the first charter deals, was in the parish of St George and belonged until 1149 to the five or six Augustinian canons of the secular college of St George's. It has been suggested that Geoffrey himself may have been a canon of that college. Weight is added to that suggestion by the fact that it is known that Walter the Archdeacon was Provost of the college and that Robert de Chesney, author of the last of these charters and by then Bishop of Lincoln, had also been one of its canons.

The college of St George's came to an end in 1149, in which year it was made over to Oseney Abbey. Geoffrey's various attempts at dedicating the *History of the Kings of Britain* and his praise of Alexander, Bishop of Lincoln, in vii.1–2, had gained him no preferment. Alexander himself had died in 1148. Soon after Alexander's death, Geoffrey added a third literary enterprise to the *History* and the 'Prophecies of Merlin' which he had incorporated in it. This was the *Life of Merlin*,[9] written in Latin verse and dedicated to that Robert de Chesney who, as we have seen, had been one of the Canons of St George's in Oxford and was Bishop of Lincoln from 1148 to 1167, as successor to Alexander. In this poem Geoffrey is named twice, as *Gaufrido de Monemuta* four lines from the end and as *Galfridum Monemutensem* in the *explicit*.

In the early months of 1151, just before the death of Walter the Archdeacon, Geoffrey became Bishop Elect of St Asaph, in what is now Flintshire. He was ordained priest at Westminster in mid-February 1152 and consecrated at Lambeth a week later by Archbishop Theobald.[10] There is no evidence that he ever visited his see, and indeed the wars of Owain Gwynedd make this most unlikely. Towards the end of 1153 he was one of the bishops who witnessed

the Treaty of Westminster between Stephen and Henry Fitz-
Empress.[11] If the doubtful evidence of the Welsh chronicles is
accepted, then he died in 1155.[12]

It frequently happens that we do not know even the name of the
author of a medieval masterpiece. When we are given a name, that
is often the sum of our knowledge. With Geoffrey of Monmouth
we are much better placed. The facts set out in the last few paragraphs justify us in adding certain tentative conclusions to what we
actually know about Geoffrey's life. To have called himself
Galfridus Monemutensis he must have had some vital connexion with
Monmouth, probably that of birth. Everything in his writings and
his thinly-sketched biography points to his having been a Welsh-
man, or perhaps a Breton born in Wales. There must have been
some biographical reason for his constant preoccupation with
Caerleon-on-Usk, situated some twenty miles only south-west of
Monmouth. Over a period of twenty-three years, from 1129 to
1151, he seems to have been connected closely with events in
Oxford. That he twice signed himself *magister* may imply some
teaching function, although the University of Oxford did not yet
exist. That in five of his signatures as we have them, the first dated
1129 – seven years, that is, before the completion of the *History of
the Kings of Britain*, with its long panegyric of Arthur of Britain –
and the second, let us remember, a forgery, he should have added
Artur, [*Arthur*], *Arturus*, *Arturo* and *Artour* to his first name may
possibly imply that his father's name was Arthur.[13]

For twenty-three years of his life, during which period he wrote
three works which have come down to us, the evidence is, then, that
Geoffrey was resident in Oxford; and for the last four he seems to
have lived in London. Much is known of the Oxford of the first
half of the twelfth century. What was formerly a prosperous
market-town had declined sadly at the time of the Norman invasion.
By the early twelfth century, however, Oxford was flourishing
once more, although it was still far from being a University. In a
letter dated *c.* 1117 Theobald d'Estampes called himself *magister*

Oxenefordiae, using the same title as Geoffrey. The Oseney Chronicle says that the theologian Robert Pullen came over from Paris in 1133 to give a series of lectures, and many other contemporary scholars seem to have been connected with the place. Beaumont Palace was built just outside the North Gate by Henry I, who often visited it; and there Richard Cœur de Lion was born in 1157. Stephen held council in Oxford in 1136; and to that council came Robert, Earl of Gloucester, the eldest bastard of Henry I and step-brother to Matilda. In 1142 Matilda herself took refuge in Oxford Castle and was besieged there by Stephen, eventually making her celebrated escape across the ice and through the snow to Abingdon.[14]

These were eventful times in Oxford and one can imagine that Geoffrey must have met many distinguished visitors there and often been interrupted in his duties in St George's Chapel and in his literary pursuits.

3. GEOFFREY'S SOURCES

Where did Geoffrey of Monmouth find his material? This question is infinitely more important than any argument as to where he was buried, or whether or not one of the charters which he was supposed to have signed is a thirteenth-century forgery. There are two simple answers to the question, simple in the sense that they are naïve: these are that he took his material from a little book which a friend had given to him; and alternatively that he made his material up.

We have seen how, at the beginning of his *History*, Geoffrey stated categorically that Walter the Archdeacon presented him with 'a certain very ancient book written in the British language' and that he then proceeded to translate the book into plain, straight-forward Latin. This source-book is mentioned again casually in xi.1; and then referred to a third time in the short epilogue which appears at the end of some versions of the *History*, with the variation that its antiquity is not stressed and we are given the new information that Walter had fetched it *ex Britannia*. The essential problem of Walter's very ancient book is that we do not possess it. As Sir John Lloyd wrote, 'no Welsh composition exists which can be reasonably looked upon as the original, or even the groundwork, of the *History of the Kings of Britain*'.[15]

The first obvious comment is that the fact that we do not possess this book does not rule out its possible one-time existence. It would have been a manuscript, of course, and maybe a unique copy; and far more medieval manuscripts have been destroyed than have come down to us.

Acton Griscom, inspired to some extent by an address given by Sir Flinders Petrie[16] to the British Academy on 7 November 1917, had a second theory. This was that, while it is agreed that Geoffrey's 'very ancient book' no longer exists, we may have in our possession, without realizing it, evidence of the book's one-time existence.[17] In various collections in England and Wales there are to be found at least fifty-eight manuscripts and two fragments of manuscripts which contain early Welsh chronicles. All of them, admittedly, are later in date than the *History of the Kings of Britain*, but it does not follow that some of the material incorporated in them does not pre-date Geoffrey's work. It is now accepted that he had at his disposal something closely related to MS. Harl. 3859 in the British Museum, the contents of which are Nennius' *Historia Brittonum* with the *Cities and Marvels of Britain*, the *Annales Cambriae* and the medieval Welsh king-lists and genealogies. He also knew something of Taliesin's panegyrics to Urien Rheged; much of the material underlying *Culhwch and Olwen*; and the *Life of Saint David* and certain other hagiographical material.

There is a third possibility. Despite his categorical statement about the 'very ancient book', was Geoffrey perhaps thinking symbolically?[18] By this 'ancient book' did he really mean the knowledge of early British history which his friend Walter the Archdeacon had culled from a lifetime of talking to fellow enthusiasts and of extensive reading, he being so 'well-informed about the history of foreign countries', which knowledge he had shared with

Geoffrey during the long years of their acquaintanceship? Some
support is given to this idea by the statement in xi.1, concerning
the battle of Camlann, in which Arthur received his mortal wound,
that Geoffrey 'heard it, too, from Walter of Oxford, a man most
learned in all branches of history'.

In the last few years, a fourth and most striking suggestion has
been made about Geoffrey of Monmouth's History. In a book
published in 1951, Jacob Hammer printed a variant version of the
Historia, which differs in many ways from the standard or Vulgate
text.[19] Hammer's suggestion was that this variant version was an
adaptation of what Geoffrey himself had written, made by some
other contemporary author. Concerning this variant version,
Robert A. Caldwell has now put forward a startling theory. This
is that the variant version possibly preceded the standard text.
'The former, therefore,' he writes, 'looks like an early draft put
together from original sources, the latter like a deliberate revision.'[20]
The variant version lacks the dedications, the acknowledgements
to Walter the Archdeacon, and the references to the 'very ancient
book'. The only mention which it contains of Geoffrey himself is
at the end in a colophon, which may be false.[21] We come then to
this point: if we are prepared to ignore the evidence of the colophon
and the variant version's lack of antiquity, it is conceivable that
someone else wrote the variant version and that Geoffrey merely
adapted it; in short that Jacob Hammer's variant version, written
admittedly in Latin and not in British, is itself Geoffrey's source, his
'certain very ancient book'. To push Professor Caldwell's argument to the extreme, the source of Geoffrey of Monmouth's
Historia may be a contemporary book by a person whom, for want
of a better name, we can call the pseudo-Geoffrey. It would then
remain for us to discover the sources used by the pseudo-Geoffrey.

We have, then, a choice of possibilities: that Geoffrey had a
source-book and that this book has disappeared without leaving
any other trace; that Geoffrey's source-book is lost indeed, but that
we can trace his use of at least one written Old Welsh source in his

reproduction of the names preserved in the dynastic genealogies of MS. Harl. 3859 and in the Nennian list of the Cities of Britain; that Geoffrey's essential source was really oral tradition, personified, as it were, in his friend Walter the Archdeacon (himself, no doubt, a widely-read man); or that behind the Geoffrey of Monmouth of the Vulgate text of the *History* there lies a pseudo-Geoffrey who had earlier written the variant text, an arch-hoaxer, who not only left no clue whatsoever to his own personality but was happy to see his *History* fathered on to Geoffrey. We are free to accept any one of these theories, to attempt a combination of two or more of them, to try to discover some intermediary position between some pair of them, or, indeed, to reject them all.

What nobody who has examined the evidence carefully can ever dare to say is that Geoffrey of Monmouth, or the pseudo-Geoffrey, simply made up his material. It is true that William of Newburgh, writing about 1190, less than forty years after Geoffrey's death, condemned his fellow-chronicler out of hand. 'It is quite clear', maintained William, 'that everything this man wrote about Arthur and his successors, or indeed about his predecessors from Vortigern onwards, was made up, partly by himself and partly by others, either from an inordinate love of lying, or for the sake of pleasing the Britons.'[22] One is sometimes tempted to agree with William of Newburgh. After all, the *History of the Kings of Britain* rests primarily upon the life-history of three great men: Brutus, grandson of Aeneas; Belinus, who sacked Rome; and Arthur, King of Britain. This particular Brutus never existed; Rome was never sacked by a Briton called Belinus; and Geoffrey's Arthur is far nearer to the fictional hero of the later Arthurian romances, of whom he is the prime but not the 'onlie begetter', than to the historical Arthur of whom we learn a few scanty details in Nennius and elsewhere.[23] In short, most of the material in the *History* really is fictional and someone did invent it. What is more, Geoffrey is a great believer in circumstantial detail. In the description of the decisive battle between Arthur and Lucius Tiberius, for example, he gives us precise information about the positioning of the divisions on each side, the number of men engaged and the names of the divisional commanders. Then come, in direct speech in the Vulgate version, Arthur's address to his troops and that of Lucius Tiberius to the Roman army. One is tempted to say that this is romanticized history with a vengeance, until one remembers that the battle never took place and that it is merely romantic fiction.

Fortunately there is ample evidence to sway us in the opposite direction. The list of proper names and place-names given at the back of this volume includes 871 head-words. A large proportion of these are the names of historical people and of places actually on the map. Much of this background material is twisted almost beyond recognition; but in earliest essence it has some element of truth. Geoffrey did not invent it, nor did the pseudo-Geoffrey: *ergo* one or other of them must have taken it from somewhere.[24] In addition to the debt which he acknowledged to Walter's 'very ancient book' and to the book of the 'Prophecies of Merlin' which he said he translated, also from British, to please Alexander, Bishop of Lincoln, Geoffrey made many cross-references in the Vulgate text to such writers as Cicero, Juvenal, Lucan, Apuleius, Bede, King Alfred, etc. He can also be shown to have drawn upon Livy, Orosius and Virgil. For the variant version Jacob Hammer has made a long list of such cross-references to the Old Testament and to the New, and then to twenty-eight separate Latin writers.[25] Finally, there is the archaeological evidence, the fact that strange light has been thrown upon certain of the alleged fancies of Geoffrey of Monmouth by subsequent archaeological discoveries. The connexion of Vortigern and his son Pacentius with Ireland (viii.14) is, for example, allegedly supported by the ogham stones with Vortigern's name on them which have been discovered at Ballybank and Knockaboy.[26] As fate caught up with him, Vortigern, in Geoffrey's account (viii.2), fled to the fortified camp of Genoreu, on the hill called Cloartius, in Erging, by the River Wye. Here 'Gonoreu' is Ganarew and 'Cloartius' a misspelling for the modern

Little Doward, with its hilltop camp, all of it very near to Monmouth.[27] There is the remarkable story of how Merlin brought Stonehenge piecemeal from Mount Killaraus in Ireland to Salisbury Plain (viii.10–14) and its resemblance to the parallel account of the carrying of the bluestones by sea and overland from the Prescelly mountains which is given by modern archaeologists.[28] In v.4 Geoffrey tells how the Venedoti decapitated a whole Roman legion in London and threw their heads into a stream called Nantgallum or, in the Saxon language, Galobroc. In the 1860s a large number of skulls, with practically no other bones to accompany them, were dug up in the bed of the Walbrook by General Pitt-Rivers and others.[29]

We are presented, then, with a well-nigh insoluble mystery. Whether the author of the *Historia Regum Britanniae* was Geoffrey of Monmouth himself or some curious pseudo-Geoffrey, it remains true that much, if not most, of his material is unacceptable as history; and yet history keeps peeping through the fiction. We can perhaps give Acton Griscom the last word here: 'How much allowance must be made for expansion and embellishment', he wrote, 'is admittedly hard to determine, because, first and foremost, Geoffrey was bent on turning chronicle history into literature.'[30] From the great number of borrowings which, as I point out in my notes, he makes from the *De excidio Britanniae* of Gildas and the *Historia Brittonum* of Nennius, his debt to these two early chroniclers is certainly a considerable one. Some scholars have suggested that our search for sources might well begin and end there.

4. THE WORK ITSELF

In Geoffrey's long and eventful account of the history of the Britons there are, as we have seen, three personalities which dominate: Brutus himself, the imaginary founder of the nation, and the father-figure; Belinus, who, with his brother Brennius, is supposed to have captured and sacked Rome; and Arthur of Britain, with his beautiful

wife Guinevere, Mordred who betrayed him, and his four brave
knights, Cador of Cornwall, Gawain son of Loth, Bedevere the
Cup-bearer and the Seneschal Kay. Some 82 pages of the *History of
the Kings of Britain*, in this translation of the Vulgate text, are devoted to these three, and Arthur himself fills more than a fifth of the
book. In between the adventures of Brutus, Belinus, Arthur, and
their supporting chieftains, come a host of lesser figures and a
succession of curious episodes: some of them more than touched
with reality, others purely fictional; some of them well-known
Romans, others half-forgotten Britons, but many of them still
familiar enough today to all who are interested in the literature and
the early history of our island: the giant Gogmagog; Locrinus who
married Gwendolen but loved the Saxon woman Estrildis; Hudibras; Bladud and the founding of Bath; King Lear and his three
daughters; Gorboduc; the brothers Ferrex and Porrex; Lud who
built London; Cassivelaunus; Julius Caesar; Cymbeline; Claudius;
Vespasian; Constantine; King Cole; Vortigern; Hengist and
Horsa; Octa; the prophecies of Merlin the magician; Utherpendragon; the moving of Stonehenge from Ireland to Salisbury
Plain; the seduction of Ygerna of Tintagel; Loth; Lucius Tiberius;
Gormont and Isembard; and, finally, the coming of Saint Augustine.

The first half of Geoffrey's book is a well-ordered chronicle of
what might well appear to be remote but nevertheless historical
events, were it not for their very strangeness, the imaginative
treatment given to some of them, and their factual extravagance in
certain fields of history where we are too well informed from other
sources to allow ourselves to be misled.

It is not until vi.17 that we read of the discovery by Vortigern's
messengers of the boy Merlin, the soothsayer son of an incubus and
of a princess who had entered a nunnery, a discovery to be followed
a little later by the long interpolation devoted to Merlin's prophecies. If we have been deceived before, and Merlin is the first really
other-worldly element in the book, then we now at once realize
how far away we are from anything which can ever approach real

history. As a direct result of the magic arts of Merlin, Arthur himself is born, and there follows the most striking part of Geoffrey's *History*: the long series of extraordinary episodes which form the life-history of the most outstanding of all British heroes, from his mysterious conception in the castle of Tintagel to his mortal wounding but not death at the battle of Camlann. After holding our attention for so long, Arthur then steps out of the story as mysteriously as he had entered it. At one moment we are told that 'Arthur continued to advance, inflicting terrible slaughter as he went.' A few lines later Geoffrey tells us laconically that 'Arthur himself, our renowned King, was mortally wounded and was carried off to the Isle of Avalon, so that his wounds might be attended to' (xi.2). He is never mentioned again, apart from two trifling cross-references in xii.2 and xii.6, until, nearly at the end of the book, the Angelic Voice announces to Cadwallader that 'God did not wish the Britons to rule in Britain any more, until the moment came which Merlin had prophesied to Arthur' (xii.17).

Merlin the magician and Arthur the all-conquering British King: it was these two personages who were to give Geoffrey of Monmouth his place in the development of European literature. 'Here,' wrote Professor Lewis Jones, 'was just what a romantic age was thirsting for, and Arthur immediately became the central figure of the most popular and most splendid of the romantic cycles . . . a hero whose deeds challenged comparison with those of Alexander and Charlemagne.'[31] Geoffrey may be said to have created the figure of the prophet Merlin as he appears in later romance, even though, according to Celtic scholars, it can now be regarded as certain that he derived the outline of the Merlin story from anterior Welsh sources.[32] Behind Geoffrey's new literary Arthur, on the other hand, lies a long tradition of historical references, going back in ultimate essence to the ninth-century chronicler Nennius.[23]

If we leave Brutus on one side, it is an interesting exercise to set face to face Geoffrey's other two major heroes: Belinus, who sacked

Rome, and Arthur, who was forced to turn back when he had reached the passes over the Alps; and then to consider why the former has had no appeal for later writers, while the latter has enjoyed a European, and, indeed, a world, success which still continues unabated today. We must note, first of all, that, as a personality and as a character, Geoffrey's Arthur is nearer to Belinus than is the later and more literary Arthur of Chrétien de Troyes. What is there about Geoffrey's Arthur which was to make him a world figure? In Geoffrey's book, Arthur's story is coupled with that of Merlin; but so was Vortigern's. From his coronation at the age of fifteen Geoffrey's Arthur was all-conquering; but so was Belinus. Arthur fought with a giant on St Michael's Mount; but Corineus had been a famous baiter of giants in his day. Arthur's wife Guinevere was a very beautiful woman; but there are many other striking beauties in Geoffrey's book. The truth is that Geoffrey's Arthur differs from Belinus and the other characters in the *Historia* by the air of other-worldliness and mystery attached to his person from before his birth; by his identification with the new ideal of chivalry in Western Europe, e.g. at the plenary court which he held at Caerleon-on-Usk, and by the attractive, up-to-date nature of his four favourite knights, Cador, Gawain, Bedevere and Kay; by the fact that he did not die, but was carried away to the Isle of Avalon, there to await the moment when he would fulfil Merlin's prophecy by reappearing in history; and finally, most important and pervading all the rest, by the romantic way in which Geoffrey chose to describe his every action.[33]

To help us to accept some of his flights of fancy, Geoffrey has a number of favourite devices. From time to time, he provides cross-references to allegedly contemporary events in other parts of the world, and, in particular, allusions to Old Testament and Roman history. 'At that time,' he adds, when describing the reign of Cunedagius, 'Isaiah was making his prophecies; and on the eleventh day after the Kalends of May Rome was founded by the twin brothers Remus and Romulus' (ii.15). He shows us the extent of his reading by an occasional modest remark about some other historian. 'However, since Gildas the historian has dealt with this quarrel at sufficient length,' he writes of the disagreement between Lud and Nennius, 'I prefer to omit it, for I do not wish to appear to be spoiling by my homelier style what so distinguished a writer has set out with so much eloquence' (i.17). Or again: 'Cadwallader, the son of Cadwallo, succeeded his father in the government of the realm. This was the youth whom Bede called Cliedvalla' (xii.14). Geoffrey's text is larded with toponymic conundrums, made the more exciting by the interlocking of Celtic and English roots. The capital of Britain, for example, according to Geoffrey, was first called 'Troia Nova'. This degenerated into 'Trinovantum', but Lud changed the name to 'Kaerlud' or 'Lud's City', from which last the word 'London' was formed (i.17). As a supreme touch, Geoffrey occasionally rejects some more than usually indigestible story, thus attempting to show his historical sense and to prove to us that there were bounds to his credulity. When discussing the building of the fortress of Paladur, now called Shaftesbury, by King Rud Hud Hudibras, son of Leil, he adds: 'There the Eagle spoke, while the wall was being built. If I believed its Sayings to be true, I would not hesitate to hand them down to history with my other material' (ii.9). This fine show of critical judgement is spoilt by the fact that, at the very end of the History, when the Angelic Voice has spoken and Alan of Brittany is called upon to make the fateful decision as to whether or not he should support the exiled Cadwallader in his attempt to recapture Britain, it is to the Auguries of the Eagle that he turns. 'Alan thereupon took a number of books, such as the one about the Auguries of the Eagle which had prophesied at Shaftesbury and those on the oracular Sayings of the Sybil and of Merlin' (xii.18). Once he had translated the Prophecies of Merlin, no doubt Geoffrey's judgement of what was credible or not became less severe.

5 . GEOFFREY THE ARTIST

Those critics who have studied the *History of the Kings of Britain* down the centuries, from William of Newburgh to Jacob Hammer, have been so preoccupied with the problem of Geoffrey's sources and so anxious to condemn him as a historian, that they have had little time to consider him as an artist.

About his own Latin style Geoffrey is modest, but one senses that his modesty is assumed and that in effect he was pleased with what he had written. To compare his medieval Latin with the classical mastery of Caesar, Cicero or Tacitus is clearly to ask too much. However familiar he may have been with texts written in classical Latin, and however fluently he may have spoken and written medieval and ecclesiastical Latin himself, it is after all a derived tongue which he is using, a second or third stratum overlying what was once a vernacular language, now kept alive as something more artificial. For all that, his vocabulary is extensive and his sentences ring with a note that is vibrant and true, even if their word-order is sometimes nearer to modern French than to classical Latin. According to the changes of circumstance, he writes with a variety of styles, now quiet and descriptive, now impassioned, sometimes in a long and languorous strain, on other occasions with a soldierly pithiness and a terse abruptness. His dullest passages by far are the tortured addresses to Robert of Gloucester, Waleran of Mellent and Alexander of Lincoln. He makes no claim to be a writer of purple passages. '. . . I have been content with my own expressions and my own homely style', he tells us in his opening dedication, 'and I have gathered no gaudy flowers of speech in other men's gardens. If I had adorned my page with high-flown figures of speech, I should have bored my readers, for they would have been forced to spend more time in discovering the meaning of my words than in following the story.' From time to time he must have put down his grey-goose quill, to pause a moment and savour a more than usually neat expression. 'Among the wise he was himself wise,' he writes of

the youthful Brutus, 'and among the valiant he too was valiant'
(i.3). Once, when Arthur had delivered a powerful harangue, Hoel,
King of the Armorican Britons, rose to reply. 'Your speech,' he
said to Arthur, 'adorned as it was with Ciceronian eloquence, has
anticipated exactly what we all think' (ix.17). After all, it was
Geoffrey of Monmouth who wrote all these speeches delivered by
Arthur and the other chieftains of Britain and Rome.

From the very beginning Geoffrey makes it clear that he is
writing to be read by the solitary reader, not to be declaimed aloud
in serial form and listened to with less than half an ear by inatten-
tive audiences who come and go and who, indeed, may well vary
completely from recital to recital. There are none of the calls for
silence so common in medieval vernacular literature, none of the
three-fold repetitions felt necessary in the *chansons de geste*. 'If I
had adorned my page with high-flown figures of speech, I should
have bored *my readers*. . . .' The silent reader is more appreciative
of the artistry of the writer than can ever have been the tired
pilgrims round their camp-fire on the Via Tolosana, or the young
lords and ladies flushed with food and drink who lingered at the
high table in the banqueting-hall. What, then, are Geoffrey's virtues as an artist? He has a long and spindly tale to tell, stretching
over nineteen hundred years, a period as long as from the death of
Christ down to our own decade. J. A. Giles once compiled a family
tree of all these Kings of Britain, from Brutus down to Cadwallader:
there are no fewer than ninety-nine of them. Yet Geoffrey keeps
our interest throughout. With the exception, perhaps, of the inter-
polated prophecies, the story has a wonderful shape to it. Geoffrey's
material is under tight control. He refers to and fro, drops his
threads and nimbly picks them up again. No two of his innumerable characters are alike. The tempo of his royal progress varies
from page to page. Sometimes we move through a hundred years
in almost as many words; at other times the tale stands motionless
while Geoffrey elaborates a point or paints a mighty picture. The
great panoramas of the later romances are already here, notably the

plenary court at Caerleon-on-Usk. The *History* is a succession of
battles no less than a sequence of kings; yet each battle is different,
each has its carefully sketched-in backcloth: for example the
ambush at the opening to a lush valley in which Belinus caught the
swiftly-marching Romans (iii.9), or the sally made by Brutus from
the castle of Sparatinum down into the gorge of the River Akalon,
where the unarmed troops of Pandrasus were moving up in open
order (i.5). For every battle we are, as we have seen, given the most
precise information: numbers of men in each division engaged,
deployment of cavalry, names of divisional commanders; it might
be Livy describing the battle of Cannae. As I have pointed out
already, the finer points of circumstantial detail are everywhere set
clearly before us. This was to be abused more and more by the
later writers of romance, and Rabelais made savage fun of their
excesses in his five books.

Geoffrey has few figures of speech. 'The Greeks woke up at the
groans of the dying, and when they set eye on those who were
about to butcher them they were stupefied, like sheep suddenly
attacked by wolves' (i.9). 'Those who were wounded where the
battalions met in conflict fell to the ground as if they had been
standing corn cut by the reapers' sickles' (iii.3). This is trite enough.
He tries apostrophe and the historic present. Where he excels is in
his use of direct speech: the exhortation before battle, the *oraison
funèbre*, the sober debate in the council chamber. His characters
roar and rant, they wheedle and persuade, they are in turn noble or
revengeful, magnanimous or implacable. Dialogue, as such, does
not exist; but there are interlocking speeches. Much has been
written of the psychological treatment of certain characters in
medieval writings: the state of mind of Ganelon as he commits the
greatest act of treachery since the kiss of Judas; the lament of the
Chatelaine de Vergi as she dies of a broken heart. Geoffrey has
little time for this. He paints landscapes for us, and now and then
seascapes. He never attempts a physical portrait, female or male.
There is pathos in plenty, the horror of weltering blood, the gay

colours of the plenary court, the curious plainsong of the prophecies, the other-worldly touches brought by Merlin. There are
superb word-pictures, as when Corineus wrestles with Gogmagog
on some great windswept cliff in Cornwall and finally hurls the
monster 'far out to sea . . . on to a sharp reef of rocks, where he
was dashed into a thousand fragments and stained the waters with
his blood' (i.16); when Utherpendragon steps out into the dark
night on his way to meet the trusting Ygerna in the dim torchlight
of her own castle (viii.19); or when Merlin dismantles the stones
of the Giants' Ring (viii.11). There is no humour. Geoffrey's young
women do not live for us, least of all Guinevere; but two of his old
crones stick in our memory, Tonuuenne, mother of Brennius and
Belinus (iii.7) and the hag of the Mont-Saint-Michel. There are
giants in plenty, but none of the spiteful little dwarfs and hunch-
backs of the later romances.

Three major threads go to form the pattern of Geoffrey's
design: the variation of bare genealogy, chronicle entry, dynastic
portrait and vast panoramic anecdote; the dominating personalities of first Brutus, then Belinus and finally Arthur; and the gradual
crescendo movement up to Arthur's victory over Lucius Tiberius.

How much of all this is Geoffrey of Monmouth and how much
the pseudo-Geoffrey, how much is Vulgate text and how much
variant version, this can be deduced only from a careful comparison of the two redactions. Maybe Geoffrey of Monmouth
wrote them both and was his own double-ganger. J. S. P. Tatlock
wrote of the *History* in general: 'It is hard to think of a single
medieval work of any extent with such foresighted, indeed classical
symmetry; it recalls the structure of good tragedy.'[34] As Robert A.
Caldwell concludes, the problem of the two versions 'deserves
further study in all its facets. But until it has been demonstrated
that Geoffrey was not the father of the work which has so long
passed under his name, we may continue to give him the credit for
his audacious and brilliant performance'.[35]

In his opening sentence Geoffrey uses the words 'the history of the Kings of Britain'. It might perhaps be a salutary exercise to pause a moment at this point and to ponder just what he meant by the word *historia*, or indeed what medieval French writers meant by *histoire*, *historie* and *estoire*, all of them so close etymologically to our modern word 'story' and semantically so far away from the modern connotations of the word 'history'. Jacob Hammer traced no fewer than 137 references to the *Aeneid* in his variant version of the *Historia*. Is the *Aeneid* a history? Is the *Odyssey* a history? Are we less ready to criticize Homer and Virgil for the liberties they take with historical fact? For that matter, are we sure that we know exactly what we mean by historical fact? Perhaps if we ceased to think of the *Historia Regum Britanniae* as a history and called it instead a prose-epic, we might be more just to Geoffrey as an artist.

6. GEOFFREY OF MONMOUTH DOWN THE CENTURIES

Whatever curious elements of truth the book might contain, Geoffrey of Monmouth's *History of the Kings of Britain* was, as we have seen, severely criticized by more orthodox historians writing well within the author's own century. As romanticized history on the other hand, as a source-book for the imaginative writing of others, as an inspiration for poetry, drama and romantic fiction down the centuries, it has had few if any equals in the whole history of European literature.

The results of the appearance of Geoffrey's *History* in 1136 were immediate and striking. A great number of copies of the text were made. Acton Griscom listed 186 Latin manuscripts which are still extant today, including 48 complete texts and two fragments of the twelfth century;[36] and since he made his list in 1929 a number of other manuscripts have been discovered.[37] A long series of mentions, many of them, it is true, of a deprecating and derogatory nature, began to appear in the Latin, English and French works of the more serious-minded chroniclers of the time, from Robert de

Torigni's *Chronica* down to Ranulf Higden's *Polychronicon*.[38] Numerous adaptations and paraphrases were prepared in Latin prose and verse. Next came a succession of vernacular *Bruts*. Apart from the various Welsh versions known as *Brut y Brenhinedd* (the 'Brut of the Kings'), going back to the thirteenth century, the most famous of these are the lost *Estoire des Bretuns* and parts of the extant *Estoire des Engles* by Geoffroi Gaimar, both mid-twelfth century, the *Brut* of Robert Wace and the English *Brut* of Layamon (c. 1200). Meanwhile Geoffrey's *Historia* had begun to be incorporated in the works of a long line of English chroniclers, from Alfred of Beverley, writing c. 1150, down to John Stow at the end of the sixteenth century.

The French writers of romances soon recognized a fellow-spirit in Geoffrey of Monmouth. Between 1167 and 1184 Marie de France was writing her *Lais*, the most clearly Arthurian of which is *Lanval*. Meanwhile Chrétien de Troyes, the most famous of all the French medieval poets who took their inspiration from the *matière de Bretagne*, was composing his long series of Arthurian verse-romances, *Erec et Enide*, *Cligès*, *Lancelot*, *Yvain* and *Perceval*. In France Chrétien was followed by Raoul de Houdenc with his *Meraugis de Portlesguez*, Renaud de Beaujeu with his *Li biaus Descouneuz* and Heldris de Cornuälle with *Le roman de Silence*; and in Germany by Wolfram von Eschenbach with *Parzival* and by Hartmann von Aue with *Erec* and *Iwein*. In short, the Arthurian verse-romance was soon in full spate. It was not long before this led to a series of prose adaptations, *Le roman de Laurin*, the so-called Arthurian Prose Vulgate and then back again in England to Sir Thomas Malory's *Morte d'Arthur* of 1469, between which date and that of Layamon's *Brut* the only English Arthurian work of any merit had been *Sir Gawayne and the Grene Knight* of 1360–70.

It was in England that had come the first frontal attack on Geoffrey of Monmouth and all that he stood for, this already in the twelfth century, from the chroniclers William of Newburgh and Giraldus Cambrensis. A second frontal attack came from the

English antiquarians of the sixteenth century: Polydore Vergil and William Camden. As far as pure literature was concerned, this second condemnation had the same encouraging effect as the first. A new and lengthy series of works was inspired either directly by Geoffrey, or through Holinshed and the other sixteenth-century compilers. This included Thomas Sackville and Thomas Norton's *Gorboduc* (1565), or *The Tragedie of Ferrex and Porrex*, as it was called in the 1570 version; William Warner's *Albion's England* (1586); Thomas Hughes's *The Misfortunes of Arthur*; Spenser's *Faerie Queene*; Shakespeare's *Cymbeline* and *Lear*; Michael Drayton's *Polyolbion* (1612); Milton's *History of Britain* (1670); Dryden's *King Arthur, or the British Worthy*, and Sir Richard Blackmore's *Prince Arthur* (1695) and *King Arthur* (1697). Wordsworth published his *Artegal and Elidure* in 1820 and Tennyson his *Idylls of the King* between 1859 and 1885.

The twentieth century has seen the founding of the International Arthurian Society, with its objective of studying dipassionately all literature devoted to the historical or the literary Arthur. In the 1975 number of its annual bulletin, the Society listed 980 active members in 33 countries and printed a critical bibliography of 424 books, articles and reviews dealing with Arthurian matters which had been published during the calendar year 1974.

More than eight hundred years have passed since Geoffrey of Monmouth finished his *History of the Kings of Britain*. Despite William of Newburgh and Giraldus Cambrensis, in defiance of Polydore Vergil and William Camden, the world of today seems more than ever interested in

> The sage enchanter Merlin's subtle schemes;
> The feats of Arthur and his knightly peers;
> Of Arthur, who, to upper light restored,
>   With that terrific sword
> Which yet he brandishes for future war,
> Shall lift his country's fame above the polar star![39]

No doubt much of the influence is now indirect, in the sense that

Tennyson turned to Sir Thomas Malory rather than to Geoffrey of Monmouth; but without Geoffrey's *History* there would have been no *Morte d'Arthur*, and no *Idylls of the King* either.

7. EDITIONS OF THE *HISTORIA*

Anyone who has any dealings with Geoffrey of Monmouth is immediately made aware of the difficulty of finding a reliable version of the original Latin text:

'No critical, or even reasonably accurate text of the *Historia Regum Britanniae* has hitherto been published,' lamented Acton Griscom in 1929. 'The several printed texts ... are not the accurate reproductions of manuscripts they claim to be; for even the later, nineteenth century, imprints are no more than copies of a sixteenth-century edition, itself full of errors and prepared with an almost total lack of critical judgment.'[40]

'It is deplorable,' wrote R. W. Chambers, 'that we should still be depending for our text of Geoffrey upon the whim of a sixteenth-century printer.'[41]

To some degree this has been put right by Acton Griscom himself, by Edmond Faral and by Jacob Hammer, but much work remains to be done, and much, indeed, is being done at the moment.

There are now in existence eight printed texts of the Latin *Historia*:

1. 1508. Edited by Ivo Cavellatus and printed by Josse Bade in Paris. Cavellatus used four Paris manuscripts, none of which has been identified. He said that he 'collated' them: that is, formed a composite text from them, and then 'corrected' it. Of this editor Acton Griscom wrote: '... his editorial changes, compared with available manuscript evidence, appear in most cases to be downright error. ...'[42] Cavellatus divided the text into nine books and each book into a series of chapters.

2. 1517. A reprint of the text of Ivo Cavellatus, made by Josse Bade in Paris, with a few minor changes in the reading.

3. 1587. Edited and printed by Jerome Commelin in Heidelberg. This is the text of one or other of Josse Bade's two editions, 'collated' with a fifth manuscript, also not identified, which Commelin's acquaintance, Paul Knibbe, had brought from Belgium. Of Commelin's edition Acton Griscom wrote: '. . . his text is full of obvious misreadings and errors'.[43] Commelin was the first to divide the text into twelve books.

4. 1844. Edited by J. A. Giles and published by David Nutt, London, in the series *Scriptores Monastici*. Despite the protestations of the editor, this version is little more than the Commelin text of 1587, with a considerable number of new errors added.[44]

5. 1854. Edited by A. Schulz, Halle. This is a reproduction of the text of J. A. Giles.

In short, prior to the labours of Acton Griscom, all that the world possessed in print of the Latin text of Geoffrey's *Historia* was the extremely faulty 1508 version of Cavellatus, with various strata of subsequent errors heaped upon it.

6. 1929. Edited by Acton Griscom, London. This is a most careful copying of Camb. Univ. Libr. MS. 1706, with, at the foot of each page, the variants of Berne, Stadtbibliothek, MS. 568 N.I. 8 and MS. Harlech 17, with, beneath that again, a literal translation of the Welsh text of Jesus College, Oxford, MS. LXI. This edition shows the old division into twelve books, for the convenience of cross-reference.

7. 1929. Edited by Edmond Faral, in *La Légende Arthurienne*, Vol. III, pp. 64–303, Paris. This is Trinity College, Cambridge, MS. 1125, with, at the foot of the page, the variants of Berne, Stadtbibliothek, MS. 568 N.I. 8; Leyden, Univ. Libr., MS. B.P.L. 20; and Paris, Bibl. Nat., f. lat. 6233. Faral's text is not divided into books.

8. 1951. Edited by Jacob Hammer, Cambridge, Massachusetts. This edition offers the variant version as it appears in five rather late manuscripts, variant, that is, in distinction from the standard or Vulgate version of the *Historia*, as explained on p. 16. It is divided into eleven books.[45]

Of these eight editions of the Latin text, only two need be considered by a modern translator, those of Acton Griscom and Edmond Faral, unless, indeed, he wishes to present a composite version, which would be pointless. For my own translation I have chosen to use Griscom's text, that is Camb. Univ. Libr., MS. 1706.

8. EARLIER TRANSLATIONS

There exist three English translations of the *Historia*.

1. 1718. *The British History, translated into English from the Latin of Jeffrey of Monmouth, with a large Preface concerning the Authority of the History*, by Aaron Thompson, London, cxi+410 pp. This is a translation of Commelin's 1587 edition, although Thompson claims to have looked at Josse Bade's 1517 edition and to have consulted several manuscripts. At the end of the book is printed an 'Explication of the ancient names of countries, cities, rivers, mountains, etc., mentioned in this history' and then a short index.

2. 1842. *The British History of Geoffrey of Monmouth, in twelve books, translated from the Latin by A. Thompson, Esq., a new edition, revised and corrected* by J. A. Giles, London, xxvii+282 pp., including an *index raisonné* of 24 pp. This translation was later reprinted as *Six Old English Chronicles*, by J. A. Giles, London, 1848. In his introduction to the 1842 edition, Giles says that 'the translation of Thompson has been followed, revised and corrected wherever the phraseology appeared to be unsuited to the more accurate ears of today'. There is little evidence of correction; but the English has certainly been brought up to date.

3. 1896. *Histories of the Kings of Britain by Geoffrey of Monmouth*, translated by Sebastian Evans, Temple Classics, London, 370 pp., later reprinted by Everyman's Library, London, 1912, xxvi+223+27 pp. This is a translation of the 1854 edition of Schulz, made into curious pseudo-Spenserian English. The Everyman reprint has an introduction of 18 pp. by Lucy A. Paton, a one-page bibliography and a translator's epilogue.

In effect, directly or indirectly, all three of these versions are made from Commelin's very faulty text of 1587. My own impression is that Thompson's translation is by far the most sound. All three translators adopt the division of the *Historia* into twelve books and a great number of chapters. The translations of Thompson and Giles are, of course, out of print. There is no doubt that Evans made much more use of Thompson and Giles than he was prepared to admit. In a number of passages I have doubted Evans's understanding of the Latin; he omitted sentences which he considered unseemly; and I myself find his attempts at period English regrettable. It should be added that in 1963 Everyman's Library brought out a revision of Sebastian Evans's translation, prepared by Charles Dunn, with an introduction by Gwyn Jones.

9. THIS TRANSLATION

What follows is a faithful translation into contemporary English of the *Historia Regum Britanniae* as contained in Camb. Univ. Libr. MS. 1706 and as printed by Acton Griscom in 1929. I have omitted nothing. Where the manuscript has an obvious haplography, I have added a few words from Edmond Faral's 1929 edition of Trinity College, Cambridge, MS. 1125, e.g. in vii.4, where *Mox adibit in oculos eius et faciem* becomes *Mox adibit [ipse cadaver et, dum superstabit, anhelabit] in oculos eius et faciem*.[46] Having written the *-bit* of *adibit*, the scribe of MS. 1706 let his eye run on to the last three letters of *anhelabit*, and so omitted six words. English is often much less concise than Latin, so that *In culturas mortalium irruent . . .* becomes *They will sweep down on to the fields which men have cultivated . . .* (vii.4). In many places I have found it desirable to insert pronouns and to repeat proper names, in order to make the meaning clear, and *Saltu quoque facto . . .* (vii.4) becomes *Then the Fox will leap at the Boar. . . .* On one point I agree wholeheartedly with Sebastian Evans.[47] Where Geoffrey's Latinized names represent persons well-known to English readers, I have printed the standard English form e.g. *Guenhuueram* (ix.9), *Ganhumaram* (x.13), *Ganhumare* (xi.1) and *Ganhumere* (x.2), in its various spellings and cases, becomes *Guinevere*. Where I have used a Latin name, I have chosen one particular spelling and not departed from it. My index of proper names and place names, on pp. 291 ff. gives full details of the scribal variants.

There has been much debate about the division of the *Historia* into twelve, eleven or nine books, and then the breaking down of each book into chapters.[48] Whatever devices the various scribes and editors have adopted here, it seems reasonably clear that these subdivisions were not made by Geoffrey himself. I have divided my translation into eight main parts, according to the subject-matter, and given a clear title to each part.[49] These titles are repeated as a running-head at the top of my verso pages; and at the top of my recto pages there is printed an indication of the point reached in the narrative; a really full *index raisonné*, the first ever printed of Geoffrey's book, is given at the end of the volume.

Geoffrey of Monmouth was writing for contemporary readers and not playing some curious antiquarian game in his language, as Sebastian Evans seems to have imagined. I have therefore avoided most sedulously such outmoded expressions as *sithence*, *withal* and *albeit*; and I have reduced such mathematical conundrums as 'twice ten cities and twice four more' (i.2) to simple modern figures. From my experience of copying medieval manuscripts I know how arbitrary are the paragraph divisions made by the scribes; and the divisions into paragraphs in this translation are my own. The sole object of my translation is to enable modern English readers who have no Latin, or whose Latin is not equal to the task of struggling with the original, to understand and enjoy a reputable text of the *History of the Kings of Britain*, which R. W. Chambers once called 'one of the most influential books ever written in this country'[50] and J. A. Giles 'a work from which nearly all our great vernacular poets have drawn the materials for some of their noblest works of fiction and characters of romance'.[51]

10. ACKNOWLEDGEMENTS

My wife, Barbara Reynolds, first introduced me to Dr E. V. Rieu,
the Founder Editor of the Penguin Classics, this in May 1962, at a
time when she was bringing out in the same series the *terza rima*
translation of Dante's *Paradiso* which had been left unfinished by
the late Dorothy L. Sayers when she died on 17 December 1957.
I had read much of the correspondence which passed between my
wife and Dr Rieu; I had shared in many stimulating conversations
with Dr Sayers in our home in Cambridge and in Witham when she
was busy with her translation of the *Inferno* and the *Purgatorio*; and
I had myself exchanged many letters with her when she was engaged
on her translation of *La chanson de Roland*. The task of translating
Geoffrey of Monmouth's *Historia Regum Britanniae* from twelfth-
century Latin into English prose, while it has its own knotty
problems, is clearly a much simpler one than that of putting the
Divina Commedia into English verse: but my first and chief ack-
nowledgement must surely be to these three.

My immediate sponsor for this translation has been Mrs Betty
Radice, who replaced Dr Rieu as the Editor of the Penguin Classics.
My debt to her has been a real one, particularly at the beginning of
my undertaking and in the final stages, and I express my gratitude
for the encouragement which she has given me and for much practical advice. Dr Rachel Bromwich, editor of *Trioedd Ynys Prydein*
and my good friend for many years, read part of my book in type-
script and made many most valuable suggestions. The late Mr E. R.
Harries, M.C., Librarian of the Flint County Library, lent me books
from the admirable collection of Arthurian material which he put
together over the years. Miss Sylvia Bruce, of the editorial department of Penguin Books Ltd, checked with meticulous care all that
I had written. Mrs Patricia Cartledge did much of my typing. To
all four of them I am grateful. Apart from my relations with the
seven people whom I have mentioned, I have prepared my translation in some isolation and solitude, during the brief periods of

leisure left to me in a busy life. The authors of the books listed in my short bibliography have been my silent collaborators. Perhaps my greatest inspiration was to have been present at the reception given in honour of Dr Rieu on 22 January 1964 on the occasion of his retirement from the editorship of the Penguin Classics, to have talked there with him and Sir Allen Lane and to have inspected with some awe all the volumes in the series which had been published up to that date, spread out on the grand piano in the Great Drawing Room of the Arts Council building.

LEWIS THORPE

Nottingham
13 June 1976

Notes to the Introduction

1. The date is much debated. As I show in n.7, the evidence of the various dedications led *Griscom* to decide that the book was completed in April 1136. Cp. *Faral, Rom.*, pp. 16–17: ' Or, on le montrera, la première rédaction complète de l'Historia parut, au plus tôt, en avril ou mai 1136.' *Parry-Caldwell*, p. 80, more or less agree. *Tatlock* prefers 'the inclusive date 1130–1138', p. 437.

2. *Lloyd, Hist.*, pp. 523–4, *Lloyd, Art.*, pp. 466–8 and *Tatlock, passim*, all maintain that Geoffrey was of Breton stock. The name '*Arthur*', which Geoffrey used in several of his signatures, is stated to have been rare in England and Wales at this time and common in Brittany. Since 1075 Monmouth had been held by a Breton family, first by Wilhenoc, who later founded Monmouth Priory and became a monk there, and then by his nephew William FitzBaderon, who must have been in power at about the time of Geoffrey's birth – if, indeed, Geoffrey was born in Monmouth. It has been maintained that in the *History of the Kings of Britain* Geoffrey shows more sympathy with the Bretons than with the Welsh. *Parry-Caldwell*, p. 73, do not agree.

3. In iii.10 Geoffrey tells us how Belinus founded the city of Caerleon, on the bank of the River Usk, near the Severn Sea. Originally it was called '*Kaerusc*', but when the Romans came its name was changed to the '*Urbs Legionum*', this because the legions used to winter there. Gurguint Barbtruc, the son of Belinus, also did much for Caerleon-on-Usk and when he died he was buried there (iii.12). In the days of King Lucius the British were converted to Christianity and their three pagan archflamens were replaced by three archbishops, one based on London, the second on York and the third on the city of Caerleon, 'the site of which last, by the River Usk in Glamorgan, is still shown by its ancient walls and buildings' (iv.19). During the persecutions by Diocletian and his emissary Maximinianus Herculius, many Christians were martyred in Britain, including 'Julius and Aaron, two townsfolk of the City of the Legions' (v.5). In the days of Aurelius, the Archbishop of the City of the Legions was called Tremorinus (viii.10), and when he died that same King replaced him

by Dubricius (viii.12). It was Dubricius, Archbishop of Caerleon, who crowned the youthful Arthur (ix.1) and who addressed Arthur's troops before the Battle of Badon (ix.4). When Dubricius, become Primate of all Britain and Legate of the Papal See (ix.12), finally retired, he was succeeded as Archbishop of Caerleon by David, who was Arthur's uncle (ix.12); and when David himself died, soon after the crowning of Constantine (xi.3), he was replaced by Kinoc, priest of the church of Llanbadarn. Merlin mentioned the City of the Legions at the beginning of his prophecies (vii.3), and it was there that Guinevere became a nun (xi.1). For Geoffrey's reason for fabricating a non-existent archbishopric at Caerleon and making it Arthur's capital, see *Brooke*, pp. 201–10. In earlier Welsh sources Arthur's capital is invariably at Celliwig in Cornwall (see *Bromwich*, *T.Y.P.*, p.3).

4. See p. 51 = '*quendam britannici sermonis librum vetustissimum*'. This book in early British is mentioned a second time on p. 258, (see n.5, below) and again in an epilogue to the *History*, which, as it does not appear in MS. Camb. Univ. Libr. 1706, is printed as n.1 on p. 284 = '*librum istum britannici sermonis quem Gualterus Oxenefordensis archidiaconus ex Britannia advexit*'. Opinions are sharply divided as to what '*britannici sermonis*' and '*ex Britannia*' mean in these quotations. Cf. *Parry–Caldwell*, p. 81 and p. 81, n.1. In ii.1, '*Unde adhuc gens patrie lingua britannica sese Kambros appellat*', the words '*lingua britannica*' can only mean 'in the Welsh language'. There is surely no evidence that Walter the Archdeacon was ever in Brittany! In the twelfth century '*britannicus*' can mean either Welsh or Breton, for the two languages had still diverged very little since the sixth-century settlement of Brittany by South Welsh and west country emigrants. I have translated 'in the British language' and 'from Britain'.

5. See p. 51 = '*Walterus, Oxenefordensis archidiaconus, vir in oratoria arte atque in exoticis hystoriis eruditus*'. The second reference is on p.258 = '... *ut in prefato britannico sermone invenit & a Waltero Oxenefordensi in multis historiis peritissimo viro audivit*...' For the third reference see n.4 above.

6. *Faral, Rom.*, pp. 10–11, stresses this fact.

7. This dedication varies in the different manuscripts of the *Historia*. In the great majority of manuscripts, the work is dedicated solely

to Robert, Earl of Gloucester. In at least seven manuscripts, including MS. Camb. Univ. Libr. 1706, which has been followed in this translation, a second dedicatory paragraph and a second dedicatee, Waleran, Count of Mellent, are added to the paragraph of dedication to Robert, Earl of Gloucester. One manuscript, Berne, Stadtbibl. 568, is unique in that it has the double dedication, but that the words 'Stephane, rex Anglie' appear in place of 'Roberte, dux Claudiocestrie', and then, later on, 'Roberte, consul Claudiocestrie' in place of 'Galeranne, consul Mellenti'. There is a fourth version of the Historia, e.g. in Bibl. Nat., MS. lat. 6233, which contains no dedication at all. From a careful analysis of the historical implications of these variants, Griscom, pp. 42–98, concludes that the text of MS. Camb. Univ. Libr. 1706 is the earliest version which we have, and that it was completed in April 1136. (See also A. Griscom, 'The date of composition of Geoffrey of Monmouth's Historia: new manuscript evidence', in Speculum, I, 1926, pp. 129–56, a first draft of part of his book.) The single address, 'consul auguste', at the beginning of xi.1. has, on the contrary, been taken by some to prove that the sole dedication to Robert, Earl of Gloucester, was the original one. Hammer, Var., p. 3, cannot accept 'the method of classification by the dedications', but Parry–Caldwell, p. 80, n.2, stress that their view is 'that the dedication can be relied upon only for the external, not for the textual, history of the work'.

8. In Salter, Oxf. there are listed seven charters which bear Geoffrey's signature. These are: I. The foundation charter of Oseney Abbey, extant in two cartularies, one in Christ Church, Oxford, and the other Brit. Mus., Cotton MS. Vitellius E.XV, and dated c. 1129. Walter the Archdeacon signed 'Waltero archidiacono' and Geoffrey 'Galfrido Artur'.II. A charter of St John's College, Oxford, dated c. 1125–35, in which Robert d'Oilli II confirmed gifts of land in Walton to the secular canons of St George's in the castle of Oxford. Walter the Archdeacon signed 'Waltero archidiacono' and Geoffrey 'Galfrido Arthur'. III. A deed in the Godstow Cartulary, f° 5, (Exch. K. R., Misc. Books, n° 20), dated January 1139, in which Walter the Archdeacon granted to Godstow an exemption from certain archidiaconal payments. Geoffrey signed 'mag. Galf. Arturus'. IV. A deed in the same cartulary, f° 96, in which Walter the Archdeacon made to Godstow a grant of

land in Shillingford. Geoffrey signed 'Galfrido Arturo'. v. Another deed in the same cartulary, f° 142, dated 1149–50, in which Walter renewed his agreement that certain tithes which he had permitted his villeins in Walton to pay to the church of St Giles in Oxford should still be paid to that church, now that it had become the property of Godstow. Geoffrey signed 'magistro Galfrido Artour'. vi. A grant of land in Knolle in the same cartulary, dated early 1151, by Richard Labanc. This is signed 'Gaufridus episcopus sancti Asaphi & Walterus Oxenefordie archidiaconus', etc. Walter died in 1151 and Geoffrey is known to have been consecrated on 21 February 1152, so that 'episcopus' here means 'episcopus electus'. vii. A charter by Bishop Robert de Chesney in the Thame cartulary, dated late 1151. Geoffrey signed 'Gaufridus electus sancti Asaphi'. Walter was dead and the new Archdeacon of Oxford, Robert Foliot, signed in his place. In Lloyd, Art., p. 464, n.5, that author wrote of H. E. Salter and his Geoffrey of Monmouth charters that 'in 1929 he added an eighth (Early Oxford Charters, no. 60)'. In effect, charter no. 60 in Salter's book, Facsimiles of early charters in Oxford muniment rooms, Oxford, 1929, for that is what Lloyd means, is a photographic reproduction of v above. Lloyd then failed to notice that charter 101 in this same book is signed by Geoffrey as 'Galfrido Arthur' and by Walter the Archdeacon as 'Waltero archidiacono', that it is ii above and that Salter shows it to be a thirteenth-century forgery. What is more, charter 102 also is signed by 'Galfrido Artur' and really is additional to the seven, but it, too, is a thirteenth-century forgery. In short, instead of increasing the total from seven to eight, by removing two, Salter's book reduces the number of genuine charters signed by Geoffrey from seven to six.

9. The Vita Merlini, ed. by J. J. Parry, Univ. of Illinois Studies in Language and Literature, Urbana, 1925; and Life of Merlin, ed. with introduction, text, translation and commentary by Basil Clarke, Univ. of Wales Press, Cardiff, 1973.

10. See Councils and ecclesiastical documents relating to Great Britain and Ireland, by A. W. Hardan and W. Stubbs, Vol. 1, p. 360, Oxford, 1869, where the relevant passage from the Profession Rolls at Canterbury reads: 'Anno ab Incarnatione Domini MCLI. [i.e. 1152],

Theobaldus, Cant. Archiepiscopus et totius Angliae Primas etc., VII cal. Martii sacravit Galefridum electum Ecclesiae Sancti Asaph in Episcopum apud Lamhetham, accepta prius ab eodem secundum consuetudinem scripta de subjectione et obedientia sibi exhibenda professione, praesentibus et comministrantibus sibi suffraganeis Willelmo Norwicensi Episcopo et Waltero Roffensi; ordinavit autem ad presbyterum eundem precedenti Sabbato, i.e. XV. cal. Martii, apud Westmonasterium'.

11. See *Foedera, Conventiones, Literae*, etc., by T. Rymer and R. Sanderson, London, 1704–35, Vol. 1, p. 14. Geoffrey's signature appears as '*Galfrido de S. Asaph episcopo*'.

12. For example, the *Brut y Tywysogion*, Peniarth 20 Version, edited by T. Jones, Cardiff, 1952, which records the death of 'Geffrei, Bishop of Llandaff,' against MCLIV (= 1155).

13. See *Lloyd, Hist.*, p. 524: '. . . there is evidence that he used it [= the name Arthur] in the days of his obscurity, and reason, therefore, to suppose that his father's name was Arthur'.

14. The material in this paragraph is well known, e.g. *Tatlock*, p. 27. What I have written, however, bears resemblance to a page or two in an unpublished essay which Miss E. M. R. Ditmas, author of the novel *Gareth of Orkney*, had the kindness to let me read some years ago, and it is only just that I should mention her name here.

15. *Lloyd, Hist.*, p. 526.

16. Professor Sir W. M. Flinders Petrie, 'Neglected British History', an article in *The Proceedings of the British Academy*, 1917–18, pp. 251–78, previously read as a paper.

17. *Griscom*, pp. 99–147.

18. One is reminded forcibly of the opening words of Dante's *Vita Nuova*: '*In quella parte del libro de la mia memoria . . .*' and of similar statements in the *Divina Commedia* – *Inferno*, ii.8, xv.88; *Paradiso*, xvii.91, xxiii.52, etc. The possibility is made the more likely by the fact that so many medieval texts in vernacular tongues have an intoductory statement in which the author pretended that he was translating from Latin to give assurance to his listeners or

readers, who may have had a feeling that anything in their own language could not be worth their serious attention. For example, in the thirteenth-century verse romance *Le roman de Silence*, the author, Heldris de Cornuälle, who takes his primary inspiration from Geoffrey of Monmouth's own *History*, and a secondary inspiration from the *Estoire Merlin* in the Arthurian prose-Vulgate, four times tells us that he is using a source-book, adding in one passage that he is translating from Latin. It is most unlikely that he is doing anything of the kind. What he means is that his ultimate inspiration is bookish and learned. That part of the ultimate inspiration really was in Latin made it the more impressive. See Lewis Thorpe, 'Le roman de Silence, by Heldris de Cornuälle', in *Nottingham Mediaeval Studies*, Vol. v (1961), p. 57.

19. See under *Hammer, Var.*, in the Short Bibliography at the beginning of this book (p. 46).

20. See *Parry–Caldwell*, pp. 86–8, from which this sentence is taken; and Robert A. Caldwell, 'The use of sources in the Variant and Vulgate Versions of the *Historia Regum Britanniae* and the question of the order of the versions', in *Bulletin Bibliographique de la Société Internationale Arthurienne*, Vol. 9 (1957), pp. 123–4.

21. *Hammer, Var.*, p. 264. The colophon reads: 'I, Geoffrey Arthur of Monmouth, who have been responsible for translating this history of the Britons from their language into our own, leave to those who come after me the history of the kings who succeeded in Wales from that time onwards, and the task of describing what happened to them' (my translation). Such colophons, or *explicits*, are often the work of the scribe and not of the author himself.

22. William of Newburgh, *Historia Rerum Anglicarum*, edited by R. Howlett in *Chronicles of the reigns of Stephen, Henry II and Richard I* (Rolls Series), 1884–5, *proemium*, 1, ii.

23. For an up-to-date review of these details, see *Jones, T.*

24. Sir John Lloyd has a fascinating passage in which he describes how Geoffrey took the names 'Dunvallo Molmutius' (ii. 17), 'Gurguit Barbtruc' (iii.11–12), 'Gorbonianus' (iii.16) and 'Cursalem' (ix.12)

from the Old Welsh genealogies in Brit. Mus. Harl. MS. 3859, where they appear as 'Dumngual moilmut,' 'Guurgint bar(m)b truch', 'Gorboniaun' and 'Cursalen'; how he formed the name of his heroine 'Guendoloena' (ii.4–6) from a masculine name 'Guendoleu'; and how five contemporaneous kinglets mentioned by Gildas are reduced by Geoffrey to four, 'Constantine' (xi.3), 'Aurelius Conanus' (xi.5), 'Vortiporius' (xi.6) and 'Malgo' (xi.7), who then reign successively over all Britain. See *Lloyd, Hist.*, p. 527 and n.161.

25. *Hammer, Var.*, pp. 265–9.

26. See *Griscom*, p. 100 and his references. There is nothing in this. The dating of ogham stones is notoriously difficult and the name VOR(R)TIGURN on these two specimens means simply 'great prince' and has no connexion with the British Vortigern. (See *Bromwich, T.Y.P.*, p. 392).

27. *Lloyd, Art.*, p. 461.

28. See, e.g., R. J. C. Atkinson, *Stonehenge*, London, 2nd ed., 1956, pp. 183–5; and Stuart Piggott, *Antiquity*, XV (1941), pp. 305–19, 'The Stonehenge Story'.

29. See *Griscom*, pp. 211–14 and supporting evidence. *Tatlock*, pp. 31–3, is most critical of Griscom's argument.

30. *Griscom*, p. 101.

31. *Jones, W.L.*, p. 70.

32. The theory that Geoffrey invented Merlin was disproved by H. M. Chadwick in 'Merlin in the works of Geoffrey of Monmouth', pp. 123–32 of *The Growth of Literature*, I, Cambridge, 1932. See also *Bromwich, T.Y.P.*, pp. 469 *et seq.*

33. This immediately becomes apparent, for example, if one reads first the factual treatment of the fight between Corineus and the giant Gogmagog (i.16), and then the romantic treatment of Arthur's struggle with the Spanish ogre on the Mont-Saint-Michel (x.3).

34. *Tatlock*, p. 393, quoted by *Parry–Caldwell*, p. 85.

35. *Parry–Caldwell*, p. 87.

36. *Griscom*, pp. 551–72.

37. *Hammer, Add. MSS.*

38. For an easy reference list, see *Chambers, E. K.*, pp. 258–82.

39. Wordsworth's *Artegal and Elidur*, lines 51–6, quoted by *Jones, W. L.*, p. 86.

40. *Griscom*, p. 4.

41. *Chambers, R. W.*, p. 45.

42. *Griscom*, p. 12.

43. *Griscom*, p. 14.

44. *Giles* claims to have made a great labour of collating nine manuscripts. In his discussion of the edition, pp. 14–18, *Griscom* shows how false this claim is.

45. The five manuscripts are: Exeter Cathedral Chapter Library, MS. 3514, late 13th C., = E; Trinity College, Dublin, MS. E.5. 12. (515), late 13th C. or early 14th C., = D; Brit. Mus. Harl. MS. 6358, early 13th C., = H; Nat. Libr. of Wales, Aberystwyth, MS. Parton 37, 18th C., = P; and Cardiff Publ. Libr., MS. 2.611, *c.* 1300, = C. Of these H and C are partly Variant and partly Vulgate. J. Hammer first prints C and then, for books viii to xi repeated, DEH. This edition is divided into eleven books. To these five manuscripts is now to be added a sixth, the former Phillipps MS. 26233, partly Variant and partly Vulgate, now Nat. Libr. of Wales, Aberystwyth, MS. 13210D, second half of the thirteenth century. See *Bibl. Bull. of the International Arthurian Society*, Vol. xxv (1973), pp. 147–52, 'Another manuscript of the Variant Version of the *Historia Regum Britanniae*', by Daniel Huws and Brynley F. Roberts.

46. *Faral, Lég.*, Vol. iii, text of *Historia Regum Britanniae*, §116, lines 197–8.

47. *Evans*, p. 248.

48. *Griscom*, pp. 26–30.

49. *Chambers, E. K.*, pp. 30–3, suggested much the same.

50. *Chambers, R. W.*, p. 225.

51. *Giles, Chron.*, p. viii.

Short Bibliography

of Works Used in the
Introduction and in the Notes

Bromwich, T. Y. P. Rachel Bromwich, *Trioedd Ynys Prydein: The Welsh Triads*, edited with introduction, translation and commentary, Cardiff, 1961.

Bromwich, Art. Rachel Bromwich, 'The character of the early Welsh tradition', chapter in *Studies in early British History*, edited by Nora K. Chadwick, Cambridge, 1954, 2nd ed., 1959.

Brooke. C. N. L. Brooke, 'The Archbishoprics of St David's, Llandaff and Caerleon-on-Usk', chapter in *Studies in the early British Church*, edited by Nora K. Chadwick, Cambridge, 1958.

Chambers, E. K. E. K. Chambers, *Arthur of Britain*, London, 1927.

Chambers, R. W. R. W. Chambers, 'Geoffrey of Monmouth and the *Brut* as sources of Early British history', article in *History*, III, (1918–19), pp. 225–8.

Evans. Sebastian Evans, *Histories of the Kings of Britain by Geoffrey of Monmouth*, Everyman, London, 1912.

Faral, Lég. Edmond Faral, *La Légende Arthurienne, Études et Documents*, 3 vols., Paris, 1929.

Faral, Rom. Edmond Faral, 'Geoffrey de Monmouth: les faits et les dates de sa biographie', article in *Romania*, LIII, (1927), pp. 1–42.

Giles. J. A. Giles, *The British History of Geoffrey of Monmouth, in twelve books*, London, 1842.

Giles, Chron. J. A. Giles, *Six Old English Chronicles*, London, 1885.

Griffiths. M. E. Griffiths, *Early Vaticination in Welsh, with English parallels*, Cardiff, 1937.

Griscom. Acton Griscom, *The Historia Regum Britanniae of Geoffrey of Monmouth*, London, 1929.

Hammer, Add. MSS. Jacob Hammer, 'Some additional manuscripts of Geoffrey of Monmouth's Historia Regum Britanniae', article in *Modern Language Quarterly*, III (1942), pp. 235–42.

Hammer, Var. Jacob Hammer, *Geoffrey of Monmouth. Historia Regum Britanniae. A variant version edited from manuscripts*, Cambridge, Massachusetts, 1951.

Jones, T.   Thomas Jones, 'The early evolution of the legend of Arthur', article in *Nottingham Mediaeval Studies*, VIII (1964), pp. 3–21.

Jones, W. L.   W. Lewis Jones, *King Arthur in history and legend*, Cambridge, 1911.

Kendrick.   T. D. Kendrick, *British Antiquity*, Methuen, 1950.

Lloyd, Art.   J. E. Lloyd, 'Geoffrey of Monmouth', article in *The English Historical Review*, LVII (1942), pp. 460–8.

Lloyd, Hist.   J. E. Lloyd, *A history of Wales from the earliest times to the Edwardian Conquest*, London, 1939, 2nd ed., 2 vols with the pages numbered consecutively 1–816.

Lot.   Ferdinand Lot, *Nennius et l'Historia Brittonum*, Paris, 1934.

Parry–Caldwell.   John J. Parry and Robert A. Caldwell, 'Geoffrey of Monmouth', chapter in *Arthurian Literature in the Middle Ages, a collaborative history*, edited by Roger S. Loomis, Oxford, 1959, pp. 72–93.

Piggott.   Stuart Piggott, 'The sources of Geoffrey of Monmouth', articles in *Antiquity*, XV (1941), pp. 269–86, 'The "pre-Roman" King-List', pp. 305–19, 'The Stonehenge Story'.

Salter, Oxf.   H. E. Salter, 'Geoffrey of Monmouth and Oxford', article in *The English Historical Review*, XXXIV (1919), pp. 382–5.

Tatlock.   J. S. P. Tatlock, *The Legendary History of Britain: Geoffrey of Monmouth's Historia Regum Britanniae and its early vernacular versions*, University of California Press, 1950.

Thompson.   Aaron Thompson, *The British History, translated into English from the Latin of Jeffrey of Monmouth, with a large preface concerning the authority of the history*, London, 1718.

Wade-Evans.   A. W. Wade-Evans, *Nennius's History of the Britons*, S.P.C.K., 1938.

THE HISTORY OF THE
KINGS OF BRITAIN

HEBRIDES

CAITHNESS

SHETLAND

MORAY

ORKNEYS

ALBA

Loch Lomond
Wall of Antoninus Pius
Dumbarton
Carse of Falkirk
Edinburgh
LOTHIAN

Wall of Hadrian

Carlisle
NORTHUMBRIA
WESTMORLAND
DEIRA

IRELAND

IRISH SEA

R. Ouse
York
HUMBER
Conisbrough
LINDSEY

St Asaph
Chester
Caistor
Bangor
Lincoln
Snowdon
Stafford
VENEDOTIA
Bangor
Iscoed
R. Trent
R. Soar
Leicester
KAMBRIA
R. WYE
MERCIA
Llanbadarn
Warwick
DEMETIAN
SEA
Worcester
Severn
Monmouth
Malvern
DEMETIA
Usk
Gloucester
Colchester
St. Davids
City of the Legions
Cirencester
Oxford
St. Albans
Carmarthen
Llandaff
R. Thames
LONDON
Bath
Silchester
THANET
SEVERN SEA
Amesbury
Canterbury
SOMERSET
Salisbury
Winchester
Richboro
Shaftesbury
R. Southampton
Porchester
Tintagel
CORNWALL
R. Camel
Exeter
R. Dart
Dorchester
Camelford
Totnes

ENGLISH CHANNEL

Dedication

WHENEVER I have chanced to think about the history of the kings of Britain, on those occasions when I have been turning over a great many such matters in my mind, it has seemed a remarkable thing to me that, apart from such mention of them as Gildas and Bede had each made in a brilliant book on the subject, I have not been able to discover anything at all on the kings who lived here before the Incarnation of Christ, or indeed about Arthur and all the others who followed on after the Incarnation. Yet the deeds of these men were such that they deserve to be praised for all time. What is more, these deeds were handed joyfully down in oral tradition, just as if they had been committed to writing, by many peoples who had only their memory to rely on.

At a time when I was giving a good deal of attention to such matters, Walter, Archdeacon of Oxford, a man skilled in the art of public speaking and well-informed about the history of foreign countries, presented me with a certain very ancient book written in the British language. This book, attractively composed to form a consecutive and orderly narrative, set out all the deeds of these men, from Brutus, the first King of the Britons, down to Cadwallader, the son of Cadwallo. At Walter's request I have taken the trouble to translate the book into Latin, although, indeed, I have been content with my own expressions and my own homely style and I have gathered no gaudy flowers of speech in other men's gardens. If I had adorned my page with high-flown rhetorical figures, I should have bored my readers, for they would have been forced to spend more time in discovering the meaning of my words than in following the story.

I ask you, Robert, Earl of Gloucester,[1] to do my little book this favour. Let it be so emended by your knowledge and your advice

1. Robert, Earl of Gloucester, the illegitimate son of Henry I, who died on 31 October 1147. The date of his birth is not known.

that it must no longer be considered as the product of Geoffrey of Monmouth's small talent. Rather, with the support of your wit and wisdom, let it be accepted as the work of one descended from Henry, the famous King of the English; of one whom learning has nurtured in the liberal arts and whom his innate talent in military affairs has put in charge of our soldiers, with the result that now, in our own lifetime, our island of Britain hails you with heartfelt affection, as if it had been granted a second Henry.

You too, Waleran, Count of Mellent,[1] second pillar of our kingdom, give me your support, so that, with the guidance provided by the two of you, my work may appear all the more attractive when it is offered to its public. For indeed, sprung as you are from the race of the most renowned King Charles, Mother Philosophy has taken you to her bosom, and to you she has taught the subtlety of her sciences. What is more, so that you might become famous in the military affairs of our army, she has led you to the camp of kings, and there, having surpassed your fellow-warriors in bravery, you have learnt, under your father's guidance, to be a terror to your enemies and a protection to your own folk. Faithful defender as you are of those dependent on you, accept under your patronage this book which is published for your pleasure. Accept me, too, as your writer, so that, reclining in the shade of a tree which spreads so wide, and sheltered from envious and malicious enemies, I may be able in peaceful harmony to make music on the reed-pipe of a muse who really belongs to you.

1. Waleran, Count of Mellent, or Meulan, 1104–1166, son of Robert de Beaumont, Count of Meulan, and twin brother of Robert, Earl of Leicester. For the importance of these two dedications, see p. 11 and n.7.

Part One

BRUTUS OCCUPIES THE ISLAND OF ALBION

BRITAIN, the best of islands,[1] is situated in the Western Ocean, [i.2] between France and Ireland. It stretches for eight hundred miles in length and for two hundred in breadth. It provides in unfailing plenty everything that is suited to the use of human beings. It abounds in every kind of mineral. It has broad fields and hillsides which are suitable for the most intensive farming and in which, because of the richness of the soil, all kinds of crops are grown in their seasons. It also has open woodlands which are filled with every kind of game. Through its forest glades stretch pasture-lands which provide the various feeding-stuffs needed by cattle, and there too grow flowers of every hue which offer their honey to the flitting bees. At the foot of its windswept mountains it has meadows green with grass, beauty-spots where clear springs flow into shining streams which ripple gently and murmur an assurance of deep sleep to those lying on their banks.

What is more, it is watered by lakes and rivers full of fish, and at its southern end by a narrow strait across which men sail to France. There are three noble rivers, the Thames, the Severn and the Humber, and these it stretches out as though they were three arms.

1. This description of Britain is similar in many ways to the opening chapter of Bede's *Ecclesiastical History*. It can be traced further back still, to §§ 7–9 of the *Historia Brittonum* of Nennius, written towards the end of the eighth century, where the thirty-three cities of the Britons are listed. As early as the sixth century something very similar to it appears in the *De excidio Britanniae* of Gildas, who, in his §3, writes of 'the mouths of two noble rivers, the Thames and the Severn, as it were two arms, by which foreign luxuries were of old imported', of 'eight-and-twenty cities' and of 'transparent rivers, flowing in gentle murmurs, and offering a pledge of sweet slumber to those who recline upon their banks'. (Translation by J. A. Giles, 1841, as in all the notes which follow on Gildas and Nennius.)

Into them goods from across the ocean are carried, merchandise coming from all countries by this same sea-traffic.

In earlier times Britain was graced by twenty-eight cities. Some of these, in the depopulated areas, are now mouldering away, with their walls broken. Others remain whole and have in them the shrines of saints, with towers built up to a noble height, where whole companies of men and women offer praise to God according to the Christian tradition.

Lastly, Britain is inhabited by five races of people, the Norman-French, the Britons, the Saxons, the Picts and the Scots. Of these the Britons once occupied the land from sea to sea, before the others came. Then the vengeance of God overtook them because of their arrogance and they submitted to the Picts and the Saxons. It now remains for me to tell how they came and from where, and this will be made clear in what follows.

[i.3]   After the Trojan war, Aeneas fled from the ruined city with his son Ascanius and came by boat to Italy. He was honourably received there by King Latinus, but Turnus, King of the Rutuli, became jealous of him and attacked him. In the battle between them Aeneas was victorious. Turnus was killed and Aeneas seized both the kingdom of Italy and the person of Lavinia, who was the daughter of Latinus.

When Aeneas' last day came, Ascanius was elected King. He founded the town of Alba on the bank of the Tiber and became the father of a son called Silvius. This Silvius was involved in a secret love-affair with a certain niece of Lavinia's; he married her and made her pregnant. When this came to the knowledge of his father Ascanius, the latter ordered his soothsayers to discover the sex of the child which the girl had conceived. As soon as they had made sure of the truth of the matter, the soothsayers said that she would give birth to a boy, who would cause the death of both his father and his mother; and that after he had wandered in exile through many lands this boy would eventually rise to the highest honour.

The soothsayers were not wrong in their forecast.[1] When the day came for her to have her child, the mother bore a son and died in childbirth. The boy was handed over to the midwife and was given the name Brutus. At last, when fifteen years had passed, the young man killed his father by an unlucky shot with an arrow, when they were out hunting together. Their beaters drove some stags into their path and Brutus, who was under the impression that he was aiming his weapon at these stags, hit his own father below the breast. As the result of this death Brutus was expelled from Italy by his relations, who were angry with him for having committed such a crime. He went in exile to certain parts of Greece; and there he discovered the descendants of Helenus, Priam's son, who were held captive in the power of Pandrasus, King of the Greeks. After the fall of Troy, Pyrrhus, the son of Achilles, had dragged this man Helenus off with him in chains, and a number of other Trojans, too. He had ordered them to be kept in slavery, so that he might take vengeance on them for the death of his father.

When Brutus realized that these people were of the same race as his ancestors, he stayed some time with them. However, he soon gained such fame for his military skill and prowess that he was esteemed by the kings and princes more than any young man in the country. Among the wise he was himself wise, and among the valiant he too was valiant. All the gold and silver and the equipment which he acquired he handed over to his soldiers. In this way his fame spread among all peoples. The Trojans began to flock to him and to beg him to become their leader, so that they might be

1. In essence the story of Brutus is taken from §10 of the *Historia Brittonum* of Nennius, where the birth of the hero is described; and §15, which gives the journey westwards. Cp., for example, the sentences: 'Thus reduced, he wandered forty-two years in Africa, and arrived, with his family, at the altars of the Philistines, by the Lake of Osiers. Then passing between Rusicada and the hilly country of Syria, they travelled by the River Malva through Mauretania as far as the Pillars of Hercules ...' (Nennius, §15), with the similar passage on p. 66.

freed from their subjection to the Greeks. They said that this could easily be done, for they had now increased in number in the country to such an extent that there were reckoned to be seven thousand of them, not counting the women and children.

What is more, there was a certain nobly-born youth in Greece called Assaracus who favoured their faction. He was the son of a Trojan mother, and he had the greatest faith in them, thinking that with their help he could resist the persecution of the Greeks. His own brother was harassing Assaracus, on account of three castles which his dying father had given him, and was trying to take these away from him by alleging that he was the son of a concubine. This brother was Greek on both his father's and his mother's side, and he had persuaded the King and the other Greeks to support his case. When Brutus saw how many men he now had, and realized that the castles of Assaracus were there for him to take, he agreed without misgiving to the request of the Trojans.

[i.4]   Once Brutus had been promoted to the position of leader, he called the Trojans together from all sides and fortified the castles of Assaracus. Assaracus himself occupied the open woodlands and the hills with the entire force of men and women who supported him and Brutus. Then Brutus sent to the King a letter which read as follows:

'Brutus, the leader of those who survived the fall of Troy, sends his greeting to King Pandrasus. The people sprung from the illustrious line of Dardanus have withdrawn to the hidden depths of the forests, for they have found it intolerable that they should be treated in your kingdom otherwise than as the purity of their noble blood demands. They have preferred to keep themselves alive on flesh and herbs, as though they were wild beasts, and have their liberty, rather than remain under the yoke of your slavery, even if pampered there by every kind of wealth. If, in the pride of your power, this offends you, then you should not count it against them. Rather you should pardon them, for it is the natural aim of everyone in captivity to strive to return to his former dignity. Be moved to pity for them, and deign to bestow upon them their lost liberty. Give them permission to inhabit the forest-glades which they have occupied in their attempt to escape from slavery. If you cannot grant this, then let them, with your approval, go off to join the peoples of other lands.'

When the content of this letter was explained to him, Pandrasus [i.5] was greatly surprised that people whom he had held in slavery should be so bold that they could send such messages to him. He summoned a council of his leaders and decided to collect an army and to pursue the Trojans. While he was searching the waste lands in the neighbourhood of the castle of Sparatinum where he thought they were, Brutus made a sally with three thousand men and suddenly attacked when Pandrasus was least expecting anything of the sort. Having heard of the coming of Pandrasus, Brutus had entered this castle the night before, so that he might make a surprise attack on the Greeks, as they passed by unarmed and marching in broken order. The Trojans charged them and attacked them fiercely, aiming at killing as many as they could. In their utter stupefaction the Greeks fled in all directions. With the King at their head they rushed to cross the River Akalon which flowed near by. As they forded the river they were in grave danger from the whirling current of its water. Brutus attacked them as they fled, and by his assault he slaughtered some of them in the river and others on the bank. This double death which he was inflicting gave him immense pleasure as he rushed to and fro in the battle.

Antigonus, the brother of Pandrasus, was greatly distressed when he observed what was happening. He marshalled his scattered forces into formation. Then he turned and charged swiftly at the raging Trojans. He preferred to meet death while fighting rather than turn in cowardly flight and be drowned in the muddy whirlpools of the river. He moved forward in close formation and exhorted his men to resist bravely and to hurl back with all their might the weapons which were causing such slaughter among them.

This availed him little or nothing. The Trojans were fully equipped; their enemies were virtually unarmed. Because of this the Trojans pressed on all the more boldly and the slaughter which they inflicted was very heavy. They continued to attack in this way until almost all the Greeks were killed and they had captured Antigonus and his comrade Anacletus.

[i.6]   Once Brutus had made sure of victory, he garrisoned the fortress with six hundred soldiers and then set off for the hidden recesses of the forest-groves where the Trojan people were waiting for his help. Pandrasus, on the other hand, was upset by his own flight and by the fact that his brother was captured, and spent that night in rallying his scattered forces. When the next day dawned, he set off with his re-formed army to besiege the castle, for he imagined that Brutus had himself occupied it, taking with him Antigonus and the other captives whom he had seized. As soon as he reached the walls, Pandrasus reconnoitred the site of the castle, divided his army into troops and stationed them at various places round the perimeter. Some he ordered to prevent those inside from coming out, some that they should cut off the water-courses which ran from the rivers, and others that with a great number of battering-rams and other machines of war they should shatter the fabric of the walls. They followed his instructions with good results and strove with great zeal and in every way they could imagine to harass the besieged unmercifully. When night fell they chose their bravest men to guard the camp and their tents from any stealthy attack by the enemy, while the others who were worn out by toil enjoyed peaceful sleep.

[i.7]   Those who were besieged stood on the top of the walls and strove with might and main to repel the assault-machines of the enemy with devices of their own. They struggled as one man to defend themselves by hurling down missiles and brimstone torches; and when the enemy constructed a *testudo* and dug underneath their walls, they used Greek fire and a deluge of boiling water to force them to retreat. In the end, suffering as they were from lack of food and from their day-long effort, they sent a messenger to Brutus to beg him to hasten to their assistance. They were afraid that they would become so weak that they would be compelled to abandon the fortress.

Brutus wanted very much to bring help, but he was himself greatly preoccupied by the fact that he did not have enough soldiers to permit him to join battle in the field. He relied instead upon a cunning plan, thinking that he would approach the enemy's camp in the night and that once he had tricked their guards he would slaughter them as they slept. However, this could not be achieved without the assent and the assistance of one of the Greeks. Brutus therefore summoned Anacletus, the comrade of Antigonus, drew his sword out of its scabbard and said to him: 'My fine young friend, unless you agree faithfully to what I propose and carry out what I order you to do, this is the end of your life and of that of Antigonus too. This coming night I intend to attack the Greeks' camp and to slaughter them when they least expect it. I am afraid that their sentinels may discover my intention and so hinder my plan. In so far as it is necessary for me to attack their sentinels first, I want them to be deceived by your behaviour so that I can come within striking-distance of the others in safety. You must carry out this cunning plan for me. Go to the besiegers in the second hour of the night and allay their suspicion by lying to them. Say that you have freed Antigonus from where I held him prisoner, taken him to a valley in the woods and hidden him there among the bushes. Pretend that he is unable to go any farther because of the chains with which he is shackled. Then lead them to the edge of the glade, as if they are going to free him. I shall be there with a band of armed men, ready to kill them.'

Anacletus was terrified by the sight of the sword, which threatened [i.8] him with death all the time that Brutus was speaking. He swore that he would carry out this order, if only he himself and Antigonus too were allowed to live. The bargain was struck between them, and at the second hour of the night, which had already nearly come, he started on his way towards the siege as he had been ordered. When he finally came near to the camp, the sentinels, who were keeping a watchful eye on all the obscurer spots in the neighbourhood, gathered around him on all sides. They asked him what he had come for and if he was there to betray the army. He pretended to be overjoyed at seeing them and answered them in this way: 'I am not here to betray my own people. I have escaped from the Trojans' prison. I beg you to come with me to your own Antigonus, whom I have rescued from the fetters of Brutus. He is hampered by the weight of his chains and I have told him to stay hidden in the bushes a short distance back on the edge of the forest, until I could find some of you whom I could bring back to free him.' They were not sure whether he was telling the truth or not, but one of their number appeared who recognized Anacletus, greeted him and told his companions who he was. They hesitated no longer, but called the others who were some way off to come quickly. They followed Anacletus to the wood where, according to what he had said, Antigonus lay hidden. As they made their way through the bushes Brutus attacked them with his armed bands. He charged at them and, terrified as they were, he was able to inflict frightful slaughter upon them.

Then he set out for the siege. He divided his comrades into three companies and ordered each band to go to a different part of the camp, discreetly and without making a sound. Once they were in position they were not to kill anyone until he himself had seized the King's tent with his own troop. He would then blow his horn as a signal to them.

[i.9]   When Brutus had told the Trojans what they were to do, they quietly and without more ado entered the camp; they occupied the various parts as he had ordered and awaited the promised signal. As soon as he stood in front of the tent of Pandrasus, which he was burning to enter more than all the others, Brutus gave his men the signal without waiting any longer. The moment they heard it they quickly drew their swords, went into the sleeping-quarters of

the unconscious enemy and with deadly effect dealt blow after
blow. In this way the Trojans moved forward through the camp,
showing pity to none.

The Greeks woke up at the groans of the dying, and when they
set eye on those who were about to butcher them they were
stupefied, like sheep suddenly attacked by wolves. They saw no
way of protecting themselves, for they had no time either to pick
up their weapons or to take flight. Themselves unarmed, the
Greeks ran to and fro between the armed men wherever their
panic led them; but all the time they were being cut to pieces by the
Trojans who were attacking them. Anyone who got away half-
alive was dashed against the rocks and the tree-trunks as he rushed
along in his desire for escape, and so gave up his soul together with
his blood. Anyone who, protected only by his shield or by some
other covering, rushed headlong through the pitch-dark night in
fear of death and came upon these same rocks, fell there, and as
he fell his arms or legs were shattered. He who avoided both of
these disasters was drowned in the rivers which flowed near by,
for he did not know where to flee. Hardly anyone escaped unhurt
and without suffering some mishap. What is more, as soon as they
heard of the arrival of their comrades-in-arms, the Trojans inside
the fortress hurried out and doubled the slaughter which was being
inflicted.

When Brutus had seized Pandrasus' tent, as we have said already, [i.10]
he was careful to tie the King up and keep him safe, for he knew that
he would get what he wanted more easily by keeping Pandrasus
alive than by killing him. On the other hand, those who had come
with Brutus went on with the slaughter. In the part of the camp
which had been allocated to each of them they succeeded in killing
everyone they found. It was in this way that they passed the night,
and the light of dawn revealed just how many of the people there
they had destroyed. As a result Brutus was beside himself with joy.
When all the enemy had been slaughtered, he allowed his own men
to deal as they wished with the spoils of those they had destroyed.

He himself entered the fortress, taking the King with him, and waited while the royal treasure was being distributed. When everything had been shared out, he placed a new garrison in the fortress and ordered the dead to be buried. He then reassembled his troops and returned jubilant with victory to the depths of the forest.

Their success filled his men's hearts with immense joy. Their illustrious leader called his elders together and asked them what ought to be demanded of Pandrasus. Now that the King was in their power, he would agree without reservation to any demand they might make, provided always that he were permitted to go free. They immediately began asking for all sorts of different things. Some begged Brutus to demand a part of Pandrasus' kingdom, so that they could settle there; others, on the contrary, asked for permission to emigrate and for whatever would be useful to them on their journey. When they had gone on vacillating for a long time, one of their number called Membritius stood up, called for silence and spoke as follows, while the others listened: 'Why do you hesitate about the measures which, in my opinion, ought to be adopted for your future welfare? If you want a lasting peace for yourselves and for your heirs, one thing alone must be asked for: permission to depart. If you grant Pandrasus his life on condition that he allows you to occupy a part of Greece and remain there among the descendants of Danaus, you will never enjoy lasting peace as long as the brothers, sons and grandsons of those on whom you have inflicted decisive defeat remain intermingled with you or as your neighbours. They will always remember the slaughter of their relatives and they will hate you for ever. They will take offence at the merest trifles and they will do all in their power to take vengeance. Since you command the smaller force, you will not have the strength to be able to resist the attacks of the local inhabitants. If any dispute should arise between you and them, their number will increase daily while your own will get smaller. My advice, therefore, is that you should ask Pandrasus for the hand of his eldest daughter, whom they call Ignoge, as a comfort to your leader. With her you should ask for gold and silver, ships and grain, and everything else that you will need for your journey. If we can arrange all this, we should obtain the King's permission and then sail away to other lands.'

When Membritius had finished his speech, which was longer [i.11] than what I have recorded, the entire assembly agreed with him. They decreed that Pandrasus should be brought into their midst and that, unless he agreed to what they demanded, he should be condemned to a most cruel death. He was led in straight away and was placed on a seat higher than the others.

When he had been told what tortures would be inflicted on him if he did not do the things that were demanded, he made the following reply: 'Since the gods are hostile to me and have delivered me and my brother Anacletus into your hands, I must obey your command; for, if you meet with a refusal, we shall both lose our lives, which you have the power to give to us or to take away as you choose. I consider that there is nothing better or more enjoyable than life itself. It is not therefore to be wondered at if I am willing to purchase life with my material possessions. I obey your orders, although against my will.

'I take some comfort in the knowledge that I am about to give my daughter to a young man of such great prowess. The nobility which flourishes in him, and his fame, which is well-known to us, show him to be of the true race of Priam and Anchises. Who other but he could have freed from their chains the exiles of Troy, when they were enslaved by so many mighty princes? Who other but he could have led them in their resistance to the King of the Greeks; or have challenged in battle such a vast concourse of warriors with so few men, and led their King in chains in the very first engagement? Since so noble a young man has been able to resist me so courageously, I give him my daughter Ignoge. I also give him gold and silver, ships and corn, and whatsoever you will consider necessary for his journey.

'If you change your present plan and prefer to stay with the

Greeks, then I grant you a third of my kingdom for you to live in. If not, then I will carry out my promises effectively; and in order that you may feel the more assured, I will remain a hostage in your hands until I have done so.'

As soon as this agreement was made, messengers were sent to all the shores of Greece to collect ships. When these were brought together, to the number of three hundred and twenty-four, they were handed over and loaded with every kind of grain. The daughter of Pandrasus was married to Brutus; and, according to what his rank demanded, each man was presented with gold and silver. Once all these things had been done, the King was set free from prison. The Trojans sailed away from his dominion with a following wind. Ignoge stood on the high poop and from time to time fell fainting in the arms of Brutus. She wept and sobbed at being forced to leave her relations and her homeland; and as long as the shore lay there before her eyes, she would not turn her gaze away from it. Brutus soothed and caressed her, putting his arms round her and kissing her gently. He did not cease his efforts until, worn out with crying, she fell asleep.

Meanwhile the Trojans sailed on for two days and one night, with a favourable wind blowing. Then they touched land at a certain island called Leogetia, which had remained uninhabited since it was laid waste by a piratical attack in ancient times. Brutus landed three hundred armed men on the island to see if anything at all lived there. They found no one, but they killed all sorts of wild animals which they had discovered between the forest pastures and the woodlands.

They came to a deserted city and there they found a temple of Diana. In the city there was a statue of the goddess which gave answers if by chance it was questioned by anyone. In the end they returned to their ships, loaded with the game which they had discovered, and described the city and the lie of the land to their comrades. They suggested to their leader that he should go to the temple and that, when he had offered sacrifices, he should inquire

of the deity of the place what land she would grant them as a safe
and permanent dwelling-place. By the common consent of all,
Brutus took with him the Augur Gero and twelve of the older men
and set out for the temple, carrying everything necessary for a
sacrifice. When they reached the place, they wrapped fillets round
their brows and, according to the age-old rite, they set up three
sacrificial hearths to the three gods: to Jupiter, that is, to Mercury
and to Diana. To each in turn they poured a libation. Brutus stood
before the altar of the goddess, holding in his right hand a vessel
full of sacrificial wine mixed with the blood of a white hind, and
with his face upturned towards the statue of the godhead he broke
the silence with these words: 'O powerful goddess, terror of the
forest glades, yet hope of the wild woodlands, you who have the
power to go in orbit through the airy heavens and the halls of hell,
pronounce a judgement which concerns the earth. Tell me which
lands you wish us to inhabit. Tell me of a safe dwelling-place where
I am to worship you down the ages, and where, to the chanting of
maidens, I shall dedicate temples to you.' This he said nine times;
four times he proceeded round the altar, pouring the wine which he
held upon the sacrificial hearth; then he lay down upon the skin
of a hind which he had stretched before the altar. Having sought for
slumber, he at length fell asleep. It was then about the third hour
of the night, when mortal beings succumb to the sweetest rest. It
seemed to him that the goddess stood before him and spoke these
words to him: 'Brutus, beyond the setting of the sun, past the
realms of Gaul, there lies an island in the sea, once occupied by
giants. Now it is empty and ready for your folk. Down the years
this will prove an abode suited to you and to your people; and for
your descendants it will be a second Troy. A race of kings will be
born there from your stock and the round circle of the whole earth
will be subject to them.'

When he awoke from this vision, the leader remained in doubt
as to whether it had been a dream which he had experienced or
whether the living goddess really had prophesied the land to which

he should travel. In the end he called his comrades together and
told them in full detail what had happened to him in his sleep.
They were delighted and advised him to turn back to the ships and
to travel westwards under full sail in search of what the goddess
had promised them, while the wind still blew fair. Without wasting
time they turned back to their friends and put to sea.

After ploughing through the waves in a crossing which lasted
thirty days, they arrived in Africa, still not knowing in which
direction they should steer their ships. Then they came to the
Altars of the Philistines and to the Salt-pan Lake, and from there
they sailed on between Russicada and the mountains of Zarec. In
this spot they suffered great danger from an attack by pirates, but
they beat it off and became the richer by booty and plunder.

[i.12]   After this they passed the River Malve and landed in Mauretania.
There they were harassed by lack of food and drink; they therefore
disembarked from their ships, split up into groups and ravaged
the country from end to end. Once they had re-victualled they
sailed for the Pillars of Hercules, and there those deep-sea monsters
called the Sirens made their appearance and nearly sank their ships
as they moved forward. They escaped, however, and came upon
four generations born to exiles from Troy, generations which had
accompanied Antenor in his flight. Their leader was called Corineus,
a sober-minded man, wise in counsel, yet of great courage and
audacity. If he were to come up against a giant he would overthrow
him as easily as if he were fighting against a mere boy. As soon as
they had realized that his stock was of such high antiquity, they
took him into alliance with them straight away, together with the
people over whom he ruled. Later Cornwall was called after the
name of this leader. In every battle he was of more help to Brutus
than anyone else.

Next they came to Aquitaine, where they entered the estuary
of the Loire and cast anchor. They remained there for seven days
and explored the lie of the land. At that time Goffar the Pict ruled
in Aquitaine and was King of that country. When he learned that

a foreign people with a huge fleet had landed within the confines of his kingdom, he sent messengers to them to ask whether they brought peace or war. While the messengers were still on their way to the fleet, they met Corineus, who had just landed with two hundred men to hunt for game under the woodland trees. The messengers immediately accosted him and asked by whose permission he had entered the King's forest to kill his animals, seeing that it had been decreed from ancient time that no one should hunt there without that ruler's order. Corineus answered them that permission was completely unnecessary. Then one of their number called Himbert rushed forward, drew his bow and aimed an arrow at him. Corineus dodged the arrow, charged at Himbert and broke his head in pieces with the bow which he was carrying. Thereupon the others fled, escaping with some difficulty from the hands of Corineus, and reported the death of their comrade to Goffar.

The leader of the Poitevins, who was saddened by the news, collected a huge army together, so that he could take vengeance on them for the death of his messenger. When Brutus heard of Goffar's coming, he put his ships in a state of defence, ordering all the women and children to remain on board and then set out himself to meet the enemy with his entire force of vigorous young men.

The battle began and the fighting was fierce on both sides. When they had spent a great part of the day in slaughtering each other, Corineus felt ashamed that the Aquitanians should be so steadfast in their resistance and that the Trojans should not be able to press on to victory. He took fresh heart, called his own men over to the right of the battle, arranged them in fighting formation and charged headlong at the enemy. With his troops in close order he broke through their ranks in front and went on killing the enemy until he had worked right through their force and compelled them all to flee. He lost his sword, but by good luck he had a battle-axe: and anything he struck with this he cut in two from top to bottom. Brutus was greatly impressed by his boldness and courage. So were his comrades, and so indeed were the enemy. Corineus brandished his battle-axe among the retreating battalions and added not a little to their terror by shouting: 'Where are you making for, you cowards? Where are you running to, you slackers? Turn back! Turn back, I say, and do battle with Corineus! Shame on you! You are so many thousands and yet you run away from me who am one! Take at least this comfort in your flight: that it is I, Corineus, who am after you – I who often drive in confusion before me the giants of Etruria, thrusting them down to hell three or four at a time.'

[i.13]   At these words of his one of the Poitevin leaders called Suhard did turn back and charged at him with three hundred fighting-men. Corineus received on his outstretched shield the blow which Suhard dealt him. Then he remembered the battle-axe which he was holding. He swung it up in the air, struck Suhard on the crest of his helmet and at the spot where he made contact split him in two halves from top to bottom. Then he rushed at the others, twirling his battle-axe, and went on causing the same destruction. Up and down he ran, avoiding none of the blows which were dealt him and never pausing in his destruction of the enemy. From one he severed an arm and a hand, from another he carved the very shoulders from his body. At a single blow he struck off one man's head, while from another he cut away the legs. He was the one whom they all attacked, and he in his turn took them all on. Brutus was filled with emotion when he saw this, and he hurried forward with one of his companies to bring assistance to Corineus. A great bellow of shouting arose between the two peoples, many blows were struck and terrible slaughter was inflicted on each side.

This could not go on much longer. The Trojans were victorious: they drove King Goffar and his Poitevins backward in flight. Goffar managed to get away: he fled to the other regions of Gaul to seek help from his kinsmen and friends. At that time there were in Gaul twelve kings of equal rank, under whose dominion the whole country was ruled. They received Goffar sympathetically and promised with one accord that they would drive this foreign people out of the lands of Aquitaine.

Brutus was overjoyed at this victory. He enriched his comrades [i.14] with the spoils of those whom they had killed, marshalled them once more into companies and then marched through the country in this order, for it was his intention to sack it completely and to load his ships with all its goods. He therefore burned the cities far and wide, heaping up fire upon fire. He carried away the goods which he had looted in these cities and he even ravaged the open fields. He wrought pitiable slaughter on both townsfolk and peasantry, for his plan was to exterminate this unhappy race down to the last man. However, when Brutus had inflicted this devastation on almost all the regions of Aquitaine, he came to the place which is now called Tours, the city which, as Homer testifies, he himself afterwards founded. When he was examining places suitable for a refuge, it was here that he measured out a camp into which he might retreat if need should arise. He was driven to this by the fear caused by the arrival of Goffar, who had marched to this same neighbourhood with the kings and princes of Gaul and a huge force of armed men, so that he might do battle with Brutus. When his own camp was completely finished, Brutus waited there two days for Goffar, relying on his own prudence and the courage of the young men whom he had under command.

When Goffar learned of the presence of the Trojans in this [i.15] neighbourhood, he advanced by forced marches through the day and the night until he came close enough to see the camp of Brutus. He gazed at it grimly, and then with a sardonic smile burst forth with these words: 'How sad my destiny is! These ignoble exiles have pitched their camp in my kingdom. Arm yourselves, men! Arm yourselves, and charge through their serried ranks! In a short time we shall seize hold of these weaklings as if they were sheep and carry them captive through our kingdom.' All the men whom he had brought with him immediately armed themselves and marched, drawn up as they were in twelve columns, towards the enemy. The reaction of Brutus to this was far from that of a weakling. He placed his companies in position, and prudently instructed his troops as to what they were to do, how they should advance and how hold their ground. The result was that when they joined battle the Trojans at first had the upper hand and inflicted fearful slaughter on the enemy. Some two thousand of the Gauls fell dead, and in their terror the remainder were on the point of running away; but victory has the habit of appearing on the side where the number of men is the greater. Thus, although they had been driven back at first, the Gauls later on re-formed and attacked the Trojans on all sides, for they were three times as numerous as the others. The Gauls caused great slaughter among the Trojans and forced them to withdraw into their camp. When this victory was won, the Gauls besieged the Trojans in their camp, firm in the conviction that they themselves would never withdraw until the enemy whom they had surrounded had either offered their necks to be encircled with chains or had been cruelly tortured to death after suffering for a long time from hunger.

Meanwhile, on the next evening, Corineus had a conference with Brutus, saying that he wanted to make his way out that same night along certain little-known trackways and conceal himself until daybreak in a neighbouring wood. Brutus should leave the camp at first light and, while he was engaging the enemy, Corineus should attack from the rear and, by charging at them, bring about the overthrow of the Gauls.

This plan of Corineus' was approved by Brutus. Corineus emerged with all caution, as he had proposed, accompanied by three thousand men, and made his way into the depths of the woods. When the next day dawned, Brutus arranged his troops in battalions, opened up the gates of the camp and marched forth to battle. The Gauls immediately attacked him. They drew up their own line of battle and fought with Brutus hand to hand. Each side inflicted wounds on the other, and in both of the two armies many thousands of men immediately fell dead, for no one spared his opponent. A certain Trojan called Turnus, who was a nephew of Brutus, was there, and, apart from Corineus, no one was stronger or bolder than he. He slew six hundred men himself with his own sword, but he was killed before his time by the Gauls, who made a sudden attack on him. The city of Tours, which we have already mentioned, took its name from Turnus, for he was buried there.[1] While the troops on either side were fighting bitterly, Corineus unexpectedly attacked the enemy from the rear, coming at full speed. Thereupon the other Trojans pressed on with all the more courage and renewed the attack from the front in their effort to complete the slaughter. The Gauls were terrified as much as anything by the din raised by Corineus as he charged them from their rear, for they thought that more men had come than were really there. They left the field at full speed and the Trojans pursued them with their blows. In their pursuit the Trojans continued to slaughter the Gauls, and they did not abandon the bloodshed until they had gained victory.

Although this signal triumph brought him great joy, Brutus was nevertheless filled with anxiety, for the number of his men became smaller every day, while that of the Gauls was constantly increasing. Brutus was in doubt as to whether he could oppose the Gauls any longer; and he finally chose to return to his ships in the full glory of his victory while the greater part of his comrades were still safe, and then to seek out the island which divine prophecy had promised would be his. Nothing else was done. With the approval of his men Brutus returned to his fleet. He loaded his ships with all the riches which he had acquired and then went on board. So, with the winds behind him, he sought the promised island, and came ashore at Totnes.

1. The germ of this idea comes from Nennius, *Historia Brittonum*, §10, where we read of Brutus that 'he was exiled on account of the death of Turnus, slain by Eneas. He then went among the Gauls, and built a city of the Turones, called Turnis'.

[i.16]   At this time the island of Britain was called Albion. It was uninhabited except for a few giants. It was, however, most attractive,
because of the delightful situation of its various regions, its forests
and the great number of its rivers, which teemed with fish; and it
filled Brutus and his comrades with a great desire to live there.
When they had explored the different districts, they drove the
giants whom they had discovered into the caves in the mountains.
With the approval of their leader they divided the land among
themselves. They began to cultivate the fields and to build houses,
so that in a short time you would have thought that the land had
always been inhabited.

Brutus then called the island Britain from his own name, and
his companions he called Britons. His intention was that his memory
should be perpetuated by the derivation of the name. A little later
the language of the people, which had up to then been known as
Trojan or Crooked Greek, was called British, for the same reason.

Corineus, however, following in this the example of his leader,
called the region of the kingdom which had fallen to his share
Cornwall, after the manner of his own name, and the people who
lived there he called Cornishmen. Although he might have
chosen his own estates before all the others who had come there,
he preferred the region which is now called Cornwall, either for
its being the *cornu* or horn of Britain, or through a corruption of
his own name.

Corineus experienced great pleasure from wrestling with the
giants, of whom there were far more there than in any of the districts which had been distributed among his comrades. Among the
others there was a particularly repulsive one, called Gogmagog,
who was twelve feet tall. He was so strong that, once he had given
it a shake, he could tear up an oak-tree as though it were a hazel
wand. Once, when Brutus was celebrating a day dedicated to the
gods in the port where he had landed, this creature, along with
twenty other giants, attacked him and killed a great number of the
Britons. However, the Britons finally gathered together from

round and about and overcame the giants and slew them all,
except Gogmagog. Brutus ordered that he alone should be kept
alive, for he wanted to see a wrestling-match between this giant
and Corineus, who enjoyed beyond all reason matching himself
against such monsters. Corineus was delighted by this. He girded
himself up, threw off his armour and challenged Gogmagog to a
wrestling-match. The contest began. Corineus moved in, so did
the giant; each of them caught the other in a hold by twining his
arms round him, and the air vibrated with their panting breath.
Gogmagog gripped Corineus with all his might and broke three
of his ribs, two on the right side and one on the left. Corineus then
summoned all his strength, for he was infuriated by what had
happened. He heaved Gogmagog up on to his shoulders, and running as fast as he could under the weight, he hurried off to the
nearby coast.[1] He clambered up to the top of a mighty cliff, shook
himself free and hurled this deadly monster, whom he was carrying
on his shoulders, far out into the sea. The giant fell on to a sharp
reef of rocks, where he was dashed into a thousand fragments and
stained the waters with his blood. The place took its name from the
fact that the giant was hurled down there and it is called Gogmagog's
Leap to this day.

Once he had divided up his kingdom, Brutus decided to build [i.17]
a capital. In pursuit of this plan, he visited every part of the land in
search of a suitable spot. He came at length to the River Thames,
walked up and down its banks and so chose a site suited to his
purpose. There then he built his city and called it Troia Nova. It

    1. Totnes, on the River Dart, once a walled town, with a heavily-forti-
fied castle since the Conquest, was already an important port in Saxon times
and saw much trade with Brittany during the Middle Ages. The wharves
can still be used by vessels of up to 200 tons. It was there that Brutus had
landed. Later on in the *Historia*, Vespasian, Constantine II, Aurelius Ambrosius and Utherpendragon all came ashore at Totnes, and so did the
marauding Saxons. Totnes is, of course, some nine miles up river and
Corineus had a long way to run with his burden. Geoffrey cannot have
known this; but his distances are so often unrealistic.

was known by this name for long ages after, but finally by a corruption of the word it came to be called Trinovantum.[1]

After Lud, the brother of Cassivelaunus, who fought with Julius Caesar, had seized command of the government of the kingdom, he surrounded the capital with lofty walls and with towers built with extraordinary skill, and he ordered it to be called Kaerlud, or Lud's City, from his own name. As a result a great quarrel arose later on between him and his brother Nennius, who was annoyed that he should want to do away with the name of Troy in his own country. However, since Gildas the historian has dealt with this quarrel at sufficient length, I prefer to omit it, for I do not wish to appear to be spoiling by my homelier style what so distinguished a writer has set out with so much eloquence.

[i.18]   When the above-named leader Brutus had built the city about which I have told you, he presented it to the citizens by right of inheritance, and gave them a code of laws by which they might live peacefully together. At that time the priest Eli[2] was ruling in Judea and the Ark of the Covenant was captured by the Philistines. The sons of Hector reigned in Troy, for the descendants of Antenor had been driven out. In Italy reigned Aeneas Silvius, son of Aeneas and uncle of Brutus, the third of the Latin Kings.

1. Sir Mortimer Wheeler refers to the founding of London by Brutus, in London Museum Catalogues, No. 3, *London in Roman Times*, 1930, pp. 13–14. He has little sympathy for Geoffrey's account, or his etymology, as, indeed, was to be expected. He gives a 'quotation' from the *History* which Geoffrey never wrote.

2. This is taken direct from Nennius, *Historia Brittonum*, §11: '... Brutus, who governed Britain at the time Eli the high priest judged Israel, and when the ark of the covenant was taken by a foreign people'.

Part Two

BEFORE THE ROMANS CAME

IN the meantime Brutus had consummated his marriage with his [ii.1]
wife Ignoge. By her he had three sons called Locrinus, Kamber and
Albanactus, all of whom were to become famous. When their
father finally died, in the twenty-third year after his landing, these
three sons buried him inside the walls of the town which he had
founded. They divided the kingdom of Britain between them in
such a way that each succeeded to Brutus in one particular district.
Locrinus, who was the first-born, inherited the part of the island
which was afterwards called Loegria after him. Kamber received
the region which is on the further bank of the River Severn, the
part which is now known as Wales but which was for a long time
after his death called Kambria from his name. As a result the people
of that country still call themselves Kambri today in the Welsh
tongue. Albanactus, the youngest, took the region which is nowa-
days called Scotland in our language. He called it Albany, after his
own name.

Eventually, when these three had reigned in peace and harmony
for a long time, Humber, the King of the Huns, landed in Albany.
He met Albanactus in battle, killed him and forced the people of
his country to flee to Locrinus.

As soon as Locrinus heard the news, he persuaded his brother [ii.2]
Kamber to join him in an alliance. Locrinus called up all the young
men of his own country and went out to meet the King of the Huns
somewhere near the river which is now called the Humber. When
the two forces made contact, Locrinus forced Humber to flee.
Humber retreated as far as the river and was then drowned beneath
its waters, giving his name to the stream. Once he had gained this
victory, Locrinus distributed the spoils of the enemy among his
allies, keeping back nothing for himself except the gold and silver

which he found on board their ships. He also reserved for himself three young women of striking beauty. The first of these girls was the daughter of the King of Germany. Humber had seized this girl along with the other two at a time when he was sacking her home-land. Her name was Estrildis and she was of such beauty that it would be difficult to find a young woman worthy to be compared with her. No precious ivory, no recently fallen snow, no lilies even could surpass the whiteness of her skin. Locrinus was overcome with passion for her. He was determined to make love with her, and he even went so far as to suggest that she might marry him.

When he discovered this, Corineus was greatly annoyed, for Locrinus had promised that he would marry Corineus' own daughter.

[ii.3]   Corineus therefore went to the King and addressed him as follows, brandishing his battle-axe as he did so: 'These then, Locrinus, are the rewards you offer me in exchange for all the wounds which I have received through my allegiance to your father, at the time when he was waging war with unknown peoples? My daughter is to be passed over and you are to demean yourself to the point where you will be prepared to marry some barbarian woman or other! You will not do this unpunished – as long, that is, as strength is left to this right hand of mine which has torn the joy of living from many a giant up and down the Tyrrhenian shores!' He bellowed out these words again and again, brandishing his battle-axe as if he was going to strike Locrinus.

Then the friends of the two men came between them. These friends forced Locrinus to carry out what he had promised and Corineus was pacified.

[ii.4]   Locrinus duly married Corineus' daughter, whose name was Gwendolen. For all that, he could not forget the love which he felt for Estrildis. He had a cave dug beneath the town of Trinovantum and there he shut Estrildis up, putting her in the care of his servants with orders that she should be treated with all honour, for despite everything that had happened he was determined to make love with her in secret. Locrinus was so consumed with fear of Corineus that he did not dare to entertain Estrildis openly. Therefore he concealed her, as has been explained. He visited her for seven whole years, without anyone being the wiser, except those who were the deepest in his confidence. Whenever he went to Estrildis he gave it out that he intended to make some secret sacrifice to his gods; and he managed to persuade others to believe this, although it was not true. In the end Estrildis became pregnant and gave birth to an extraordinarily beautiful daughter whom she called Habren. Gwendolen was pregnant, too, and she bore a son who was given the name Maddan. This Maddan was handed over to his grandfather Corineus to be taught his early lessons.

Some time later, when Corineus was at long last dead, Locrinus [ii.5] deserted Gwendolen and took Estrildis as his Queen. Gwendolen was most indignant at this. She went off to Cornwall and there she assembled all the young men of that region and began to harass Locrinus with border forays. At last, when both sides had gathered an army together, they joined battle near the River Stour.[1] There Locrinus was struck by an arrow and so departed from the joys of this life. With Locrinus out of the way, Gwendolen took over the government of the kingdom, behaving in the same extravagant fashion as her father had done. She ordered Estrildis and her daughter Habren to be thrown into the river which is now called the Severn; and she published an edict throughout the length and breadth of Britain that this river should be called after the girl's name. Gwendolen's intention was that this everlasting honour should be done to Habren because her own husband had been the girl's father. It thus comes about that right down to our own times this river is called Habren in the British language, although by a corruption of speech it is called Sabrina in the other tongue.

1. This is usually identified as the river which 'enters the Severn some ten miles above Worcester' (*Tatlock*, p. 29). In 'Geoffrey of Monmouth, Wace and the Stour', *Modern Language Notes*, LXIX (1954), pp. 237–9, Robert A. Caldwell follows Wace in suggesting the Dorsetshire Stour.

[ii.6]   Gwendolen reigned for fifteen years after the death of Locrinus, who had himself reigned ten years. As soon as she realized that her son Maddan had grown to man's estate, she passed the sceptre of the realm to him, being content herself with the province of Cornwall for the remainder of her life.

At that time the prophet Samuel was reigning in Judea, Aeneas Silvius was still alive and Homer was considered to be a famous rhetorician and poet.

Maddan married and by his wife he became the father of two sons, Mempricius and Malin. He ruled his kingdom in peace and frugality for forty years. When he died, a quarrel over the kingship arose between the sons whom I have mentioned, for each of the two was eager to possess the whole island. Mempricius, who wanted very much to carry out his own plan, called a conference with Malin, giving the impression that he was about to come to some agreement with him. Mempricius was, however, eaten up with burning treachery and he killed his brother in the presence of the other delegates. He then took over the government of the whole island, exercising so great a tyranny over the people that he encompassed the death of almost all the more distinguished men. He hated all his own family; and, by main force or by treachery, he did away with anyone who he feared might succeed him in the kingship. What is more, he deserted his own wife, by whom he had become the father of a much-admired young man called Ebraucus, and he abandoned himself to the vice of sodomy, preferring unnatural lust to normal passion. At last, in the twentieth year of his reign, when he was out on a hunting expedition, he became separated from his companions in a certain valley. There he was surrounded by ravening wolves and eaten up in miserable circumstances.

At that time Saul was reigning in Judea and Eurysthenes in Sparta.

[ii.7]   After the death of Mempricius, his son Ebraucus, who was very tall and a man of remarkable strength, took over the government of Britain and held it for thirty-nine years. He was the first after

Brutus to sail a fleet to the shores of Gaul. He made war upon the provinces of the Gauls, slaughtering their menfolk and sacking their cities. By the time he came back victorious he was enriched with a vast booty of gold and silver. At a later date he founded a city on the farther side of the Humber, which city he called Kaerebrauc after himself, that is to say the City of Ebraucus.

At that time King David was reigning in Judea and Silvius Latinus was King in Italy. In Israel, Gad, Nathan and Asaph were the prophets.

Ebraucus also founded the city of Alclud over in Albany; and the castle of Mount Agned, which is now called the Maidens' Castle and the Dolorous Mountain.

What is more, by the twenty wives which he had, he was the [*ii.8*] father of twenty sons and of thirty daughters. For forty years he ruled over the kingdom of Britain with great firmness. The names of his sons were as follows: Brutus Greenshield, Margodud, Sisillius, Regin, Morvid, Bladud, Lagon, Bodloan, Kincar, Spaden, Gaul, Dardan, Eldad, Ivor, Cangu, Hector, Kerin, Rud, Assaracus and Buel. The names of his daughters were: Gloigin, Ignogin, Oudas, Guenlian, Guardid, Angarad, Guenlodoe, Tangustel, Gorgon, Medlan, Methahel, Ourar, Mailure, Kambreda, Ragan, Gael, Ecub, Nest, Chein, Stadudud, Cladus, Ebrein, Blangan, Aballac, Angoes, Galaes (the most beautiful of the young women who lived at that time in Britain or in Gaul), Edra, Anor, Stadiald and Egron. The father sent all his daughters to Italy to Silvius Alba, who was king after Silvius Latinus. There they were married to the more noble of the Trojans whose offers of marriage were being refused by the Latin and Sabine women. With their brother Assaracus as leader the sons took a fleet to Germany. There, with the help of Silvius Alba, they subdued the people and seized the kingdom.

The Brutus who was surnamed Greenshield stayed behind, how- [*ii.9*] ever, with his father. It was he who took over the government of the kingdom after Ebraucus. He reigned for twelve years.

Leil, the son of Greenshield, a great lover of peace and justice, succeeded him. Leil took advantage of the prosperity of his reign to build a town in the northern part of Britain which he called Kaerleil after himself.

This was the time when Solomon began to build the Temple of the Lord in Jerusalem and when the Queen of Sheba came to listen to his wisdom. About the same time Silvius Epitus succeeded his father Alba in the kingship of Rome.

Leil lived on for twenty-five years after mounting the throne, but towards the end he ruled the kingdom feebly. As a result of Leil's prolonged inactivity a civil war suddenly broke out in the realm. Leil's son Rud Hud Hudibras reigned for thirty-nine years after him. Once the civil war was over, Hudibras restored peace once more to the people. It was he who built Kaerreint: that is, Canterbury. He also founded Kaerguenit, or Winchester, and the fortress of Paladur, which is now called Shaftesbury. There the Eagle spoke, while the wall was being built. If I believed its Sayings to be true, I would not hesitate to hand them down to history with my other material.

At that time Capys, the son of Epitus, was reigning in Rome; and Haggai, Amos, Joel and Azariah were making their prophecies. [ii.10] Hudibras' son Bladud finally succeeded him and ruled the kingdom for twenty years. It was he who built the town of Kaerbadum, which is now called Bath, and who constructed the hot baths there which are so suited to the needs of mortal men. He chose the goddess Minerva as the tutelary deity of the baths. In her temple he lit fires which never went out and which never fell away into ash, for the moment that they began to die down they were turned into balls of stone.[1]

At that time Elijah prayed that it should not rain upon the earth, so that for three years and six months no rain fell.

1. Geoffrey makes no mention of the legend that Bladud was a leper whose initial enthusiasm for Bath arose from the fact that the water and the impregnated mud there had cured him. Cp. R. A. L. Smith, *Bath*, 3rd ed., 1948, London, pp. 11–12.

Bladud was a most ingenious man who encouraged necromancy throughout the kingdom of Britain. He pressed on with his experiments and finally constructed a pair of wings for himself and tried to fly through the upper air. He came down on top of the Temple of Apollo in the town of Trinovantum and was dashed into countless fragments.

After Bladud had met his fate in this way, his son Leir was [ii.11] raised to the kingship. Leir ruled the country for sixty years. It was he who built the city on the River Soar which is called Kaerleir after him in the British tongue, its Saxon name being Leicester. He had no male issue, but three daughters were born to him. Their names were Goneril, Regan and Cordelia. Their father was very fond indeed of them and above all he loved Cordelia, his youngest daughter. When he felt himself becoming a really old man, he made up his mind to divide his kingdom between these three daughters of his and to marry them to husbands whom he considered to be suited to them and capable of ruling the kingdom along with them. In an attempt to discover which of the three was most worthy of inheriting the larger part of his realm, he went to them each in turn to ask which of them loved him most. When he questioned Goneril, she immediately called the gods of heaven to witness that he was dearer to her than the very soul which dwelt within her body. 'My dearest daughter,' answered Leir, 'since you have preferred me, even in my old age, to your own life, I will marry you to any young man you choose and I will give you a third part of the kingdom of Britain.' Regan, the second daughter, was determined to wheedle her own way into Leir's favour, just as her sister had done. It was her turn next to be questioned. She swore that her only possible answer could be that she loved Leir more than any other living person. Her credulous father thereupon decided to marry Regan with the same pomp that he had promised to his eldest child and to give her at the same time another third of his kingdom.

When she heard how Leir had been deceived by the blandishments of her two older sisters, Cordelia, the King's youngest daughter, made up her mind to test him by giving quite a different answer. 'My father,' she said, 'can there really exist a daughter who maintains that the love she bears her own father is more than what is due to him as a father? I cannot believe that there can be a daughter who would dare to confess to such a thing, unless, indeed, she were trying to conceal the truth by joking about it. Assuredly, for my part, I have always loved you as my father, and at this moment I feel no lessening of my affection for you. If you are determined to wring more than this out of me, then I will tell you how much I love you and so put an end to your inquiry. You are worth just as much as you possess, and that is the measure of my own love for you.'

Cordelia's father, who was angry because she had spoken in this way and apparently really meant what she had said, immediately lost his temper with her. He wasted no time in showing what his reaction was going to be. 'Since you have so much scorn for me your old father that you refuse to love me as much as your sisters do, then I in my turn will scorn you. You shall never share my kingdom with your sisters. All the same, you are still my daughter. I do not say that I shall be unwilling to marry you off to some foreigner, if fate should offer you such a husband; but this I do make clear to you, that I shall never attempt to marry you with the same honour as your sisters. Until this moment I have loved you more than the others. Now, indeed, you say that you love me less than they do.

With the advice of the nobles of his realm he proceeded there and then to give the older girls in marriage to two of his Dukes, Cornwall and Albany, and to share between them one half of the island for as long as he, Leir, should live. He agreed that after his own death they should inherit the entire kingdom of Britain.

Soon afterwards it happened that Aganippus, King of the Franks, heard Cordelia's beauty being greatly praised. He immediately sent messengers to Leir to ask if the King would let Cordelia go back with them so that he could marry her. Cordelia's father was still as angry as ever. He said that he would willingly give her to

Aganippus, but that there would be no land or dowry to go with her; for he had shared his kingdom, with all his gold and silver, between her two sisters Goneril and Regan. Aganippus' love for the girl was not damped when he received this answer. He sent a second time to King Leir to say that he had plenty of gold and silver himself, and other possessions, too, for he ruled over a third of Gaul. He wanted the girl for one reason only, so that he might have children by her. The bargain was struck. Cordelia was dispatched to Gaul and there she was married to Aganippus.

Some long time after, when King Leir began to grow weak with [ii.12] old age, the Dukes whom I have mentioned, with whom, as the husbands of his daughters, he had shared Britain, rebelled against him. They took the remainder of his kingdom from him and with it the royal power which up to then he had wielded manfully and in all glory. There was no direct break between them, however, for Maglaurus, Duke of Albany, one of Leir's sons-in-law, agreed to maintain him, together with one hundred and forty knights, so that he should not end his days alone and in obscurity.

By the time Leir had stayed two years with his son-in-law, his daughter Goneril made up her mind that he had too many attendants, especially as they kept wrangling with her own servants because they were not offered more plentiful rations each month. Goneril duly spoke to her husband about it. Then she ordered her father to content himself with the service of thirty soldiers and to dismiss the others whom he had with him. Leir was infuriated by this. He left Maglaurus and went off to Henwinus, the Duke of Cornwall, to whom he had married Regan, his second daughter. Leir was received honourably by the Duke, but a year had not passed before a quarrel arose between the two households. Regan was annoyed by this and she ordered her father to dismiss all his retainers except five who should remain to do him service. Thereupon Leir, who was greatly aggrieved by what had happened, went back again to his eldest daughter, thinking that she might take pity on him and let him stay with his full retinue. Goneril, however, had never recovered from her first burst of indignation. She now swore by all the gods in heaven that Leir should not lodge with her at all unless he contented himself with a single soldier-attendant and dismissed all the others. She upbraided her father for wanting to go about with such a huge retinue now that he was an old man with no possessions at all. She refused steadfastly to give way to his wish. For his part he had to obey her, and so the other attendants were dismissed and he was left with a single soldier.

As he sat thinking about his former glories, Leir developed such a loathing for the misery to which he had been reduced that he began to wonder whether he would not be better off with his youngest daughter across the sea. He had an unpleasant feeling that she would not be willing to do anything at all for him, seeing that he had given her away so shamefully, as I have already told you. For all that, he could not bear his poverty-stricken existence any longer and he set off across the sea to the lands of Gaul.

As he made the crossing, he observed that he was held third in honour among the princes who were on the boat. He burst into tears and sobbed aloud. 'Oh, you Fates,' he cried, 'so constant in your own sequences, you who in some fixed course steadfastly follow your own preordained journey, why did you ever raise me up to happiness only to snatch it away from me again? It is even more miserable to sit thinking of some past success than to bear the burden of subsequent failure. Indeed, the memory of the time when, attended by so many hundred thousand fighting-men, I used to batter down the walls of cities and to lay waste the provinces of my enemies saddens me more than the calamity of my own present distress, although it has encouraged those who once grovelled beneath my feet to abandon me in my weakness. Oh, spiteful Fortune! Will the moment never come when I can take vengeance upon those who have deserted me in my final poverty? Oh Cordelia, my daughter! How true were the words you spoke to me when I asked you how much you loved me! You said: "You are worth as much as you possess, and that is the measure of my own love for you." As long, then, as I had something to give, so long did I seem worth while to the other two, for it was my gifts that they cared for, not me myself. At times they were affectionate towards me, it is true, but they loved my presents more. Now that the gifts have ceased, these two have disappeared as well. How shall I dare to ask favours of you, the dearest of my daughters – I who, in my anger at those very words of yours which I have just quoted, decided to marry you off less honourably than I did your sisters? Yet, after all the kindnesses which I have done them, they are content to see me as an outcast and a beggar.'

At last Leir landed. He kept muttering these things to himself and many others like them as he travelled to Karitia, where his daughter was. He waited outside the city and sent a messenger to Cordelia to tell her into what poverty he had fallen. It was simply because he had nothing to eat and nothing with which to clothe himself that he had come to seek her compassion. Cordelia was greatly moved by what she heard and she wept bitterly. She asked how many armed attendants Leir had with him. The messenger replied that he had no one, except a certain knight who was waiting with him outside the city. Cordelia then took as much gold and silver as was necessary and gave it to the messenger, telling him to accompany her father to some other city and to bathe him, dress him and nurse him there, giving it out that he was ill. Cordelia also commanded that Leir should take into his retinue forty properly-equipped and fully-armed knights and that only when this was done should he announce his arrival to King Aganippus and his own daughter. The messenger went back immediately. He led King Leir off to another city and hid him there while he was doing all the things which Cordelia had ordered.

As soon as Leir was dressed in royal robes, equipped with royal [ii.13] insignia and accompanied by a household, he announced to Aganippus and his own daughter that he had been expelled from the realm of Britain by his own sons-in-law and that he had come to them so that he might recover his kingdom. Accompanied by their counsellors and noblemen, Aganippus and Cordelia came out to meet him. They received him honourably and they granted him the rank which he held in his own country until such time as they should have restored him to his former dignity.

[ii.14] Meanwhile Aganippus sent messengers throughout the whole of Gaul to summon all the men there who could bear arms, so that with their help he might endeavour to restore the kingship of Britain to his father-in-law Leir. When this was done, Leir marched at the head of the assembled army, taking his daughter with him. He fought with his sons-in-law and beat them, thus bringing them all under his dominion again.

Three years later Leir died; and Aganippus, King of the Franks, died too. As a result Leir's daughter Cordelia inherited the government of the kingdom of Britain. She buried her father in a certain underground chamber which she had ordered to be dug beneath the River Soar, some way downstream from Leicester. This underground chamber was dedicated to the two-faced Janus: and when the feast-day of the god came round, all the craftsmen in the town used to perform there the first act of labour in whatever enterprise they were planning to undertake during the coming year.

[ii.15] When Cordelia had ruled the kingdom peacefully for a period of five years, Marganus and Cunedagius began to cause her trouble. These were the sons of her two sisters who had been married to the Dukes Maglaurus and Henwinus. They were both young men known for their remarkable courage. Maglaurus was the father of Marganus, the first of the two; and Henwinus was the father of the second, Cunedagius. When, after the death of their fathers, these two had succeeded them in their dukedoms, they became indignant at the fact that Britain was subjected to the rule of a woman. They therefore assembled their armies and rose in rebellion against the Queen. They refused to stop their outrages; and in the end they laid waste to a number of provinces and met the

Queen herself in a series of pitched battles. In the end she herself
was captured and put in prison. There she grieved more and more
over the loss of her kingdom and eventually she killed herself. As a
result the two young men seized the island. That region which
extends beyond the Humber in the direction of Caithness submitted to the rule of Marganus; the other part which stretches
towards the setting sun south of the river was put under Cunedagius.

Two years later certain people who were tainted with subversive
ideas came to Marganus. They started to encourage him to make
trouble, telling him that it was a shame and a disgrace that he, who
was the elder, should not rule over the whole island. Marganus was
stirred up by this grievance and by others of a like nature. He led
his army through the lands of Cunedagius and began to set light
to one place after another. In this way a quarrel sprang up between
the two; and Cunedagius marched out to meet Marganus with all
his own army. When the two met in battle the slaughter which
Cunedagius inflicted was considerable and he drove Marganus in
flight before him. Cunedagius pursued Marganus as the latter fled
from province to province; and in the end he caught up with his
cousin in a remote district in Wales. There Marganus was killed
and to this day the place is called Margon by the country folk from
his name. Once he had won this victory, Cunedagius took over the
kingship of the whole island and ruled it in great glory for thirty-
three years.

At that time Isaiah was making his prophecies; and on the
eleventh day after the Kalends of May Rome was founded by the
twin brothers Remus and Romulus.[1]

After the death of Cunedagius, his son Rivallo succeeded him, a [ii.16]
peaceful, prosperous young man who ruled the kingdom frugally.
In his time it rained blood for three days and men died from the
flies which swarmed. Rivallo's son Gurgustius succeeded him.

1. *Remus and Romulus*. The text has '*a geminis fratribus Remo et Remulo*'.
Geoffrey has already twice mentioned Rome as being in existence, on p.
80.

Sisillius came after Gurgustius, then Jago the nephew of Gurgustius, then Kimarcus the son of Sisillius and after him Gorboduc.

Two sons were born to Gorboduc, one called Ferrex and the other Porrex. When their father had become senile, a quarrel arose between these two as to which should succeed the old man on the throne. Porrex was the more grasping of the two and he planned to kill his brother by setting an ambush for him. When Ferrex learned this he escaped from his brother by crossing the sea to Gaul. With the support of Suhard, King of the Franks, Ferrex returned and fought with his brother. Ferrex was killed in the battle between them and so too was all the force which had come over with him. Their mother, whose name was Judon, was greatly distressed when she heard of her son's death. She was consumed with hatred for Porrex, for she had loved Ferrex more than him. Judon became so unbalanced by the anguish which the death of Ferrex had caused her that she made up her mind to avenge the death upon his brother Porrex. She chose a time when Porrex was asleep, set upon him with her maid-servants and hacked him to pieces.

As a result of this the people of Britain were for a long time embroiled in civil war; and the island came into the hands of five kings who kept attacking and massacring each other's men in turn.

[ii.17] Some time later a certain young man called Dunvallo Molmutius came into prominence because of his personal courage. The son of Cloten King of Cornwall, he excelled all the other kings of Britain by his good looks and his bravery. Almost as soon as he had succeeded to the kingship of Cornwall after his father's death, he attacked Pinner, King of Loegria, and killed him in pitched battle. As a result Rudaucus, King of Kambria, and Staterius, King of Albany, met to make an alliance with each other. They then led their armies into Dunvallo's territory, destroyed his buildings and killed his peasantry. Dunvallo himself marched to meet them at the head of thirty thousand men and joined battle with them. When a great part of the day had been passed in fighting, Dunvallo found himself still as far as ever from victory. He summoned six hundred

of his boldest young men and ordered them to strip the arms from
those of their enemies who lay dead around them and then to put
those same arms on. He himself cast on one side the protective
clothing which he was wearing and did the same as his men. He
then led the way through the enemy lines, moving his men forward as if they had actually been enemy troops. He reached the
spot where Rudaucus and Staterius were and signalled to his
comrades to attack them. As Dunvallo's men charged forward, the
two Kings were killed and many others with them. Dunvallo
Molmutius then came back with his companions and disarmed, for
he was afraid of being attacked by his own men. He once more put
on his own arms which he had earlier cast aside. He then exhorted
his soldiers to charge at the enemy and attacked them himself with
great ferocity. Almost immediately after this he won the battle,
for his enemy was put to flight and scattered. Now at last Dunvallo
was free to march through the lands of those whom we have listed
as killed. He destroyed their cities and fortresses and forced their
people to accept his own rule. When he had completely subjugated
the entire island, he fashioned for himself a crown of gold and
restored the realm to its earlier status.

It was Dunvallo Molmutius who established among the Britons
the so-called Molmutine Laws which are still famous today among
the English. Included in the other things which Gildas of blessed
memory wrote about him many years later was this: that it was
he who decreed that the temples of the gods and the cities should
be so privileged that anyone who escaped to them as a fugitive or
when accused of some crime must be pardoned by his accuser when
he came out. Dunvallo it was, too, who decreed that the roads
which led to these temples and cities should be included in the same
law and that the ploughs of the peasantry should be inalienable.
During Dunvallo's lifetime no bandits were allowed to draw their
swords and the outrages of robbers came to an abrupt end, for no
one dared to do violence to his fellow. Dunvallo died at last, having
spent forty years in such activities since the day when he took the

crown. He was buried in Trinovantum beside that Temple of Concord which he himself had built as a symbol of his own laws.

[iii.1]   Belinus and Brennius, the two sons of Dunvallo, each of whom was determined to inherit the kingship, now began a great war of attrition against each other. Their object in this struggle was to decide which of the two should be crowned King of the realm. They fought a great number of battles with each other, but at length their friends intervened to make peace between them. These friends decided that the kingdom should be divided between the two of them in such a way that Belinus should be crowned King of the island and hold Loegria, Kambria and Cornwall, he being the elder, for Trojan custom demanded that the highest office offered by the inheritance should go to him. They also decided that Brennius, on the other hand, who was the younger, should be subject to his brother but should rule Northumbria from the Humber as far north as Caithness. A treaty was therefore drawn up to embody these points of agreement and for five years the two of them ruled the country peacefully and justly.

The spirit of discord is, however, perpetually on the watch for a chance to put an end to a state of prosperity. Certain ingenious liars came to Brennius and put the following argument to him. 'How can you be so cowardly,' they asked, 'as to let yourself be domineered over by Belinus, when the fact that you have the same father and mother and the same nobility of birth makes you his exact equal? To this you can add that on the many occasions when Cheulfus, the leader of the Moriani, has tried to gain a foothold in the country, it has been you who have shown in a long series of battles that you could stand up to him and who have driven him back out of your territory. Why do you not break this agreement which does you so little honour? Marry the daughter of Elsingius, King of the Norwegians, and with his help recover your lost dignity.'

When they had corrupted the mind of Brennius with these arguments and with others of a like nature, the young man agreed to do what they suggested. He went off to Norway and married the King's daughter, just as he had been advised by the hangers-on about whom I have told you.

When this came to the ears of his brother Belinus, the latter [*iii.2*] was most indignant that Brennius should have acted against him in this way without any prior consultation. Belinus marched into Northumbria, seized the cities of the people born in those parts and garrisoned them with his own men.

The news of what his brother Belinus had been doing was immediately reported to Brennius. He fitted out a fleet and hurried back towards Britain, bringing with him a vast army of Norwegians. As he sailed on across the sea, expecting no immediate attack and with a favourable wind behind him, he was assailed by Ginchtalacus, King of the Danes, who had followed in his wake. Ginchtalacus was passionately in love with the girl whom Brennius had married. He was so incensed by what had happened that he had prepared a fleet and an army and was now pursuing Brennius as fast as his ships could sail. In the sea-battle which ensued Ginchtalacus seized the ship on which the girl was, threw grappling-irons on board and dragged it away into the middle of his own fleet.

As the two sides joined battle in scattered formation and forced their way through the deep sea, a squall got up and suddenly head winds began to blow. Their ships were dispersed and cast ashore upon different coasts. The Danish King was driven along by the hostile fury of the winds. He ran before them for five days and then he landed with some trepidation on the Northumbrian shore, taking the girl with him. He had no idea to what country this untoward accident had carried him. When the local inhabitants discovered what had happened, they seized the two of them and took them to Belinus, who was on the sea-shore awaiting his brother's arrival. There were three other ships alongside that of Ginchtalacus, one of them belonging to Brennius' fleet. When the new arrivals revealed their identity to King Belinus, he was delighted. Belinus was all the more pleased that this should have

happened to him at a moment when he was so determined to take
vengeance on his brother Brennius.

[iii.3]   A few days passed and then Brennius managed to reassemble his
ships and land on the coast of Albany. When he learned that his
wife and certain of his men had been captured and that his brother
had wrested the kingdom of Northumbria from him during his
absence, Brennius sent messengers to Belinus to demand that his
territory and his bride should both be handed back to him. He
swore that if this were not done he would ravage the whole island
from sea to sea and that, what is more, he would kill his brother if
only the opportunity arose of meeting him on the field of battle.
When Belinus learned this, he flatly refused what was demanded.
He called together the entire military force of the island and advanced into Albany ready to meet Brennius in battle.

As soon as Brennius heard that what he had asked for had been
refused and that his own blood-brother was marching against him
in this way, he went forward to meet Belinus in a forest called
Calaterium, determined to do battle with him there. The two of
them took up their positions in the same open field and divided
their troops into companies, so as to be ready to engage at close
quarters those advancing against them. They spent the greater part
of the day in their conflict, for on both sides the men who were
fighting hand-to-hand were extremely brave. Much blood was shed
on this side and that, and the weapons which they brandished so
lustily inflicted deadly wounds. Those who were wounded where
the battalions met in conflict fell to the ground as if they had been
standing corn cut by the reapers' sickles. In the end the Britons were
victorious. The Norwegians fled to their ships with their lines of
battle slashed to pieces. Belinus followed hard behind them as they
ran, cutting them down without pity. Fifteen thousand men fell
in that battle, and of those left alive not one thousand escaped un-
wounded. With great difficulty Brennius himself managed to escape in a single ship, to which good fortune led him as he ran. He
sailed off to the coast of France; but the others who had come

over with him found hiding-places wherever chance led them.

As soon as he had won this victory Belinus summoned all his [*iii.4*] leaders to York, for he wanted to discuss with them what he should do with the King of the Danes. The King had sent word from his prison that he would be prepared to submit himself and his kingdom, together with the Danes themselves, to Belinus, and to pay tribute every year, if only he were permitted to depart in freedom with the woman he loved. To this he added that he would confirm the pact by an oath and by giving hostages. When the leaders had been assembled and this matter had been put to each of them, they all agreed that Belinus should accede to Ginchtalacus' petition, on the condition laid down. Belinus had no objection. Ginchtalacus was released from prison and he and the woman he loved went back to Denmark.

Now that there remained no one in the whole realm of Britain [*iii.5*] who was prepared to resist Belinus, he took over the kingship of the entire island from sea to sea and ratified the laws which his father had drawn up. He proclaimed that justice should be administered fairly throughout his kingdom. Above all he decreed that cities and the roads leading to cities should have that right of sanctuary which Dunvallo had established. The roads themselves were a bone of contention, for no one knew just where their boundaries should be. The King was very keen to remove every ambiguity from this law. He summoned workmen from all over the island and ordered them to construct a road of stones and mortar which should bisect the island longitudinally from the Cornish sea to the shore of Caithness and should lead in a straight line to each of the cities on the route. He then ordered a second road to be built, running west to east across the kingdom from the town of St Davids on the Demetian Sea over to Southampton and again leading directly to the cities in between. He built two more roads in a diagonal pattern across the island, to lead to the cities for which no provision had been made. Then he consecrated these highways in all honour and dignity, proclaiming it to be an integral part of his code of laws that punishment should be meted out to any person who committed an act of violence upon them. If anyone wishes to know the full details of the highway code established by Belinus, he must read the Molmutine Laws which the historian Gildas translated from Welsh into Latin, and which King Alfred later re-wrote in the English language.

[iii.6]   While Belinus was thus governing his kingdom in peace and tranquillity, his brother Brennius was driven away to the coast of France, as I have just explained above. Brennius was greatly dis-couraged, for he found it hard that he should have been expelled from his own country and have no possibility of ever returning to enjoy the rank which he had lost. He was unable to make up his mind as to what he should do. With a retinue of only twelve knights he visited the Gallic leaders and explained his misfortune to each of them in turn, but he did not succeed in persuading any of them to help him. In the end he came to Segnius, the leader of the Allo-broges, who received him honourably. Brennius stayed some time with Segnius and came to be so friendly with him that no one else in that leader's entourage was as influential as he. Brennius showed such wisdom, both in peace and in war, no matter what was the business in hand, that Segnius came to love him as a father loves a son. Brennius was comely to look at, tall and well-proportioned; and, as you would expect, he was highly skilled at hunting and hawking. He insinuated himself so far into the friendship of Duke Segnius that the latter finally decided that Brennius should marry his only daughter. If, as the years passed, no male heir should be born to Segnius, then the Duke bequeathed to Brennius after his death his own lordship over the Allobroges: this together with the hand of his daughter. If a son were to be born to Segnius, then he promised to help Brennius in his attempt to seize the kingdom of Britain. All this was agreed to not only by Duke Segnius but also by all the leading warriors who bore allegiance to him, so far had Brennius established himself in their esteem. The girl was married to Brennius straight away. The nobles of the country were made

subject to him and the royal throne became his. The year in which
these agreements were come to had not yet run its entire course
when the Duke's last day dawned and death claimed him. Brennius
immediately took steps to put under an even closer obligation to
himself those leaders with whom he had already become so friendly.
He shared among them Duke Segnius' treasure, which had been
hoarded since the time of his remote ancestors. What was even
more attractive to the Allobroges, Brennius was most liberal in
distributing food, and kept open house to everybody.

Once Brennius had made himself popular with all about him, he [iii.7]
pondered in secret how he could take vengeance on his brother
Belinus. He explained his position to the people under his rule;
and they all agreed to follow him, to whichever kingdom he might
choose to lead them. Without wasting time he collected a huge
army together and then made a treaty with the Gauls by which he
was allowed to pass in peace through their provinces on his way
towards Britain. He fitted out a fleet on the Normandy coast, put
out to sea at a moment when the winds were favourable, and so
landed on the island of Britain.

The moment his brother Belinus learned of the coming of
Brennius, he mustered the young men of his entire realm and
marched forth to do battle with the invader. As the battalions on
the two sides stood waiting in orderly array, ready to join battle
the very next instant, the mother of the two leaders, who was still
alive, came hurrying through the serried ranks. Her name was
Tonuuenna and she was passionately keen to see the son on whom
she had not set eyes for so long. With trembling steps she came to
the place where Brennius stood, threw her arms round his neck
and kissed him repeatedly with all a mother's love. She bared her
breasts before him and in a voice broken with sobbing she spoke to
him as follows: 'Remember, my son, remember these breasts
which you once sucked! Remember the womb of your mother,
in which the Creator of all things fashioned you as a man-child
from stuff that was not yet human, bringing you forth into the

world while the birth-pangs tore at her vitals because of you. Remember all the care and anxiety which I endured for your sake: and then grant me my request. Forgive your brother. Curb the anger which is consuming you. You ought to have no ill-feeling for Belinus, for he has done you no harm. As for your pretext that you were expelled from your own country by his doing, if you will only consent to examine the truth of the matter carefully you will find nothing in it that you can possibly call injustice. Indeed, Belinus did not drive you into an exile where something worse still was going to befall you. On the contrary, he forced you to abandon a humble position so that you could raise yourself to a greater one. Once you were his subject and you held only part of this kingdom. Now that you have lost that part, you have made yourself the equal of Belinus, for you have seized the kingship of the Allobroges. What else did Belinus do to you, apart from promoting you from your position as a petty princeling to that of a mighty king? Add to this the fact that the quarrel which arose between the two of you was started by you yourself, not by him: for you were passionately determined to rebel against him and in this you relied upon the help of the King of Norway!'

Brennius was moved by what his weeping mother had said. Calmly and quietly he obeyed her. He took off his helmet and went with her to meet his brother. When Belinus saw him coming with a peaceful look on his face, he threw down his own weapons and ran forward to put his arms round Brennius and kiss him. There and then they became firm friends. Their troops disarmed and they all entered the town of Trinovantum together. The two discussed with each other what they should do next. They decided to put one common army into the field, to lead this army into Gallic territory and to subject to their joint dominion all the provinces of that country.

[iii.8]   Twelve months later Belinus and Brennius crossed over to Gaul and began to ravage the countryside there. When this became known to the Gallic tribes, all the Frankish princes came together to meet the invaders and fought against them. Belinus and Brennius were victorious and the Franks fled in all directions, with the men of their battalions gravely wounded. Once they had won the pitched battle, the Britons and the Allobroges were relentless in their pursuit of the Gauls. They captured their kings and forced them to surrender. They garrisoned the towns which they had captured and in one year they conquered the entire kingdom. When they had forced all the provinces of Gaul to submit, they set out for Rome with the whole of their immense army and began to plunder cities and farming communities up and down Italy.

At that time Gabius and Porsenna were the two Consuls in [iii.9] Rome and the jurisdiction of the country was in their hands. As soon as these two realized that no people was strong enough to resist the fury of Belinus and Brennius, they first sought the Senate's approval and then came to the invaders to sue for peace and friendship. With them they brought many gifts of gold and silver, together with a tribute to be repeated each year if only they were permitted to retain their own possessions in peace. The two Kings took hostages from the Consuls and then showed them mercy, leading their own troops off to Germany.

No sooner had Belinus and Brennius begun harassing the German people than the Romans repented of the treaty just described. Their courage revived and they marched forth to help the Germans. When the Kings learned this they were greatly incensed by it. They consulted each other to see how they could possibly fight two peoples at once. So great a force of Italian citizens had arrived that the Britons had much cause for anxiety. After due consultation with his brother, Belinus remained in Germany with his Britons and pressed on with the war against that enemy. Brennius, for his part, marched towards Rome with his own armies, so that he might take vengeance on the Romans for having broken the treaty.

When they heard this news, the Italians deserted the Germans. They hurried forward in an attempt to out-march Brennius, hoping in this way to arrive back in Rome. Belinus was informed of this and he disengaged his army. Once the next night was over he set out at full speed and occupied a certain valley through which the enemy had to pass. Belinus hid in ambush along the bottom of this valley and waited for the enemy to arrive. At dawn on the next day the Italians reached the place in question, as they pressed on with the journey which they had undertaken. When they saw before them the valley which was glittering with the arms of their foes, they were immediately filled with consternation, for they thought that it was Brennius who was there with his Senonian Gauls. The moment the enemy came in sight Belinus made a sudden charge at them and attacked them with great ferocity. Without more ado the Romans rushed headlong from the battle-field, for when attacked so unexpectedly they had been marching in broken order and without having put on their armour. Belinus pursued them mercilessly, never pausing in his slaughter until night came on and prevented him from completing the massacre.

After this victory, Belinus followed the tracks of Brennius, who had now been besieging Rome for three days. The two brothers joined forces and attacked the city from all sides, doing their utmost to breach its walls. In their effort to cause even greater dismay, they erected gibbets in front of the city gateway and announced to the besieged that they would hang from the gallows-tree the hostages whom the Romans had given, if these last would not agree to surrender. However, the Romans persevered in their endeavour. They were determined to defend themselves and took no pity on their sons and grandsons. First they destroyed the attackers' siege-machines with counter-weapons, or indeed with identical devices; then they drove the invaders back from the walls with every conceivable kind of missile. The two brothers observed this. In the very insolence of their burning rage they ordered twenty-three of the noblest of their hostages to be hanged in full sight of their relations. The Romans resisted all the more boldly. Encouraged by messengers from Gabius and Porsenna, who reported to the besieged that the Consuls would arrive to relieve them on the following day, the Romans next determined to sally forth from the city and to do battle with their enemies. Just as they were ordering their lines of counter-attack with great skill, lo and behold! the two above-mentioned Consuls, who had reassembled their scattered troops, marched in ready for the fight. They moved forward in close file and suddenly attacked the Allobroges and the Britons. With the help of the townsfolk who had sallied forth, the Consuls succeeded in causing great slaughter in the early stages. When the two brothers saw the carnage which was being inflicted on their troops, they were very worried. They began to harangue their men and to re-form their lines of battle. By means of repeated waves of attack the two Kings drove the enemy backwards. Finally, when thousands of those engaged had been killed on either side, victory went to the two brothers. Gabius was killed and Porsenna was captured. The city was invested and the invaders distributed all the hidden treasures of the citizens among their own troops.

Once he had won this victory, Brennius stayed on in Italy, [iii.10] where he treated the local people with unheard-of savagery. I have not attempted to describe his other activities there or his eventual death, for the histories of Rome explain these matters. Had I myself done so, I should have made this work inordinately prolix and by going a second time over ground which had been covered by others I should have turned aside from my purpose.

Belinus, for his part, returned to Britain and for the remaining days of his life governed his homeland in peace. He restored existing cities wherever they had fallen into decay and he founded many new ones. Among the others which he founded was a certain city on the bank of the River Usk, near to the Severn Sea: this was the capital of Demetia and for a long time it was called Kaerusc. When the Romans came the earlier name was dropped and it was re-named the City of the Legions, taking its title from the Roman legions who used to winter there.

In the town of Trinovantum Belinus caused to be constructed a gateway of extraordinary workmanship, which in his time the citizens called Billingsgate, from his own name. On the top of it he built a tower which rose to a remarkable height; and down below at its foot he added a water-gate which was convenient for those going on board their ships. He ratified his father's laws everywhere throughout the kingdom, taking pleasure in the proper administration of his own justice. As a result, in his time there became available to the populace such an abundance of wealth as no previous age had ever witnessed and no subsequent era was ever to acquire. Finally, when his last day dawned and carried him away from this life, his body was cremated and the ash enclosed in a golden urn. This urn the citizens placed with extraordinary skill on the very top of the tower in Trinovantum which I have already described.

[iii.11]   Gurguit Barbtruc, the son of Belinus, succeeded him. He was a modest man and a wise one. In all his activities he imitated the deeds of his father, being himself a lover of peace and justice. When his neighbours rebelled against him, he took fresh courage from the example of his father, fought dreadful wars against them and reduced them once more to the subjection which they owed him. Among many other things it happened that the King of the Danes, who had paid tribute to Belinus while he was still alive, refused to pay it to Gurguit, saying that he owed him no allegiance. Gurguit bore this ill. He took a fleet to Denmark, fought the most frightful battles against the local inhabitants, killed the King and reduced the country to its former state of subservience.

[iii.12]   On that same occasion, when Gurguit Barbtruc was returning home via the Orkney Islands after his victory, he came upon thirty ships full of men and women. Gurguit asked what they were doing there. Their leader, whose name was Partholoim,[1] went up to Gurguit, did obeisance to him and asked for his pardon and

1. Partholoim is a confused memory from Nennius, *Historia Brittonum*, §13: 'Long after this, the Scots arrived in Ireland from Spain. The first that came was Partholomus, with a thousand men and women. . . .'

peace. Partholoim then described how he had been expelled from certain regions in Spain and how he was now cruising in those waters in search of a land where he might settle. He then asked Gurguit for some small region in Britain which he might occupy, so that he need no longer continue this hateful wandering over the sea. A year and a half had passed since he had been expelled from his homeland and had set sail across the ocean with his comrades. When Gurguit Barbtruc learned that these men came from Spain and were called Basclenses, and when he understood just what they wanted of him, he ordered his representatives to go with them to the island of Ireland, which at that time was a completely uninhabited desert. He granted the island to them. They have increased and multiplied there and they still hold the island today.

Gurguit Barbtruc's death was a peaceful one. He was buried in the City of the Legions, which, ever since his father's death, he had done so much to adorn with walls and public buildings.

Guithelin received the crown of the kingdom after Gurguit. He [*iii.13*] ruled it liberally and temperately all his life through. His wife was a noblewoman called Marcia, who was skilled in all the arts. Among the many extraordinary things she used her natural talent to invent was a law she devised which was called the *Lex Martiana* by the Britons. King Alfred translated this along with the other laws; in his Saxon tongue he called it the Mercian Law. When Guithelin died the government of the kingdom remained in the hands of this Queen and her son, who was called Sisillius. Sisillius was then only seven years old and his youth prevented him from taking the kingship into his own hands.

For this reason his mother, who was extremely intelligent and [*iii.14*] most practical, ruled over the entire island.

When Marcia closed her eyes for the last time, Sisillius was crowned King and began to govern. His son Kinarius became King after him. Then came Danius, the brother of Kinarius. When Danius died the crown passed to Morvidus, son of Danius by his mistress Tanguesteaia. Morvidus would have been famous for his prowess had he not indulged in the most outrageous cruelty. Once he had lost his temper he spared no one, committing mayhem on the spot, if only he could lay his hands on his weapons. For all this he was handsome to look at and he distributed gifts most open-handedly. In the whole land there was no one who was as brave as he, or who could resist him in a fight.

[iii.15]   In his time a certain king of the Moriani landed in Northumbria with a strong force and began to ravage the countryside. Morvidus assembled the young men of his entire kingdom, marched forth against the invader, and met him in battle. He himself was more effective in the fight than the greater part of the army which he commanded. Once he had proved victorious not a soul was left alive whom he did not slaughter, for he ordered them all to be dragged before him in turn and he satiated his lust for blood by killing them one by one. When he became so exhausted that he had to give up for a time, he ordered the remainder to be skinned alive and in this state he had them burnt.

In the midst of these bestialities and other similar outrages a calamity occurred which put an end to the iniquity of Morvidus. A monster of unheard-of savageness appeared from the direction of the Irish Sea and began to devour one after the other all those who lived on the neighbouring sea-coast. As soon as this news reached the ears of Morvidus, he went to meet the monster and fought with her single-handed. When he had used all his weapons against her without effect, she rushed at him with her jaws wide open and swallowed him up as though he had been a tiny fish.

[iii.16]   Morvidus had five sons. Gorbonianus was the eldest and succeeded to the throne. At that time there was no man alive who was more just than he or a greater lover of equity, and none who ruled his people more frugally. Throughout the whole of his life it was his custom to pay due honour to the gods and to insist upon common justice for his people. In all the cities in the realm of Britain he restored the temples of the gods and he also built many new ones. As long as he lived a great abundance of wealth flooded into the island, such, indeed, as was enjoyed by none of the neighbouring countries. Gorbonianus encouraged the country-folk to till their ground and he protected them from the oppressions of their overlords. He rewarded his young soldiers with gold and silver, making it unnecessary for any of them to molest his comrade-in-arms. In the midst of these and many similar actions which bore witness to his innate goodness, he paid his debt to nature, closed his eyes for the last time, and was buried in the town of Trinovantum.

Archgallo, the brother of Gorbonianus, wore the crown after [iii.17] him; and in all that he did he was as different as he could be from his brother. Whenever he could he made it his business to do away with the noble and to exalt the base. He stole their wealth from the rich and in this way he heaped up untold treasure. The leaders of the realm refused to endure this any longer. They rose in rebellion against him and deposed him from the throne of the kingdom. Then they promoted in his place his brother Elidurus, who was afterwards called the Dutiful because of the compassion which he showed to Archgallo.

When Elidurus had been King for some five years, he came upon his deposed brother one day when he was hunting in the Forest of Calaterium. Archgallo had wandered about through certain of the neighbouring kingdoms, seeking help so that he might recover his lost honour. He had found no support there and, coming to the point where he could no longer bear the poverty which had overtaken him, he had returned to Britain with a retinue reduced to ten knights. He was travelling through the above-named Forest, seeking those whom he had in earlier times called his friends, when his brother Elidurus came upon him unexpectedly. The moment he saw him, Elidurus ran up to him, embraced him and kissed him repeatedly. When he had spent some time lamenting the misery to which Archgallo was reduced, Elidurus took him to one of his cities called Alclud and there he hid him in his own bedroom. He then pretended to be ill and sent messengers through the kingdom for a whole year to request the princes under his jurisdiction to come to visit him. They all assembled in the town where he lay and he ordered them each in turn to come into his bedroom without making a sound, saying that if they came in a crowd the noise of so many voices would make his head ache. Each believed his story and obeyed his order, entering his house one after the other. Elidurus ordered his servants, who had been forewarned of this, to seize each man as he came in and to cut off his head if he would not swear allegiance a second time to his brother Archgallo. Elidurus submitted them all in turn to this treatment and by playing on their terror reconciled them all to Archgallo. When this oath had been ratified, Elidurus led Archgallo to York and there he took the crown from his own head and placed it on that of his brother. It was for this reason that he was called the Dutiful, because of the brotherly love which he had shown towards Archgallo. The latter reigned for the next ten years, but without reverting to his earlier evil behaviour. On the contrary, he now set himself to suppress the unworthy and to raise up the deserving. He left the individual to enjoy what belonged to him and his administration of justice was equitable. After a time he fell into a coma; and when he died he was buried in the town of Leicester.

[iii.18]   Thereupon Elidurus was restored to his former honour and made King once more; but while he was following virtuously in the footsteps of his eldest brother Gorbonianus, his two remaining brothers, Ingenius and Peredurus, collected an army together from all sides and marched forward to do battle with him. The two were victorious: they seized Elidurus and shut him up in a tower in the town of Trinovantum, setting a guard to watch over him. Then they divided his kingdom into two. The part which stretches westwards from the River Humber fell to Ingenius; and the other half, with the whole of Albany, to Peredurus. Seven years later Ingenius died and the entire kingdom came under the rule of Peredurus. Once promoted in this way, he proceeded to govern the realm benignly and moderately, with the result that he was thought even more of than his brothers who had reigned before him. No mention was ever made of Elidurus. Then death, which spares no man, came upon Peredurus unawares and snatched him away from life. Elidurus was immediately freed from prison and raised to the throne a third time. He passed his days in virtue and justice and then closed his eyes for the last time, leaving to his successors an example of brotherly love.

Once Elidurus was dead, a son of Gorbonianus accepted the [iii.19] crown and emulated his uncle by his good sense and prudence. There was nothing at all of a tyrant about him; he behaved justly and compassionately towards his people, never deviating from the path of righteousness. Marganus, the son of Archgallo, reigned next. He accepted the quiet behaviour of his relatives as his guiding light and ruled the British race in all tranquillity. His brother Enniaunus succeeded him. This King was so different from Marganus in the way in which he governed the people that in the sixth year of his reign he was deposed from his royal position. He had no time for justice, preferring the methods of a tyrant, and it was this which caused his removal from the throne. Enniaunus was replaced by his cousin Idvallo, the son of Ingenius, and he, warned by the fate of his predecessor, was just and righteous in all that he did. Runo, the son of Peredurus, succeeded Idvallo. Then came Gerennus, the son of Elidurus; and after Gerennus his own son Catellus. After Catellus came Millus, then Porrex, then Cherin. Three sons were born to Cherin: Fulgenius, Edadus and Andragius, who all reigned one after the other. Next came Urianus, the son of Andragius, and then in turn Eliud, Cledaucus, Clotenus, Gurgintius, Merianus, Bledudo, Cap, Oenus, Sisillius and Beldgabred. This last surpassed all the musicians of ancient times, both in harmony and in playing every kind of musical instrument, so that he was called the god of minstrels. After him reigned his brother Archmail. Eldol came after Archmail, then Redon, then Redechius, then Samuil, then Penessil, then Pir, then Capoir. Digueillus, the son of Capoir, came next, a man modest and prudent in all his actions and one who cared above all for the fair administration of justice among his people.

[iii.20]   Heli, the son of Digueillus, succeeded him, ruling the kingdom for forty years. Heli had three sons: Lud, Cassivelaunus and Nennius. Lud, the eldest of these, accepted the kingship after his father's death. He was famous for his town-planning activities. He re-built the walls of the town of Trinovantum and girded it round with innumerable towers. He ordered the citizens to construct their homes and buildings there in such a style that no other city in the most far-flung of kingdoms could boast of palaces more fair. Lud was a warrior king, lavish in arranging feasts. However many other cities he might possess, this one he loved above all and in it he passed the greater part of each year. As a result it was afterwards called Kaerlud and then, as the name became corrupted, Kaerlundein. In a later age, as languages evolved, it took the name London, and later still, when the foreign invaders landed and conquered the country, it was called Lundres. When Lud died his body was buried in the above-named city, near to the gateway which in the British tongue is still called Porthlud after him, although in Saxon it bears the name Ludgate.

Two sons were born to Lud: Androgeus and Tenvantius. In view of their youth, they were in no position to govern the kingdom; and Lud's brother Cassivelaunus was preferred in their stead. As soon as he was crowned King he gained such high esteem for his bounty and his prowess that his fame was spread abroad through far-distant kingdoms. As a result the kingship of the entire realm came into his hands, instead of into those of his nephews. However, Cassivelaunus had such a sense of family solidarity that he did not wish the young men to be cut off from the kingship, and he allotted a large share of his realm to the two of them. He granted the town of Trinovantum and the duchy of Kent to Androgeus; and to Tenvantius he gave the duchy of Cornwall. Cassivelaunus himself remained in authority over both of them and over the princes of the entire island, for he was the overlord by virtue of his crown.

Part Three

THE COMING OF THE ROMANS

MEANWHILE it happened, as can be read in the histories of Rome, [iv.1]
that, after he had conquered Gaul, Julius Caesar came to the sea-
coast of the Ruteni. From there he gazed across at the island of
Britain and enquired of those standing about him what land it was
and what folk inhabited it. When he had been told the name of the
kingdom and of the inhabitants, he went on gazing out to sea. 'By
Hercules!' he exclaimed. 'Those Britons come from the same race
as we do, for we Romans, too, are descended from Trojan stock.
After the destruction of Troy, Aeneas was our first ancestor, just as
theirs was Brutus, that same Brutus whose father was Silvius, the
son of Ascanius, himself the son of Aeneas. All the same, unless I am
mistaken, they have become very degenerate when compared with
us, and they can know nothing at all about modern warfare, living
as they do beyond the deep sea and quite cut off from the world. It
will be a simple matter to force them to pay tribute and to swear
perpetual obedience to the majesty of Rome. First of all I must send
a message to them, to order them to pay tax, just as other peoples
do homage to the Senate without their having been approached or
attacked by the people of Rome, for we must not shed the blood
of our kinsmen, nor offend the ancient dignity of our common
ancestor Priam.'

Caesar dispatched this message in a letter addressed to King
Cassivelaunus. The latter was most indignant and sent back an
answer worded as follows:

'Cassivelaunus, the King of the Britons, sends his greetings to [iv.2]
Gaius Julius Caesar. The cupidity of the Roman people, my dear
Caesar, is really quite beyond belief. They have an insatiable thirst
for anything made of gold or silver, to the point that they cannot
leave even us alone, although we live over the edge of the world

and far beyond the perilous seas. They even have the nerve to stretch out their greedy fingers towards our small revenues, which up to now we have enjoyed in peace. This does not satisfy them: they want us to surrender our liberty and to endure perpetual bondage by becoming subject to them. What you have sought from us, Caesar, is an insult to yourself, for a common inheritance of noble blood comes down from Aeneas to Briton and to Roman alike, and our two races should be joined in close amity by this link of glorious kinship. It is friendship which you should have asked of us, not slavery. For our part we are more used to making allies than to enduring the yoke of bondage. We have become so accustomed to the concept of liberty that we are completely ignorant of what is meant by submitting to slavery. If the gods themselves try to take our freedom from us, we shall still do our utmost to resist them with all our strength in our effort to preserve that freedom. If you start attacking the island of Britain, as you have threatened, you must clearly understand, Caesar, that we shall fight for our liberty and for our kingdom.'

[iv.3]   The moment he had read this letter Gaius Julius Caesar prepared his fleet. He had to wait for a following wind before he could put into effect the threats which he had sent to Cassivelaunus. When the wind came which he wanted, Caesar immediately hoisted his sails and landed with his army in the estuary of the River Thames.

As soon as the Romans had come ashore in their boats, Cassivelaunus marched to meet them with the whole of his force. He reached the town of Dorobellum and there he took counsel with the princes of his kingdom as to how he could best drive the enemy back. With him was Belinus, the commander-in-chief of his army, with the help of whose planning and advice the whole kingdom was governed. Androgeus, Duke of Trinovantum, and Tenvantius, Duke of Cornwall, the two nephews of Cassivelaunus, were also there; and so, too, were three Kings holding sway under Cassivelaunus: Cridous of Albany, Gueithaet of Venedotia and Brittahel of Demetia. These men had brought their troops with them ready for the fray. Their advice was that Caesar's camp should be attacked immediately, and that they should charge at him and drive him away before he could occupy any city or fortress. If he once managed to invest some fortified place in the land, then in their opinion the task of expelling him would be all the more difficult, for he would know where to find refuge for his troops. Everyone agreed with this and they all marched forward to the sea-shore, where Julius Caesar had set up his camp and his tents.

The two armies were drawn up in battle-array and the Britons engaged the enemy in hand-to-hand combat, matching javelin with javelin and sword-thrust with sword-thrust. On both sides the wounded fell in heaps, with the weapons of war sticking in their entrails. The earth was drenched with the blood of the dying, as when a sudden south-west wind drives back the ebbing tide.[1] At the spot where the lines of battle were most closely interlocked it chanced that Nennius and Androgeus, with the men of Kent and the citizens of the town of Trinovantum who were under their command, fell upon the battalion which was guarding the Emperor's person. As the two sides made contact the Emperor's company came very near to being scattered by the close ranks of the invading Britons. They all fought together in a confused mêlée and Nennius had the extraordinary luck of meeting Julius in person. As he rushed at Caesar, Nennius rejoiced in his heart at the fact that he would be able to deal at least one blow at so great a man. Caesar saw Nennius charging at him. He warded his opponent off with his shield and struck him on his helmet with his naked sword. Caesar lifted his sword a second time with the intention of following up his first blow and dealing a fatal wound. Nennius saw what he was at and held out his own shield. Caesar's sword glanced off Nennius' helmet and cut into his shield so deeply that, when they

1. It has been suggested that this is a possible reference to Geoffrey's childhood, during which he would perhaps have seen the Severn Bore. Cp. *Tatlock*, pp. 76–7.

had to abandon their hand-to-hand fight because of the troops who crowded in on them, the Emperor could not wrench his sword out. Having acquired Caesar's sword in this way, Nennius threw away his own, dragged the other weapon out and hurried off to attack the enemy with it. Everyone whom Nennius struck with this sword either had his head cut off or else was so seriously wounded as Nennius passed that he had no hope of recovery. As Nennius raged up and down in this way the Tribune Labienus came to meet him, but Nennius killed him on the spot. So passed the greater part of the day. The Britons pressed forward with their ranks undivided. As they charged boldly on, God favoured them and victory was theirs. Caesar withdrew to a line between his camp and the ships, for his Romans were being cut to pieces. That night he re-formed his ranks and went on board his ships, glad enough to make the sea his refuge. His comrades dissuaded him from continuing the fight and he was happy to accept their advice and to return to Gaul.

[iv.4]   Cassivelaunus was delighted with his victory. He first gave thanks to God;[1] then he summoned to him those who had shared his victory and rewarded each man with princely gifts, according to the prowess he had shown. He was, however, stricken with grief, for his brother Nennius had been severely wounded and was lying with little hope of recovery. Julius had struck him in the battle, as described above, and his wound could not be treated by the doctor. Some fifteen days after the battle he died suddenly. When he had closed his eyes they buried him in the town of Trinovantum, by the north gate. At his funeral they placed beside him in his coffin the sword of Caesar, which he had carried off in his shield during the fight. The sword was called Yellow Death, for no man who was struck by it escaped alive.

[iv.5]   When they saw Julius Caesar turn his back to the enemy in this way and retire in disorder to their own sea-coast, the Gauls did their utmost to rebel and throw off the dominion he had over them. They were under the impression that he was now so reduced in

    1. Cassivelaunus was, of course, a pagan.

power that they no longer needed to fear him. One single rumour
was on all men's lips: that the whole sea was seething with the ships
of Cassivelaunus, who was following Caesar in his flight. The
bolder spirits among the Gauls reached the point where they were
debating how they could drive Caesar out of their territory. Julius
Caesar learned this: he had no wish to fight a war on two fronts
against a people roused to fury. He preferred to open his treasure-
chests and to call upon certain of the chief nobles in an effort to
pacify them by bribing them each in turn. To the *plebs* he promised
freedom, to those who had been disinherited he promised their lost
possessions, and he even went so far as to promise liberation to the
slaves. He who had once raged like a lion, as he took from them their
all, now went about bleating like a gentle lamb, as with muted voice
he spoke of the pleasure it caused him to be able to give everything
back to them again. This soft caressing behaviour continued until
all were won over again and he had recovered his lost power.
Meanwhile no day passed without his going over in his mind his
own flight and the victory won by the Britons.

Two years passed. Then Caesar prepared to cross the sea a second   [*iv.6*]
time, in order to avenge himself upon Cassivelaunus. As soon as
the latter heard of this, he garrisoned his cities everywhere; and
wherever their walls were ruined he repaired them. In every sea-
port he stationed fully-equipped soldiery. What is more, below the
water-line in the bed of the River Thames, up which Caesar would
have to sail if he were to approach the town of Trinovantum,
Cassivelaunus planted stakes as thick as a man's thigh and shod
with iron and lead, so that Caesar's ships would be gutted as they
moved forward.[1] Every man of military age in the island was

1. Nennius, §20, describes the 'iron spikes' placed in the Thames by the
Britons. Bede, in his *Ecclesiastical History*, written in the third decade of the
eighth century, describes how the Britons 'had constructed a defence system
of sharpened stakes which ran along the bank, and under the water across
the ford. Traces of these stakes can still be seen; cased in lead and as thick as
a man's thigh, they stand fixed and immovable in the river-bed'(Bk I, ch. 2,
translation of L. Sherley-Price, Penguin Classics, 1955).

conscripted; barracks were built for them on the water's edge; and then Cassivelaunus awaited the enemy's coming.

[iv.7]   Once he had prepared all that he needed, Julius Caesar embarked with so many troops that no one could count them, for he was eager to inflict a signal defeat upon a people who had beaten him. Had he been able to land with his fleet undamaged, no doubt he would have achieved his aim; but as he cruised up the Thames in the direction of the above-mentioned city of Trinovantum his ships ran upon the stakes which I have described and so suffered their moment of sudden jeopardy. Thousands of soldiers were drowned as the river-water flowed into the holed ships and sucked them down. When Caesar discovered what was happening he made every effort to furl his sails and then ran ashore as fast as he could. Those survivors who by the skin of their teeth had escaped from so great a peril now clambered with Caesar on to dry land.

Cassivelaunus observed all this from his vantage-point on the river bank. That so many were dying as they sank in the water rejoiced his heart, but he was worried by the fact that the others were saving themselves. He signalled to his troops and charged down upon the Romans. Despite the danger which they had endured in the river, once they reached dry land the Romans withstood the onslaught of the Britons bravely enough. Bolstered up by their own courage, they inflicted no small slaughter; but the carnage they themselves suffered was greater than the damage they did. They had been sorely tested in the river; and now they moved forward with their ranks thinned. The Britons on the other hand were reinforced, as each hour passed, by the moving up of additional troops, until they outnumbered the Romans by three to one; and thus they were victorious over their weakened enemy.

When Caesar saw that he was beaten, he fled to his ships with the few men left to him and gained the safety of the open sea without being hindered. He hoisted his sails to take the timely winds which rose, and so reached the shore of the Moriani. There he took shelter in a certain tower which he had had built in a place called Odnea before setting out this time to Britain. He could not trust the loyalty of the fickle Gauls, for they might well rise against him a second time, as they are said to have done before, when it was first known that he had shown his back to the Britons. It was against this eventuality that he had constructed the tower as a refuge, so that he could resist an insurgent people should they rise against him as he had foreseen.

Cassivelaunus was greatly elated when he had won this second [iv.8] victory. He issued an edict that all the British leaders should assemble with their wives in the town of Trinovantum to do honour to their country's gods who had given them victory over so mighty an Emperor. They all gathered together without delay. Sacrifices of various kinds were made and many cattle were killed. They offered forty thousand cows, a hundred thousand sheep and so many fowl of every kind that it was impossible to count them. They also sacrificed three hundred thousand wild animals of various species which they had caught in the woods. When they had done honour to the gods, they feasted on the viands left over, as the custom was on sacrificial occasions. What remained of that day and night they spent in various sporting events. While these sports were going on, it happened that two well-known youths, one the King's own nephew and the other the nephew of Duke Androgeus, wrestled together man to man and then disagreed as to who had gained the upper hand. The name of the King's nephew was Hirelgdas and the other man was called Cuelinus. First they wrangled with each other, then Cuelinus drew his sword and cut off the head of the King's nephew. The court was in a ferment over this death and the news of it reached Cassivelaunus. He was greatly upset by the death of his relative and he ordered Androgeus to bring Cuelinus before him in his court, stipulating that once Cuelinus had appeared he should undergo such sentence as the leaders might pronounce, lest Hirelgdas should go unavenged, always provided, of course, that he had been killed unjustly. Androgeus guessed what the King intended to do. He answered that he had a court of his own and that any case brought against his men ought to be tried there. If Cassivelaunus was determined to have the law on Cuelinus, then by age-old custom he ought to seek justice in the town of Trinovantum. When Cassivelaunus realized that he could not have satisfaction for his case, he threatened Androgeus and swore that he would ravage his duchy with fire and sword unless he agreed to his claim. Androgeus lost his temper and refused to obey the order. Cassivelaunus lost his temper, too, and rushed off to ravage the lands of Androgeus. Through his relatives and friends Androgeus kept in daily contact with the King, in an attempt to persuade him to end his fit of temper, but when he realized that nothing he could do would appease the rage of Cassivelaunus, Androgeus turned instead to thinking how he could best resist the King. In the end he despaired of finding any other solution and decided to seek the help of Caesar himself. He sent a letter to Caesar, couched in the following terms:

'Androgeus, Duke of Trinovantum, who once sought the death of Gaius Julius Caesar, now hopes that he is in the best of health. I am sorry that I opposed you at the time when you were fighting against my King. If I had refused to take part in that campaign, then you would have beaten Cassivelaunus. Since his success in that battle he has become so arrogant that he has now made up his mind to drive me into exile from my own land – me, with whose help he won his victory. That is how he thinks my efforts should be rewarded! I saved his inheritance for him, and now he is trying to disinherit me. Twice I have restored his kingdom to him, and now he wants to leave me destitute. It was I who re-established his hold over all his possessions, by fighting against you. I swear by all the gods in heaven that I have never deserved his anger, unless indeed it can be said that I did deserve it simply by refusing to hand over my nephew, whom he wants to condemn to an unjust death. Let me explain to you what I am accused of, so that in your wisdom you may understand it the more fully. It so happened that, in our joy over the victory, we arranged some religious ceremonies in the name of the gods of our country. When we had completed the sacrifices which we felt we owed to the gods, our young men competed together in certain sports which they arranged between themselves. Among the competitors our two nephews, the King's and my own, were encouraged by the example set them by the others to meet each other in a wrestling-match. My nephew won. The other man lost his temper most unsportingly and ran to hit my nephew, who avoided the blow and seized his opponent by the fist in which he was gripping his sword, hoping to wrest it from him. The King's nephew fell on the point of his own sword and then collapsed, having received a fatal stab-wound. When the King heard of this, he ordered me to hand my boy over so that he might be punished for manslaughter. This I refused to do. Cassivelaunus then invaded my dukedom with his entire army at his back and began to harry it unmercifully. It is for this reason that I ask for your compassion and that I seek your help, so that through you I may be restored to my position of honour and that through me you may become master of Britain. You need not hesitate over anything that I have suggested, for there is no thought of treachery in my mind. Human beings are conditioned by the chance happenings of history: it follows that those who have been enemies sometimes become friends and that those who have run away may yet achieve victory.'

Julius read this letter. He was advised by his staff that he could not [iv.9] go to Britain solely upon the Duke's verbal invitation, but that hostages must be sent to him, so that, with these to rely on, he might make his landing with a greater feeling of security. Androgeus immediately sent his own son Scaeva to Caesar, together with thirty young nobles who were his own close relatives. Caesar was reassured by this handing over of hostages and reassembled his troops. The wind blew strongly from the east and he landed in Richborough. Meanwhile Cassivelaunus was beginning to besiege

Trinovantum and was already sacking the villas on the outskirts of the city. When he heard of the arrival of Julius, he abandoned the siege and hurried to meet the Emperor. As he marched into a valley near Durobernia, he saw there the Roman army busy pitching its camp and putting up its tents. It was Androgeus who had led them to this spot, for he wanted them to occupy the town of Trinovantum in secret. Immediately the Romans saw that the Britons had come, they armed themselves at great speed without losing a moment and then drew up their men in companies. The Britons, for their part, put on their arms and arranged themselves in companies, too. Androgeus himself lay hid with five thousand armed men in a certain forest-glade which they had chosen, ready to run to Caesar's help and to make a sudden unexpected charge against Cassivelaunus and his companies.

When the two sides came together in this way they immediately started hurling death-dealing weapons at each other and exchanging equally mortal blows with their swords. The companies of men charged at each other and much blood was shed. On both sides the wounded fell to the ground just as autumn leaves drop from the trees. As they assaulted each other, Androgeus emerged from his grove and made a rear-attack upon Cassivelaunus' battle-line, on which the whole contest depended. In a short time this line of soldiers had to give ground, for on the one side it had been devastated by the attack of the Romans a little earlier on, and now, on the other side, it was being hard pressed by fellow Britons. The forces of Cassivelaunus were scattered. He turned in flight and ran from the battle-field.

Nearby there stood a rocky hill, with a thick hazel-wood at the top. Now that he had been defeated on the level ground, Cassivelaunus fled to this hill and his men went with him. Once he had occupied the hill-top he defended himself manfully and slew such of the enemy as pursued him. Both the Romans and the troops of Androgeus had followed close behind Cassivelaunus' companies and had continued to mangle them as they fled. Up the

hill they came, charging time and time again, but they could not
reach the top. The rocks on the hill-side and the very steepness of
the ridge afforded such good cover to the Britons that by occasional
sallies from the summit they could kill off a number of the enemy.
Caesar besieged the hill throughout the whole of that night, for
darkness was already coming on. He cut off all means of retreat.
Since he could not conquer the King by force of arms, his plan was
to reduce him by hunger. How remarkable the British race was at
that time! Twice it had put to flight the man who had subjected to
his will the entire world. Even now, when driven off the battle-
field, the Britons went on resisting the man whom the whole world
could not withstand. They were ready to die for their fatherland
and for their liberty. This is why Lucan praised them, when he
wrote about Caesar:

Territa quesitis ostendit terga Britannis.[1]

Two days now passed without Cassivelaunus' having anything
to eat. He began to fear that hunger would beat him and that he
would be captured by Caesar. Cassivelaunus therefore sent a
message to Androgeus, asking the Duke to make peace for him with
Julius, for otherwise the majesty of the race into which he,
Androgeus, had been born would come to an end with the capture
of its King. In the same message Cassivelaunus made it clear that he
had done nothing to justify Androgeus in seeking to destroy him,
although, indeed, he had caused him some disquiet. When the
envoys had delivered their message, Androgeus said: 'The leader
who is as fierce as a lion in peace-time but as gentle as a lamb in time
of war is not really worth much. By all the gods of heaven and
earth, my lord and master who used to order me about now pleads
with me! Is he really ready to make peace with Caesar and do him
homage – he whom Caesar once begged for peace? He should have
foreseen that the man with whose help he once drove so great an

1. *Pharsalia*, II, 572 = 'he ran away in terror from the Britons whom he
had come to attack'. Geoffrey has the later spelling '*quesitis*' for '*quaesitis*'.

Emperor out of his realm might one day bring that same Emperor back again. I ought not to have been treated so unjustly, for I was in a position to offer my service not only to him but to someone else if I wanted to. The man who piles insults and injuries upon the comrades-in-arms by whose very help he has triumphed is nothing but a fool. Victory is not won by any particular commander, but rather by those who shed their blood for him in the fighting. All the same, if I can, I will make peace for him, for the injury he did me is sufficiently avenged by the fact that he has begged me for mercy.'

[iv.10]   Immediately after this Androgeus went to Julius, put his arms round that leader's knees and said the following things to him: 'You have revenged yourself sufficiently on Cassivelaunus. Now have mercy on him. What is there left for him to do but render homage to you and pay tribute to the majesty of Rome?' Caesar did not answer, so Androgeus spoke again. 'All that I promised you, Caesar, was this, that I would help you to humble Cassivelaunus and to conquer Britain. Well, Cassivelaunus is beaten, and, with my help, Britain is in your hands. What more do I owe you? The Creator of all things does not intend that I should permit my leader to be bound in fetters, now that he has asked mercy of me and assured me of retribution for the injury which he has done me. I cannot allow you to kill Cassivelaunus while I myself remain alive. If you do not accept my advice, I shall not scruple to give him all the help I can.'

Julius' resolution was blunted by his fear of Androgeus. He made peace with Cassivelaunus, and the latter promised to pay a yearly tribute. The tax which he pledged himself to pay was three thousand pounds of silver. Julius and Cassivelaunus then became friends and gave each other presents. Caesar wintered in Britain and crossed back over the sea to Gaul the following spring. Some time later he collected an army together from every source and every race of mankind, and then marched to Rome to attack Pompey.

[iv.11]   Six years passed and then Cassivelaunus died and was buried in

York. Tenvantius, Duke of Cornwall, the brother of Androgeus, succeeded Cassivelaunus, for Androgeus himself had gone off to Rome with Caesar. Tenvantius was therefore crowned King and he governed his realm diligently. He was a warlike man and he insisted upon the full rigour of the law. After him his son Cymbeline was raised to royal eminence, a powerful warrior whom Augustus Caesar had reared in his household and equipped with weapons. This King was so friendly with the Romans that he might well have kept back their tribute-money, but he paid it of his own free will.

In those days was born our Lord Jesus, by whose precious blood was redeemed the human race, which hitherto had been bound by the Devil's chain.

When he had ruled Britain for ten years Cymbeline became the [iv.12] father of two sons, the older of whom was called Guiderius and the second one Arvirargus. As his life drew towards its end, Cymbeline handed over the government of his kingdom to Guiderius. Guiderius refused to pay the Romans the tribute which they demanded and as a result Claudius, who had been raised to the position of Emperor, crossed over to the island. With him there came his chief of staff, who in his own language was called Lelius Hamo. It was this man who planned all the battles which had to be waged. Hamo landed in the city of Porchester and began to block up its gate with a wall, in order to stop the citizens coming out. He wanted to weaken them by hunger and in this way to force them to surrender to him, or else he planned to kill them off mercilessly.

As soon as the coming of Claudius Caesar was known, Guiderius [iv.13] conscripted every armed man in his kingdom and marched against the Roman forces. Once battle was joined he at first caused great havoc amongst the enemy, killing more of them with his own sword than the greater part of his own army. Claudius was already retiring to his ships, and the Romans were on the point of being routed, when the crafty Hamo threw off the armour which he was wearing, put on British arms, and began to fight against his own men as though he were a Briton. Then he encouraged the

Britons to charge in pursuit, promising them a speedy victory. He had learned their language and their habits, for in Rome he had been brought up among British hostages. In this way Hamo got nearer and nearer to Guiderius; and when he finally managed to reach the King's side he killed the unsuspecting man with the blade of his sword. He then edged away through the enemy's assault-troops and re-joined his own men, having won an execrable victory.

The moment Arvirargus, the brother of Guiderius, realized that the latter was dead, he took off his own arms and put on those of the King, rushing here and there in the battle and exhorting the Britons to make a stand, just as if he really were Guiderius himself. The Britons did not know the fate of their King. At the bidding of Arvirargus they made a stand, and as they fought on they slaughtered a great number of the enemy. The Romans finally gave in, running away shamefully from the battle-field in two groups. Claudius for his part sought the safety of his ships, while Hamo, who had been prevented from reaching them, fled into the forests. Arvirargus thought that Claudius had gone with Hamo and so he hurried off after him, pursuing him relentlessly from place to place until he came to grips with him and his men on the sea-coast at a place now called Hampton, from Hamo's own name. There was a port at this place, convenient for those who wished to land; and there were merchant ships drawn up on the shore there. Hamo did his utmost to climb on board these ships, but Arvirargus intervened and killed Hamo out of hand. From that day to this the haven has been called Southampton.

[iv.14]   While this was going on, Claudius had reassembled his troops. He attacked the aforementioned city of Porchester, which in those days was called Kaerperis. He soon broke down its walls and defeated its citizens. Arvirargus took refuge in Winchester and Claudius followed him there. Claudius besieged the city and strove to capture it with various war-machines. When Arvirargus saw that he was beleaguered, he mustered his troops, threw open the city gates and went forth to do battle. Just as Arvirargus was about to lead his men in a charge, Claudius sent envoys to him, asking that they might make peace, for he was afraid of the King's courage and of the bravery of the Britons, and he preferred to subdue them by plot and diplomacy rather than incur the hazard of a battle. He therefore proposed peace to Arvirargus, promising to give him his own daughter, if only he would recognize that the kingdom of Britain was under the sway of Rome. His nobles persuaded Arvirargus to abandon his plans for battle and to accept the proposals of Claudius. Their argument was that it could be no disgrace for him to submit to the Romans, since they were the acknowledged overlords of the whole world. Arvirargus was swayed by these arguments and by others of a similar nature. He accepted their advice and submitted to Claudius. Claudius soon sent to Rome for his daughter. With the help of Arvirargus he subdued the Orkneys and the other islands in that neighbourhood.

At the end of that winter the messengers returned with Claudius' [iv.15] daughter and handed her over to her father. The girl's name was Genvissa. Her beauty was such that everyone who saw her was filled with admiration. Once she had been united to him in lawful marriage, she inflamed the King with such burning passion that he preferred her company to anything else in the world. As a result of this Arvirargus made up his mind to give some special mark of distinction to the place where he had married her. He suggested to Claudius that the two of them should found there a city which should perpetuate in times to come the memory of so happy a marriage. Claudius agreed and ordered a town to be built which should be called Kaerglou or Gloucester. Down to our own day it retains its site on the bank of the Severn, between Wales and Loegria. Some, however, say that it took its name from Duke Gloius, whom Claudius fathered in that city and to whom he granted control of the duchy of the Welsh after Arvirargus. Once the city was built and the whole island was at peace, Claudius returned to Rome, leaving the governorship of the islands of this province in the hands of Arvirargus.

At that time Peter the Apostle founded the church at Antioch. Later he came to Rome and held the bishopric there, sending Mark the Evangelist to Egypt to preach the Gospel which he had written.

[iv.16]   When Claudius had gone away Arvirargus began to show his prowess and to develop his own policy. He re-built his cities and castles and ruled the people of his kingdom with such firm application of the law that he was feared by far-distant kings and peoples. As a result he became arrogant and looked down on the majesty of Rome. He refused to continue his homage to the Senate, arrogating all things to himself instead. When this was discovered, Vespasian was sent by Claudius either to bring about a reconciliation with Arvirargus or else to force him back into subjection to Rome. As Vespasian was preparing to land in Richborough, Arvirargus went to meet him and forbade him to come into port. Arvirargus had brought such a large force of armed men with him that he scared the Romans and they were afraid to come ashore lest he should attack them. Vespasian therefore withdrew from that port, turned his sails and came ashore near Totnes.

Once Vespasian was on dry land he marched to Kaerpenhuelgoit, now called Exeter, and prepared to blockade that city. When Vespasian had besieged Exeter for seven days, Arvirargus arrived with his army and attacked him. The armies of both contestants were badly mauled all that day, but neither gained the victory. The next morning Queen Genvissa acted as mediator and the two leaders made peace. They sent their troops over to Ireland. Once winter had passed Vespasian returned to Rome, while Arvirargus remained in Britain.

At last, as old age came upon him, Arvirargus began to show deference to the Senate and to rule his kingdom in peace and quiet. He confirmed the old traditional laws and passed a number of new ones. He gave the most valuable gifts to anyone he considered worthy of them. His fame spread throughout the whole of Europe and the Romans esteemed him and feared him at the same time. In Rome he was talked about more than any other king. Juvenal tells in his book of how a certain blind man, who was chatting with Nero about a turbot which had been caught, said to the Emperor:

> Regem aliquem capies, aut de themone Britanno
> Decidet Arvirargus.[1]

No man was fiercer than Arvirargus in war and none more gentle in time of peace. Nobody was more agreeable to be with or more open-handed in distributing gifts. When he reached the end of his days he was buried in Gloucester, in the very temple which he had dedicated in honour of Claudius.

Marius, the son of Arvirargus, succeeded him in the kingship. [iv.17] He was a man of great prudence and wisdom. A little later on in his reign a certain King of the Picts called Sodric came from Scythia with a large fleet and landed in the northern part of Britain which is called Albany. He began to ravage Marius' lands. Marius thereupon collected his men together and marched to meet Sodric. He fought a number of battles against him and finally killed him and won a great victory. In token of his triumph Marius set up a stone[2] in the district, which was afterwards called Westmorland after him. The inscription carved on it records his memory down to this very day. Once Sodric was killed and the people who had come with him were beaten, Marius gave them the part of Albany called Caithness to live in. The land had been desert and untilled for many a long day, for no one lived there. Since they had no wives, the Picts asked the Britons for their daughters and kinswomen; but the Britons refused to marry off their womenfolk to such manner of men. Having suffered this rebuff, the Picts crossed over to Ireland and married women from that country. Children were born to these women and in this way the Picts increased their numbers. This is enough about them, for it is not my purpose to describe

1. Juvenal, I, iv, 126–127 = 'either you will capture a certain king, or else Arvirargus will tumble from the British chariot-pole,' i.e. will be deposed. The MS. has the spelling 'themone', and replaces 'excidet' by 'decidet'.

2. The source of Geoffrey's information and the whereabouts of this stone are discussed by Tatlock, p. 20.

Pictish history, nor, indeed, that of the Scots, who trace their descent from them, and from the Irish, too.

Once he had established absolute peace in every part of the island, Marius began to develop a close relationship with the Roman people, paying willingly the taxes which were demanded of him. Encouraged by the example of his father, he fostered justice and peace, the maintenance of the laws and decent behaviour in all matters throughout his kingdom.

[iv.18]   When Marius finally died, his son Coilus took over the government of the kingdom. From his early childhood this Coilus had been brought up in Rome. He had learnt the ways of the Romans and had conceived the greatest possible liking for them. He paid their tribute without even attempting to argue about it, for he realized that the whole world was subject to them and that their power was greater than that of individual countries or any one province. He therefore paid what was demanded and was left to rule in peace over his possessions. None of the British kings ever held the nobles of their realm in greater honour, for Coilus either left them alone in peace or else rewarded them with frequent gifts.

[iv.19]   A single son was born to Coilus. His name was Lucius. When Coilus died and Lucius had been crowned King of the country, the latter imitated all his father's good deeds, with the result that he was considered by everyone to be a second Coilus. His great wish was that he should end in even greater esteem than he had begun; and he therefore sent a letter to Pope Eleutherius to ask that he might be received by him into the Christian faith.[1] The miracles which were being wrought by young Christian missionaries among different peoples had brought great serenity to Lucius' mind. He was inspired with an eager desire for the true faith. What he asked for in his pious petition was granted to him: for the Holy Father, when he heard of the devotion of Lucius, sent him two learned and religious men, Faganus and Duvianus, who preached the Incarnation of

1. The story of the letter written to the Pope by King Lucius is told in Bede's *Ecclesiastical History*, Bk I, ch. 4.

he Word of God and so converted Lucius to Christ and washed him
lean in holy baptism. On all sides the peoples of the local tribes
urried to follow their King's example. Cleansed of their sins by
his same baptism, they were made members of the Kingdom of
God. Once the holy missionaries had put an end to paganism
hroughout almost the whole island, they dedicated to the One
God and His Blessed Saints the temples which had been founded
n honour of a multiplicity of gods, assigning to them various
ategories of men in orders.

At that time there were twenty-eight flamens in Britain and
hree archflamens, to whose jurisdiction the other spiritual leaders
nd judges of public morals were subject. At the Pope's bidding,
he missionaries converted these men from their idolatry. Where
here were flamens they placed bishops and where there were arch-
lamens they appointed archbishops. The seats of the archflamens
ad been in three noble cities, London, York and the City of the
egions, the site of which last, by the River Usk in Glamorgan, is
till shown by its ancient walls and buildings. The twenty-eight
ishops were placed under the jurisdiction of these three cities,
nce the superstitions practised there had been purged away.
arishes were apportioned off, Deira being placed under the
Metropolitan of York, along with Albany, for the great River
Humber divides these two from Loegria. Loegria itself was placed
nder the Metropolitan of London, together with Cornwall. The
evern divides these last two provinces from Kambria or Wales,
vhich last was placed under the City of the Legions.

At last, when they had arranged everything to their liking, the [iv.20]
nissionaries journeyed back to Rome and asked the most holy
ather to ratify all that had been done. He gave them his approval;
nd they then returned once more to Britain. In their company came
 great number of other religious men, and by their teaching the
aithful among the Britons were soon fully established as Christians.
Their names and deeds can be found in the book which Gildas wrote
bout the victory of Aurelius Ambrosius. All this Gildas set out in a

treatise which is so lucidly written that it seemed to me unnecessary
that it should be described a second time in my more homely style

[v.1]   When this famous King Lucius saw that worship of the true faith
had increased within his kingdom, he was very pleased indeed. He
turned to better use the goods and the lands which the idolatrous
temples had hitherto owned, permitting them to remain in the
hands of the churches of the faithful. Feeling that he ought himself
to find the money for some mark of distinction that should be
greater than this, he rewarded the churches with even larger lands
and houses, and increased their power by giving them every possible privilege. In the end Lucius died in the town of Gloucester
while still occupied with these matters and with other moves
which formed part of his plan. In the year 156 after the Incarnation
of our Lord he was buried with all honour in the church of the
Archdiocese. He had no heir to succeed him, so that after his death
dissension arose between the Britons, and the power of Rome was
weakened.

[v.2]   Once the fact of the death of Lucius was known in Rome, the
Senate sent Severus as its delegate, and two legions with him, to
restore the country to Roman domination. The moment Severus
landed, he joined battle with the Britons and forced some of them
to submit to him. He did all that he could to harass those whom he
was unable to conquer, by making terrifying assaults which he
thought likely to end their resistance. In the end he drove them
beyond Deira into Albany, where, with Sulgenius as their leader,
they resisted with might and main, often inflicting immense
slaughter on both the Romans and their own countrymen, for
Severus took with him as auxiliaries all the island peoples he could
find, and as a result frequently left the field as victor. The Emperor
was annoyed at this revolt by Sulgenius. He ordered a rampart to
be constructed between Deira and Albany, to prevent Sulgenius
from pressing his attack closer home.[1] A tax was levied and they

1. This is the wall of Hadrian and Severus. Geoffrey is unaware of the
existence of the wall of Antoninus between the Clyde and the Forth.

built their wall from sea to sea. For many years afterwards it held back the attacks of the enemy.

When Sulgenius was no longer able to resist Severus, he crossed the sea to Scythia, hoping to be restored to power with the help of the Picts. He collected together all the young men of that country, returned to Britain with a huge fleet and besieged York. As soon as this was known among the various tribes, the greater part of the Britons deserted Severus and joined Sulgenius. Severus did not let this deter him from his undertaking. He assembled his Romans and those Britons who were still faithful to him, marched off to the siege and fought with Sulgenius. Just at the moment when the battle which he had brought about was reaching its height, Severus was killed, with many of his men, and Sulgenius was mortally wounded. Severus was later buried in York, which his legions had occupied.

Severus left two sons, Bassianus and Geta, the latter born to a Roman mother and Bassianus to a British woman. Once the father was dead the Romans raised Geta to the kingship, favouring him because he was Roman on both sides. The Britons refused to accept Geta and chose Bassianus, for he was related to them through his mother's line. The two brothers thereupon fought each other. Geta was killed and Bassianus seized the kingship.

At that time there lived in Britain a certain young man called [v.3] Carausius. He was born of humble parentage, but he had shown his courage in many battles. He went to Rome and asked permission of the Senate to employ a fleet of ships to defend the coast of Britain against invasion by the barbarians. If this permission were granted him, he promised that his achievements would be so many and so great that in effect he would do more to exalt the State of Rome than if the very kingship itself of Britain were handed over to Rome. Once he had deluded the Senate with his promises, he obtained what he had asked for and returned to Britain with his commission sealed.

Carausius soon collected some ships together, gathered round

himself a great force of the young men of the country and put out
to sea. He sailed along all the coasts of the kingdom, making the
greatest possible upset among the inhabitants. Then he landed in
the neighbouring islands, laid waste to the open fields, sacked the
cities and the towns, and plundered those who lived there of all
that they had. While he was behaving in this way, all those who
lusted after someone else's possessions flocked to join him. In a
short time he had so great a force under command that no local
leader could resist him. His head became so swollen by what he had
done that he instructed the Britons to make him their king, promising that he would massacre the Romans and wipe them out of
existence and so free the whole island from that foreign race. He
was given what he asked for.

Carausius' next move was to fight with Bassianus, kill him and
take over the government of his kingdom. It was the Picts who
betrayed Bassianus, the men whom Duke Sulgenius, his own
mother's brother, had introduced into Britain. At the height of the
battle – at the very moment when they should have come to the
help of Bassianus – corrupted as they were by the promises and
bribes of Carausius, they deserted the King and attacked his allies.
The other side was thrown into confusion, for they could not tell
enemy from ally. They fled from the field of battle and the victory
went to Carausius. Once he had won the day Carausius gave the
Picts a tract of land where they might settle in Albany, and there
they remained through the centuries to come, intermarrying more
and more with the Britons.

[v.4]   As soon as the usurpation of Carausius had been reported in
Rome, the Senate sent Allectus as legate, with three legions, to kill
the tyrant and to restore the kingdom of Britain to the domination
of Rome. From the moment that he landed Allectus wasted no time.
He fought with Carausius, killed him and took over the government of Britain. Then he massacred as many of the Britons as he
could, on the plea that they had broken their alliance with the State
of Rome and joined forces with Carausius. The Britons bore this

ll. They promoted Asclepiodotus, Duke of Cornwall, to the
kingship, leagued together in the common cause, marched upon
Allectus and challenged him to battle. He was in London at the
time, busy celebrating a feast-day for the gods of his own country.
As soon as he heard of the coming of Asclepiodotus, he interrupted
his sacrifice, took the field against him with all his force and attacked
him with great ferocity. It was Asclepiodotus who was victorious.
He scattered the troops of Allectus, forced him to flee, and in the
pursuit killed many thousands of his men and the leader himself.

As soon as it was realized that Asclepiodotus was the victor,
Livius Gallus, one of Allectus' fellow-officers, withdrew what
remained of the Romans into the city. He closed the gates, garrisoned the towers and the other defence-works, and made plans
to resist Asclepiodotus, or at least to avoid the death which threatened him. The moment Asclepiodotus realized what had been done,
he lost no time in laying siege to the city. He sent word to all the
leaders of Britain that he had killed Allectus and many of his
soldiers and that he was now besieging Gallus and the remnants of
the Romans inside London. He begged each and every one of them,
as a matter of great urgency, to come and help him as quickly as
possible, for now that they were besieged the whole race of Romans
might easily be exterminated from Britain, if only, as he said, the
British leaders would attack them with their united strength.

The Demeti marched in answer to his summons, with the
Venedoti, the Deiri, the Albani and all the other Britons without
exception. As soon as they had all assembled, and Duke Asclepiodotus had inspected them, he ordered a great number of siege-
machines to be constructed so that they could batter down the city
walls. Without a moment's delay each man obeyed him to the limit
of his strength and courage, and they made a bitter assault on the
city. They quickly tore down the walls, and once they had forced
an entrance they set about killing the Romans. When the Romans
saw that they were being slaughtered one after the other, they
persuaded Gallus to surrender together with his men and to beg

mercy of Asclepiodotus, so that they might be allowed to depart
with their lives. Almost all their number had been killed already,
leaving one single legion, which was resisting as best it could.
Gallus agreed to their request, surrendering himself and his men to
Asclepiodotus. Asclepiodotus himself was prepared to have mercy
on them; but the Venedoti advanced in formation and in one day
decapitated the lot of them, beside a brook in the city which from
the name of their leader was afterwards called Nantgallum in
Welsh, or in Saxon Galobroc.[1]

[v.5]   Once he had triumphed over the Romans in this way, Asclepiodotus took the crown of the kingdom and with the assent of the
people placed it on his own head. For the next ten years he governed
the country with true justice and peace, checking the cruelty of
robbers and the knife-attacks of thieves.

It was in the days of Asclepiodotus that the persecution by the
Emperor Diocletian began. By this persecution the Christian faith,
which had remained whole and inviolate since the time of King
Lucius, was almost entirely obliterated in the island. Maximianus
Herculius, the general commanding the tyrant's armies, came over
to Britain. By his orders all the churches were knocked down and
all copies of the Holy Scriptures which they could discover were
burnt in the market squares. The priests who had been elected and
the faithful who were committed to their care were butchered side
by side, hurrying off, as it were, in a thronged and eager fellowship
towards the joys of the Kingdom of Heaven, as if to their own
appointed resting-place. God, however, increased His mercy
towards us. In this time of persecution, in order that the people of
the British Isles should not lose their way completely in the im
penetrable darkness of black night, He, of His own free gift, lit
for them the brightest lamps of His holy martyrs. Even now their

1. See p. 19 for details of General Pitt-Rivers' excavation of the Walbrook
but it must be stressed, as in n. 29, that *Tatlock* does not accept the con
clusions come to by Acton Griscom. See also R. Merrifield, *The Roman
City of London*, 1965, p. 37 and p. 76, n. 16.

THE DIOCLETIAN PERSECUTIONS

ombs and the places where they suffered would kindle an immense
low of divine charity in the minds of all who saw them, had they
ot been forgotten by their fellow-countrymen, through the
itiable perversity of the barbarians. Among the people of either
ex who, with the greatest possible courage, stood firm in the
attle-line of Christ, were Albanus, who suffered at St Albans, and
lius and Aaron, two townsfolk of the City of the Legions.[1]
lbanus, glowing bright with the grace of charity, first hid his
onfessor Amphibalus in his own house, when the latter was
osely pursued by his persecutors and on the point of being taken;
ad then changed clothes with him and offered himself to Death's
nal parting, thus emulating Christ who laid down His own life
or His sheep. The other two, torn limb from limb and mangled
ith unheard-of cruelty, rose aloft towards the delectable gates of
erusalem, bearing with them the crown of their martyrdom.

At that time Coel, Duke of Kaelcolim, that is to say Colchester, [v.6]
arted a rebellion against King Asclepiodotus. He killed the King
a a pitched battle and took for himself the distinction of the royal
rown. When this was made known to them, the Senate rejoiced
t the death of a King who had caused trouble to the power of
ome in all that he did. Mindful as they were of the setback which
ey had suffered when they had lost the kingdom, they sent as
gate the Senator Constantius, a wise and courageous man, who
ad forced Spain to submit to Roman domination and who had
bboured more than anyone else to increase the power of the State
f Rome.

When Coel, King of the Britons, heard of the coming of
onstantius, he was afraid to meet him in battle, for the Roman's
eputation was such that no king could resist him. The moment
onstantius landed in the island, Coel sent his envoys to him to sue

1. According to Bede, *Ecclesiastical History*, Bk I, ch. 7, Julius and Aaron
ere 'Legionum Urbis cives', which J. A. Giles and J. Stevenson both trans-
ted as Chester. The Diocletian persecution is also described by Gildas,
§9–11, but for him Julius and Aaron were citizens of Carlisle.

for peace and to promise submission, on the understanding that he
should retain the kingship of Britain and contribute nothing more
to Roman sovereignty than the customary tribute. Constantiu
agreed to this proposal when it reached him. Coel gave him hostage
and the two signed a treaty of peace. Just one month later Coe
developed a most serious illness which killed him within eigh
days.

After Coel's death Constantius himself seized the royal crown
and married Coel's daughter. Her name was Helen and her beauty
was greater than that of any other young woman in the kingdom
For that matter, no more lovely girl could be discovered anywhere
Her father had no other child to inherit the throne, and he had
therefore done all in his power to give Helen the kind of training
which would enable her to rule the country more efficiently after
his death. After her marriage with Constantius she had by him a
son called Constantine.

Eleven years passed and then Constantius himself died at York
and bequeathed his kingdom to his son. Some few years after his
elevation to the throne, Constantine began to give evidence o
remarkable courage, for he was as fierce as a lion. He maintaine
justice among his people, moderated the rapacity of footpads, pu
an end to the oppressive behaviour of local tyrants and did hi
utmost to foster peace everywhere.

[v.7]   At that time there lived in Rome a certain dictator called
Maxentius. His ambition was to disinherit all the nobles and all the
most distinguished citizens; and he crushed the State of Rome
under the grossest possible tyranny. Those who were driven into
exile by his oppressive savagery fled to Constantine in Britain and
were received honourably by him. Once a great number of such
men had found their way in flight to Constantine, they at last
managed to fill him with hatred for the tyrant whom I have men
tioned, this by ceaselessly complaining to him in speeches like
the following one: 'How long, Constantine, do you propose to
endure this disaster which has forced us into exile? Why do you

delay our return to our native land? You are the only one of our race who is powerful enough to expel Maxentius and to give us back what we have lost. What prince can ever be compared with the King of Britain, either for the might of his lusty soldiers or for his treasures of gold and silver? We beg you to march on Rome with your army, taking us with you, and so give us back our possessions and restore our wives and children to us.'

By these happenings and other similar events Constantine was [v.8] encouraged to go to Rome. He captured the city and then was made overlord of the whole world. He had taken with him three of Helen's uncles: Ioelinus, Trahern and Marius. He arranged for these three to be elected into the rank of the Senators.

Meanwhile Octavius, Duke of the Gewissei, led a revolt against a certain proconsul in whose hands, as a Roman dignitary, the government of the island had been left. The proconsul was killed and others with him; and Octavius seized the royal throne. This event was announced to Constantine and he sent Helen's uncle Trahern with three legions to restore the island to Roman sovereignty. Trahern landed on the coast near to a town called Kaerperis in the Welsh language. He attacked the town and captured it within two days. This news spread through all the tribes and King Octavius thereupon conscripted an armed force from the whole island. He marched to meet Trahern not far from Winchester in a field called Maisuria in the Welsh language, and there he began the battle and won the victory. Trahern withdrew to his ships with his wounded troops, went on board and sailed away to Albany, the various regions of which he began to ravage. This was duly announced to King Octavius. He reassembled his men in companies, followed Trahern, and fought him in the province called Westmorland. This time Octavius was defeated, and fled. When Trahern realized that victory was his, he pursued Octavius, and gave him no respite until he had wrested from him his cities and his crown.

Octavius was greatly saddened by the loss of his kingdom. He sailed off to Norway, to seek help from King Gunbert. As an interim measure he ordered his close friends to do their utmost to assassinate Trahern. The leading figure of a certain municipality, a man who cared more for Octavius than any of the others, obeyed his commands as soon as he possibly could. One day when Trahern was on his travels some way away from the city of London, this man lay in ambush with a hundred of his own soldiers in a certain valley in the forest through which the King would have to pass. He attacked Trahern unexpectedly as he passed by, and killed him in the midst of his soldiers. When Octavius heard this news he returned to Britain, scattered the Roman forces and drove them in flight, thus regaining the royal throne. In a short time he showed such personal bravery, and acquired such a vast store of gold and silver, that he feared no man. Indeed, he held the kingship of Britain in great content from that moment onwards until the days of Gracianus and Valentinianus.

[v.9]   Years later, weakened now by old age, Octavius decided to make provision for his people. He inquired of his counsellors which of his family they proposed to raise to the kingship after his death. All he had was a single daughter, for he lacked a son to whom he might bequeath the government of the country. There were some among his counsellors who advised that he should give his daughter in marriage, and with her the kingship, to a man chosen from among the Roman nobility: this so that they might with the greater confidence expect to enjoy peace. Others, however, advised that Conanus Meridiadocus, the nephew of Octavius, should be declared heir to the throne of the kingdom; and that the King's daughter should be married off to some prince from another country, with a dowry of gold and silver.

While these things were being argued out between them, Caradocus, the Duke of Cornwall, arrived and gave it as his opinion that they should invite the Senator Maximianus and offer him the hand of the Princess together with the kingship, and so enjoy peace for ever. Maximianus was a Briton on his father's side, for he was a son of Ioelinus, the uncle of Constantine, whom I have mentioned before. From his mother and by race he was, however, a Roman, and by birth of royal blood on both sides. This solution therefore promised a lasting peace. Caradocus felt that Maximianus had a right to Britain, for he came both from the family of the Emperors and from a British origin.

Conanus, the King's nephew, was annoyed by the advice which the leader of the Cornishmen had given. He strove with all his might and main to seize the kingship, and in trying to achieve his objective he upset the entire court. Caradocus was unwilling to retreat from the position which he had taken up. He sent his son Mauricius to Rome to explain things to Maximianus. This Mauricius was handsome in stature and of great personal courage and boldness. If any criticism was ever offered of things which he had decided, he used to support his decisions by force of arms in single combat. When he appeared in the presence of Maximianus, Mauricius was properly received and honoured above the warriors who accompanied him.

At that time there existed a great rivalry between Maximianus himself and the two Emperors Gracianus and his brother Valentinianus, for Maximianus had been denied the third share in the empire which he wanted.[1] When Mauricius saw that Maximianus was being badly treated by the Emperors, he gave him the following advice: 'Why, Maximianus, are you afraid of Gracianus, when a way lies open to you by which you could snatch the empire from him? Come with me to the island of Britain and you shall wear the crown of that kingdom. King Octavius is worn out with old age and debility and seeks nothing better than to find someone to whom he may bequeath his kingdom and his daughter. He has no male heir and he has asked the advice of his leaders about whom he shall marry his daughter to and to whom he shall give his kingdom.

1. On p. 133 it is implied that Constantine I, King of Britain, became Emperor of Rome. He is not mentioned again after p. 133, except in cross-reference. Presumably he was dead by this time.

His warriors have answered his appeal and he has decided that the girl and the kingship should be offered to you. They have sent me to you so that I may tell you of this. If you will come with me, then you will be able to carry out this project, from its early stages onwards. With the treasure-house of gold and silver which exists in Britain and the horde of warlike soldiers which lives there, you will be strong enough to return to Rome, drive out the Emperors and capture the city. This was what your relative Constantine did; and many other kings of ours who have risen to be emperors have done the same.'

[v.10]   Maximianus agreed to what Mauricius had said. He came to Britain, sacking the cities of the Franks on the way, and thus collecting together a fortune in gold and silver and rallying soldiers to his banner from all directions. Soon afterwards he put to sea with a following wind and landed at Southampton. When this was announced to King Octavius, he was completely petrified with fear, for he thought that an enemy army had arrived. He called his nephew Conanus to him and ordered him to summon all the armed soldiery of the island and to march out to meet the enemy. Conanus immediately assembled all the young men of the realm and came to Southampton, where Maximianus had pitched his tents. When he saw the vast company of men arriving, Maximianus was overwhelmed with anxiety and did not know what to do. He himself was accompanied by fewer troops; and both the numbers and the boldness of the men who had come terrified him, for he could not hope to pacify them. He summoned his older advisers, with Mauricius himself, and then began to inquire what he should do in the circumstance. 'It is not for us,' answered Mauricius, 'to fight with these lusty warriors. We have not come here with the purpose of conquering Britain by force of arms. We must ask for peace and for permission to camp here until we know what the King intends. Let us say that we have been sent by the Emperors to bring a message from them to Octavius, and so humour these folk with friendly words.'

This plan pleased everybody. Maximianus took with him twelve of his leaders, white-haired men who were wiser than the others. As he went forward to meet Conanus, they held olive-branches in their right hands. When the Britons saw these men of venerable years who bore the olive as a sign of peace, they stood up respectfully to meet them and made way so that the envoys could approach the British general more freely. Soon the visitors stood in the presence of Conanus Meridiadocus. They saluted him in the name of the Emperors and the Senate and announced that Maximianus had been sent to King Octavius to deliver dispatches from Gracianus and Valentinianus. 'Why, then, does so strong a force accompany him?' asked Conanus in reply. 'This is not the usual habit of legates. It seems more like an army on the attack, which thinks to do us injury!'

'It was not considered proper for so important a man to come here ignominiously without an armed escort,' replied Mauricius, 'especially in view of the fact that Maximianus may well be hated by many kings because of the majesty of Rome and the deeds of his own forefathers. Had he come with a smaller escort, he might perhaps have been killed by those who dislike the State of Rome. He comes in peace and it is peace that he seeks. This can well be believed from his behaviour. From the moment that we landed we have acted in such a way that we have done wrong to no man. We have paid for what we have received, like peaceful folk; and when buying necessaries we have taken nothing from any man by force.'

While Conanus was hesitating as to whether he should opt for peace or war, Caradocus, Duke of Cornwall, arrived. With him came a number of other leaders, who (once they had listened to his petition) persuaded Conanus not to attack. Conanus would have preferred to make a battle of it. Nevertheless he disarmed and granted the visitors peace. He conducted Maximianus to the King in London and explained the whole circumstance point by point. Then Caradocus, Duke of Cornwall, ordered the bystanders to [v.11] withdraw. Taking his son Mauricius on one side with him, he addressed the King as follows: 'See how God has brought about, in the way which suits you, the very thing which has long been wanted by those who have managed to keep, by their true affection for you, the trust you placed in them. You ordered your leaders to advise you what you should do about your daughter and your kingdom, now that your senile condition makes it difficult for you to go on ruling your people any longer. Some recommended that you should hand over the crown to your nephew Conanus, and marry your daughter off in a seemly way in some other land. These were they who would have faced the ruin of their countrymen, if a prince speaking some foreign tongue were set in authority over them. Others would have offered the realm to your daughter and to some nobleman of our own speech who could have succeeded you after your death. The majority, however, advised that someone of the race of the Emperors should be sent for, someone to whom your daughter could be given, and the crown with her. These men assured you that a firm and abiding peace would then follow, for the might of Rome would protect them. God has now deigned to bring to your shores this young man, born, it is true, from Roman stock, yet sprung, too, from the blood royal of the Britons. If you take my advice, you will not hesitate to marry your daughter to him. Suppose you were to deny him this, what legal argument could you bring against him in the realm of Britain? He is of the blood of Constantine. He is a nephew of our own King Coel, whose daughter Helen possessed this kingdom by hereditary right, as none can deny.'

When Caradocus had made his points, Octavius agreed with him. With the consent of all, he gave the kingship of Britain to Maximianus, and his own daughter with it.

When Conanus Meridiadocus saw this, he was more angry than you would have thought possible. He went off to Albany and busied himself in raising an army, so that he could molest Maximianus. Once he had collected a force together, he crossed the Humber and ravaged the lands on both sides of that river. As soon as this was announced to Maximianus, he assembled his entire force and hurried to meet Conanus. He fought with him and left the field victorious. However, Conanus was not so reduced that he could not begin destroying the countryside once more, as soon as he had reorganized his troops. Maximianus returned to the fray, they fought again, and the King withdrew only after he had been beaten. Finally, when each had done the other as much harm as he knew how, they made peace with each other, with the blessing of their friends.

Five years passed. Maximianus developed an obsession with [v.12] power, because of the enormous amount of gold and silver that flowed in to him daily. He prepared a fleet and conscripted every armed soldier in Britain. The kingship of Britain was not enough for him; he wanted to subjugate the Gauls too. He crossed the Channel and went first to the kingdom of the Armorici, which is now called Brittany. He began to attack the Frankish race which lived there. The Franks came to meet him, under their leader Himbaldus. They fought against him, but, finding themselves in sore straits, they turned in flight. Duke Himbaldus himself had fallen, with fifteen thousand armed men who had gathered from the entire kingdom. Maximianus was delighted at the fact that he had slaughtered so many men, for he knew that after such immense casualties the country could easily be taken. He summoned Conanus to him, some way away from his troops, and said to him with a quiet smile: 'Well, we have seized one of the fairest kingdoms of Gaul. We have every reason to hope that we shall capture the rest. We must occupy their towns and strongpoints as quickly as we can, before the news of their danger penetrates into the Gallic hinterland and calls to arms the entire nation. If only we can hold this kingdom, then I have no doubt that we can subjugate the whole of Gaul. You must not let it depress you that you have permitted the kingship of the island of Britain to pass into my hands, when you had hopes of possessing it yourself. Whatever you have lost in Britain I will make good to you in this country. I will raise you to the kingship of this realm. This will be a second Britain, and once we have killed off the natives we will people it with our own race. The land produces heavy crops of corn and the rivers are full of fish. The forests are attractive and the pastures most pleasant. Indeed, in my opinion, no country is more agreeable.' Conanus bowed his head and thanked Maximianus, promising that, as long as he lived, he would be faithful in doing homage.

[v.13]   Without more ado they drew up their lines of battle and marched to Rennes, taking it that same day. The savagery of the Britons was already well known, as was the number of men they had killed. The townsfolk fled at full speed, leaving behind their wives and children. Everyone else in the cities and castles followed their example, so that the Britons marched in without meeting resistance. Wherever they came they massacred the men, sparing only the women. Finally, when they had wiped out every single male in the whole land, they garrisoned the cities and castles with British soldiers and fortified the high hills. The inhumanity of Maximianus became common knowledge throughout the other territories of the Gauls. Great terror took hold of the leaders and princes, for they seemed to have no hope, except in offering up prayers. From every country-district they fled to the cities and castles, and indeed to any places which seemed to offer them safety.

When he realized what a source of terror he was, Maximianus became even bolder. He hurried to increase the size of his army by offering lavish bribes. He enlisted the help of all who wished to steal the possessions of others, doing all that he could to buy them over with gold and silver and any other gifts that he could think of.

[v.14]   As a result Maximianus assembled what he considered to be a force large enough to enable him to conquer the whole of Gaul. At the same time he put off acting in his own peculiar savage way until the kingdom which he had captured should settle down and he should be able to re-stock it with people from Britain. With this

end in view he issued an edict that a hundred thousand ordinary men
and women should be collected together in the island of Britain and
should come out to him; and with them thirty thousand soldiers,
who might protect from any enemy-attack those who were to
remain in the country. As soon as he had achieved all this, he distributed these people among all the tribes of the Armorican kingdom. In this way he created a second Britain, which he gave to
Conanus Meridiadocus. He himself went off to the remoter parts
of Gaul, with the rest of his soldiers. He conquered that country and
the whole of Germany, too, after a number of desperate battles,
gaining the victory in every fight. He set up the capital of his
empire at Trèves.[1] Then he vented his fury upon the two Emperors
Gracianus and Valentinianus, killing the one and driving the
second out of Rome.

Meanwhile the Gauls and the Aquitanians were causing great [v.15]
trouble to Conanus and his Armorican Britons.[2] They harassed the
newcomers by attacking them time and time again. Conanus
resisted these attacks, returning bloodshed for bloodshed and
defending with great manliness the country committed to his
charge.

Once he had gained the victory, he decided to find wives for his
troops, so that heirs might be born from them who should hold the
land for ever. To prevent any mixture of blood with the Gauls, he
ordered women to come from the island of Britain and to be
married to his men. With this end in view, he sent messages to
Britain, to Dionotus, Duke of Cornwall, who had succeeded his
brother Caradocus in the kingship of Britain, telling him to take
personal charge of the business. Dionotus was a King of great
nobility and power: it was to him that Maximianus had entrusted

1. How Maximianus denuded Britain of fighting men and then established his new capital in Trèves is described by Gildas, *De excidio Britanniae*,
§§13–14.

2. If Maximianus had conquered the whole of Gaul, it is surprising now to
find the Gauls and the Aquitanians harassing Conanus.

the rule of the island while he himself was occupied with the affairs described above. He had a daughter of extraordinary beauty, whom Conanus had always wanted for his own.

[v.16]   When he saw the messenger come from Conanus, Dionotus agreed to meet his wishes. He therefore assembled from the various provinces eleven thousand daughters of noblemen, with sixty thousand others born to the lower orders, and commanded them all to come together in the city of London. In addition he ordered ships to be brought there from the different coasts, in which they could cross the sea to the husbands whom I have mentioned. This pleased many in the great crowd; but it displeased an even greater number, who loved their parents and their homeland with deeper affection. Moreover, there were some present who preferred chastity to marriage and would rather have forfeited their lives among no matter what people than have become rich in this way. Indeed, they all had their personal wishes in the matter, if only they had been able to achieve what they really wanted. However, the fleet was made ready, the women went on board the ships, and they put out to sea down the River Thames. On the last part of the journey, just as they were turning their sails towards the men of Armorica, contrary winds sprang up against the fleet, and this scattered the whole company in a very short time. The ships ran the hazard of the seas and for the most part they foundered. Those which escaped this terrible danger were driven ashore on islands inhabited by barbarians. The women were either slaughtered by the uncivilized islanders or were sold into slavery. They had fallen in with the execrable army of Wanius and Melga, who, on the order of Gracianus,[1] were killing off those who lived on this coast and in Germany. Wanius was King of the Huns, and Melga King of the Picts; Gracianus had made an alliance with them and had dispatched them to Germany to spread havoc among all who

1. Maximianus killed Gracianus and drove Valentinianus into exile. Presumably this order by Gracianus to Wanius and Melga had been made some time previously.

avoured Maximianus. As they raged along the sea-coast, they met the young women about whom I have told you, who had been driven ashore there. When the men saw how beautiful the girls were, their first intention was to have intercourse with them. When the women refused to permit this, the Ambrones attacked them and slaughtered most of them there and then.[1]

As soon as Wanius and Melga, the leaders of the abominable Picts and Huns, who favoured the cause of Gracianus and Valentinianus, learned that the island of Britain was denuded of all its armed soldiery, they hurried off in that direction as fast as they could go. First they made a treaty with the neighbouring islands and then they landed in Albany. They drew up their line of march and then invaded the kingdom, which had no one to rule or defend it. They cut the unthinking country-folk to pieces, for, as stated above, Maximianus had taken with him all the young warriors whom he could find, leaving behind the unarmed and witless peasantry. Once the leaders whom I have named discovered that these folk had no way at all of resisting, they slaughtered them wholesale, continuing to ravage the cities and provinces as though they had been so many sheepfolds.

When this great calamity was announced to Maximianus, he sent a freedman also called Gracianus with two legions to bring them help.[2] As soon as these men came to the island, they fought with the above-mentioned enemy, killed off a great number of them and drove them off to Ireland.

In the meantime Maximianus was killed in Rome by friends of Gracianus, and the Britons whom he had taken with him were either slain or scattered. Those who managed to escape fled to

1. This is the story of St Ursula, Dionotus' 'daughter of extraordinary beauty, whom Conanus had always wanted for his own'. In MS. 1706, Geoffrey does not mention her by name. Cp. *Tatlock*, pp. 236-8.

2. In the text he is '*Gracianus municeps*', clearly a different person from the Emperor Gracianus, whom Maximianus had killed some time previously. This is the Gratianus Municeps of Bede's *Ecclesiastical History*, Bk I, ch. 11.

their fellow-countrymen in Armorica, which was already called the second Britain.

[vi.1]   When the freedman Gracianus heard of the death of Maximianus he seized hold of the royal crown of Britain and made himself King. Then he began to exercise such tyranny over the people that the *plebs* banded together to attack him and eventually assassinated him.

As soon as the death of Gracianus became common knowledge throughout the other kingdoms, the enemies I have spoken of returned from Ireland and brought with them the Scots, Norwegians and Danes. These people ravaged the kingdom with sword and fire from sea-coast to sea-coast. As a result of this most cruel oppression and devastation, messengers were sent to carry letters to Rome. They begged with tears and supplication that an armed force should come to avenge them; and they promised perpetual subjection, if only their enemies could be driven far away. A legion which had played no part in the earlier disaster was immediately put under their command. Once this legion had been shipped across the ocean to the country, it met the enemy in hand-to-hand conflict. The Romans eventually slew a great number of the enemy and drove all who remained out of the territory.

As soon as the legion had freed the prostrate people from this fearful maltreatment, the population was ordered to construct a wall from one sea to the other, to divide Albany from Deira.*

1. In this passage Geoffrey is following the *De excidio Britanniae* of Gildas. The earlier writer has the two attempts to build the Wall, §15 and §18, he describes the towers built by the Romans on the south coast of Britain, §18, and he writes the sentence: 'Meanwhile the hooked weapons of their enemies were not idle, and our wretched countrymen were dragged from the wall and dashed against the ground' (§19, cp. the almost identical words on p. 147). In Gildas the first wall, mentioned by Geoffrey on p. 126, is 'made of turf instead of stone', §15; Geoffrey's second wall was 'erected by a great crowd of workmen' = 'a turba', but the Berne MS. has 'a turbis' and he may well mean 'with turves'. Like Geoffrey's second wall, that of Gildas is built 'by public and private contributions', §18.

This wall was erected by a great crowd of workmen, as a deterrent which should hold off their enemies and as a real protection for the inhabitants of the country. Albany had been completely devastated by the barbarians who had landed there, for when hostile people came they looked upon that country as a convenient lurking-place. The local inhabitants therefore pressed on with the work and finished their wall, using private funds and public ones which they had collected.

The Romans then announced to the country of Britain that they [vi.2] could no longer be troubled with such wearisome expeditions, and that they considered it an insult to Rome that a large army of this type should be importuned on land and sea for the sake of a cowardly pack of vagabond freebooters. The Britons ought, instead, to develop the habit of relying upon their own armed power; and they should themselves defend their country, their property, their wives and their children, and, what is greater than these, their own liberty and their very lives: this by fighting manfully with all their strength. In order to give themselves an opportunity of delivering this warning in full public, the Romans ordered all men of military age in the island to assemble in London, for they themselves were making ready to return to Rome. When everyone had come together, Guithelinus, the Archbishop of London, was ordered to speak. He made the following speech to them:

'When, at the command of the princes who stand around me, I am forced to address you, I feel more like bursting into tears than embarking upon a lofty discourse. I am greatly saddened by the state of deprivation and abjectness which has overtaken you since Maximianus stripped this kingdom of all its army and all its young men. You were simply the last remnants left, common people, ignorant of the ways of war, men who were busied in other matters: some in cultivating their fields, for example, others in the various makeshifts of business life. When hostile men of other nations came to attack you, they forced you to abandon your sheepfolds, just as if you yourselves had been sheep wandering about without a shepherd. Then the might of Rome restored you to your possessions. Surely you will not always put your trust in being protected by someone else! Won't you accustom your hands to brandish shields, swords, and spears against those who would be no mightier than you yourselves, if only you could throw off your laziness and your lethargy? The Romans are tired of all this perpetual travelling-about which they have to do in order to fight your enemies for you. They now elect to forgo all the tribute which you pay, rather than be harassed any longer in this way on sea and land. Given that you were only ordinary folk in the days when you possessed soldiers, do you think that for this reason you have lost all claim to manhood? Surely men can be born out of their social caste – a soldier from a farmer, for example, or a farmer from a soldier? Surely a military man can be the son of a shop-keeper, or, for that matter, a shop-keeper the son of a military man? Given the possibility of one caste being born from another, I find it hard to believe that people are such that they can actually lose their manhood. If you are men, then behave like men! Pray to Christ to give you courage and then protect your own liberty!'

When he stopped speaking, the crowd applauded him so loudly that you would have said that there and then they were inspired with courage.

[vi.3]   Next the Romans gave the pusillanimous Britons some firm advice. They left behind them models showing how weapons could be constructed; and they recommended that towers should be built overlooking the water at intervals along the sea-coast of the southern shore, where the Britons kept their shipping, for it was there that barbarian attacks were most to be feared.

However, it is easier for a kite to be made to act like a sparrow-hawk than for a wise man to be fashioned at short notice from a peasant. He who offers any depth of wisdom to such a person is acting as though he were throwing a pearl among swine.

The moment the Romans said good-bye and went away, apparently never to return, the enemies whom I have mentioned reappeared once more from the ships in which they had sailed off to Ireland. They brought with them other companies of Scots and Picts, with Norwegians, Danes and all the rest whom they had under command, and seized the whole of Albany up to the Wall. Once the departure of those who had supported the Britons became known, and the fact that they had sworn never to return, the invaders pressed on even more confidently than before with their devastation of the island. In opposition to them, slow-witted peasants were posted on the top of the walls, men useless in battle, who were unable even to run away for the very palpitation of their bellies, and who shook with fear through the days and nights, on top of their stupid perches. Meanwhile the enemy continued to ply their hooked weapons, dragging the miserable *plebs* down from the walls with them, so that they were dashed to the ground. The very suddenness of the death they endured was a stroke of luck to those who were killed in this way, for by their immediate execution they avoided the miserable torments which awaited their brothers and their children.

Oh, how God avenges himself for past sins! Alas for the absence of so many warlike soldiers through the madness of Maximianus! If only they had been there in this great disaster! No people could have attacked them whom they would not have driven away in flight. This was made clear enough as long as they remained there. In those days they occupied Britain in all tranquillity and, what is more, they added far-distant realms to their own power. Thus it is when a kingdom is handed over to the safe-keeping of its peasantry.

What more can I say? Cities were abandoned, and the high Wall too. For the inhabitants banishments, dispersions which were even more desperate than usual, pursuits by the enemy, and more and more bloody slaughters followed fast upon each other. Just as sheep are torn apart by the wolves, so were the wretched *plebs* maltreated by their enemies. Once more the miserable remnants sent letters to Agicius, the general commanding the Roman forces, to convey the following appeal:

'To Agicius, three times consul, come the groans of the Britons.'

There followed a short introduction, and then they continued their complaints as follows:

'The sea drives us into the hands of the barbarians, and the barbarians drive us into the sea. Between the two of them, we have two deaths to choose from: we can either be drowned or have our throats cut.'[1]

For all this, the messengers returned sadly home, to explain to their fellow-citizens their lack of success, for they had received no promise of help.

1. This is taken almost *verbatim* from Gildas, *De excidio Britanniae*, §20. '"To Ætius, now Consul for the third time: the groans of the Britons." And again, a little further, thus: "The barbarians drive us to the sea; the sea throws us back on the barbarians: thus two modes of death await us, we are either slain or drowned."'

Part Four

THE HOUSE OF CONSTANTINE

THE Britons took counsel, and Guithelinus, the Archbishop of London, then crossed the sea to Little Britain, called at that time Armorica or Letavia, to seek help from their blood-brothers. In those days Aldroenus ruled the country, the fourth King after Conanus, to which last Maximianus had entrusted the realm, as was explained earlier on. When he set eyes upon so reverend a man, Aldroenus received him honourably and asked the cause of his coming. 'The nobility of your bearing,' replied Guithelinus, 'is clear to see. The grief which we, your fellow-Britons, have suffered since Maximianus despoiled our island of its soldiers, ordering them to colonize this kingdom of yours, over which you rule and will continue to rule in lasting peace, can well move you to tears. All the peoples who live near our island have risen against us, for we are the poverty-stricken remnants of your own nation. They have completely ransacked our island, which was once a treasure-house of every kind of wealth. All the peoples who live there are desperately short of nourishing food, except for the relief which they can find by their skill in hunting. There has been no one to stop this, for not a single strong man, not one military leader, was left to us of our own people. The Romans are no longer interested in us, for they have refused to help us in any way at all. Deprived as we are of all other help, we have come to you for sympathy. We beg you to give us your help and to protect our kingdom, which is yours by right, from invasion by the barbarians. If you are un-willing to help, what other man is there in existence who could be honoured with the crown of Constantine and Maximianus, as your grandfathers were honoured with it, and your great-grand-fathers, too? Make ready your fleet, and come! Behold, I place the kingdom of Britain in your hands!'

'There was a time,' replied Aldroenus, 'when I would not have refused to accept the island of Britain, given that someone was prepared to offer it to me. As long as it enjoyed peace and tranquillity, there was, I think, no more fertile country in existence. Now that a series of misfortunes has befallen the country, it has become less attractive and, indeed, my fellow princes and I no longer have any interest in it. Greater than all its other evils is the harm done to it by the overlordship of the Romans: for no man is able to hold lasting power there without losing his freedom and being forced to bear the yoke of servitude. Who would not prefer to possess a smaller competency elsewhere and remain free, rather than own Britain's riches under the yoke of slavery? This kingdom, on the other hand, which is now subject to my own rule, I hold with honour and without the obloquy of doing homage to one more mighty than myself. It is for that reason that I have preferred it to all other nations, for I govern it in liberty. Nevertheless, since my grandfathers and great-grandfathers ruled over your island, I hereby agree to place my brother Constantine under your command, with two thousand soldiers, so that, if God permit that he should free the country from this barbarian invasion, he may place its crown upon his head. This brother of mine, who bears the name which I have mentioned, is skilled in military affairs and well endowed with other virtues. I will certainly transfer his services to you, with the number of men which I have promised, if you for your part are willing to accept him. I have quite made up my mind, however, that I must refuse you any greater force of soldiers, for the possibility of an attack by the Gauls threatens me daily.'

As soon as Aldroenus stopped speaking, the Archbishop expressed his thanks and Constantine was summoned. Guithelinus was delighted to see him. 'Christ is victorious!' he cried. 'Christ is King! Christ rules over us! If only Christ is on our side, then you are the King of a deserted Britain! You are our defence, our hope, our joy!'

What more is there to say? The ships were made ready on the

shore. The soldiers were chosen from the various regions of the kingdom and handed over to Guithelinus.

As soon as everything was ready, they put out to sea. They landed [vi.5] in the port of Totnes. Without losing a moment they assembled all the young men who still remained in the island, and attacked the enemy. By the skill of this heaven-sent leader they were victorious. The Britons, who until this moment had been scattered far and wide, now flocked together from all sides. A council was held at Silchester and they raised Constantine to the kingship, setting the crown of the realm upon his head. Then they gave him a wife, born of a noble family, whom Archbishop Guithelinus had himself brought up. When their marriage had been consummated, the King had three sons by her. Their names were Constans, Aurelius Ambrosius, and Utherpendragon.[1] The King handed Constans his first-born over to the church of Amphibalus in Winchester, so that he might enter a monastic order. The other two, Aurelius and Utherpendragon, he gave to Guithelinus, so that he might bring them up. Finally, when ten years had passed, there came a certain Pict, who had been in the service of Constantine. Pretending that it was necessary for him to have a private conversation with the King in a thicket, with everyone else sent away, the Pict stabbed Constantine to death with his dagger.

As soon as Constantine was dead a disagreement arose among the [vi.6] leaders as to who should be raised to the throne. Some were in favour of Aurelius Ambrosius, others of Utherpendragon, and still others of various close relatives of the royal family. Finally, while they were still arguing for this claimant and that, there came on the scene Vortigern, leader of the Gewissei,[2] who was himself

---

1. Utherpendragon (*Jesus*, Ythr ben dragwn), takes his name from the Comet and the two Golden Dragons which he had made on p. 202. Geoffrey calls him Utherpendragon from his first appearance.

2. Until recently a sweet-shop in the town of Wallingford was kept by three sisters called Vertigen who believed that their name derived from Vortigern's, although they were under no illusions about his character.

busy making every possible effort to lay hands on the crown. He paid a visit to the monk Constans. 'As you know,' he said to him, 'your father is dead and your brothers cannot be made King because of their youth. I cannot think of anyone else in your family whom the people would promote to the kingship. If you will only agree to my plan, and increase my own personal fortune, then I will persuade the people to accept the idea of extricating you from your religious order, seeing that it stands in the way of such a rank, and then of raising you to the throne.' When Constans heard this, he was greatly pleased and he promised on oath that he would do for Vortigern whatever the latter asked. Vortigern then took charge of Constans, dressed him up in royal garments and led him off to London. There Vortigern made Constans King, although hardly with the people's approval. Archbishop Guithelinus was dead by this time. No one else was present who dared to anoint Constans, seeing that he was giving up his position as monk. However, that did not make him take the crown off again when Vortigern himself, assuming the duties of a bishop, placed it on his head with his own hands.

[vi.7]   Once Constans had been crowned in this way, he handed the entire government of the kingdom over to Vortigern. He accepted Vortigern's advice without question, never taking any action himself until Vortigern had told him to do so. It was his own lack of character which made him act in this way, plus the fact that what he had learned in the cloister had nothing to do with how to rule a kingdom.

Vortigern was so encouraged by this that he began to plan in his heart how he could himself be made King. That was what he had coveted above all things for a long time, and now he saw that the moment was coming when his desire could easily be achieved. The whole kingdom had been placed under his own control, and Constans, who was called King, stood there as the mere shadow of a leader. To his own subjects he appeared as a man totally lacking in severity and judicial authority, and he inspired no fear in the

neighbouring peoples. His two brothers Utherpendragon and
Aurelius Ambrosius still lay in their cradles and could hardly be
raised to the kingship. A further accident had happened in that the
older leaders of the kingdom had died off and so Vortigern seemed
the only man available who was wise and astute, with advice to
offer that was worth anything at all. Almost all the others were
boys or young men, who had come into their honours by some
chance or other when their fathers and uncles had been killed off
in the recent fighting.

Vortigern fully understood all this. He was busy meditating how
he could most safely and cunningly depose the monk Constans
and force his own way into the latter's position. He decided to
defer this until he had first of all subjected the various tribes to his
own rule and given them a chance to become used to him. He
began to transfer the royal treasure away from Constans into his
own keeping, and the cities, too, with their garrisons, saying that
a rumour was going round that the men of the neighbouring
islands were planning an attack. Once he had achieved this, he
stationed his own supporters there to hold these cities in allegiance
to him. Still plotting the treason which he had in his heart, he next
went to Constans and told him that it was necessary for the estab-
lishment of his own household to be increased, so that he could face
in greater safety the enemies who were about to attack him. 'Have
I not put everything under your command?' answered Constans.
'Do whatever you want to, provided only that the men retain
their ultimate fidelity to me.' 'It has been reported to me', continued Vortigern, 'that the Picts intend to lead the Danes and the
Norwegians against us, in an attempt to do us the greatest possible
harm. I therefore advise, and this I consider to be the safest course,
that you should keep certain of the Picts in your own court, to act as
liaison officers between you and the rest of their nation. If it is true
that the Picts have already begun to prepare war, then these men
will spy out for you the secret weapons and the battle-plans of their
own nationals, which you can then avoid all the more easily.'

In this you can see the hidden treachery of a secret enemy. Vortigern was advising this, not in order to ensure the safety of Constans, but because he knew that the Picts were a shifty people, ready for any mean trick. When they were drunk, or when something had made them angry, they could easily be stirred up against the King and so murder him out of hand. If this were to happen, then Vortigern would have the opportunity of making himself King, as he had so often planned to do. He therefore sent messengers to Scotland to invite a hundred Pictish soldiers to come; and these he introduced into the King's retinue. Once they had arrived, he honoured them above all the other men and enriched them with all sorts of bribes. He fattened them up so much on food and drink that they accepted him as their King. They used to wander through the streets shouting his praises and bellowing: 'It is Vortigern who ought to be King! Vortigern is worthy of the sceptre of Britain! Constans is not worthy of it!' At this Vortigern would try to give them more and more, so that he might seem even more attractive to them.

When he had won the Picts over completely, Vortigern made them drunk, and then pretended that he wanted to leave Britain, so that he could acquire greater wealth. He gave it out that the little he had would not possibly suffice for him to pay the wages of even fifty soldiers. Then he went home, apparently greatly downcast, and left them drinking in the hall. When they saw this, the Picts were more depressed than one can imagine, for they thought that what he had said was true. They grumbled among themselves. 'Why do we let this man go on living?' they asked. 'Why don't we kill him, so that Vortigern can take over the royal throne? Who else in the kingdom could possibly succeed Constans? Vortigern is the man who ought to rule! He ought to be honoured and be granted every dignity, for there is no limit to the rewards which he gives us!'

[vi.8]   Without more ado they burst into the King's bedroom, and there they attacked Constans and killed him. They carried hi head to Vortigern. When he saw it he burst into tears, as if the sight had saddened him, although he had really never been so happy in his life before. He called the citizens of London together, for it was in that city that this had happened. He ordered the traitors to be bound and then to have their heads cut off while they were still tied up: this for having dared to commit so dastardly a crime. There were some who thought that this treasonable act had really been planned by Vortigern, in that the Picts would never have undertaken such a deed without his consent. Others, however, had no hesitation in acquitting him of such a crime. The matter was never cleared up. However, those in charge of the upbringing of the two brothers Aurelius Ambrosius and Utherpendragon fled with their charges to Little Britain, just in case the two should be murdered by Vortigern. King Budicius received them there and brought them up with due honour.

As soon as Vortigern realized that there was now no one at all [vi.9] in the realm who was his equal, he set the kingly crown upon his own head and assumed precedence over his fellow princes. Some time later his treason became known. The peoples of the neighbouring islands, whom the Picts had brought over into Albany, revolted against him. The Picts themselves were incensed because their comrades-in-arms had been executed on account of Constans, and they kept doing their utmost to take revenge on Vortigern. As day followed day, the King was therefore much concerned to see the casualties of his army in battle. What is more, he was haunted by the fear of Aurelius Ambrosius and his brother Utherpendragon, who, as explained already, had fled to Little Britain because of him. His ears were filled with a constantly repeated description of how they had come to man's estate and were planning to launch an enormous fleet against the kingdom which really belonged to them.

About this time there landed in certain parts of Kent three vessels [vi.10] of the type which we call longships. They were full of armed warriors and there were two brothers named Hengist and Horsa

in command of them. At that moment Vortigern was at Duro
bernia, which is now called Canterbury, for it was his custom to
visit that city very frequently. When messengers reported to him
that unknown men, and, what is more, men of huge stature, had
landed in enormous ships, Vortigern made peaceful overtures to
them and ordered them to be led into his presence. As soon as they
were brought in, he fixed his eyes on the two brothers, for they
stood out among the others because of their noble bearing and their
good looks. Vortigern examined all the others and then asked what
country they had travelled from and why they had come to the
land over which he ruled. Hengist started to reply for the others
for his greater maturity and his good sense made him their natural
leader. 'Most noble of all Kings,' he said, 'Saxony is our home
land, one of the provinces of Germany. The cause of our coming is
that we wish to offer our services to you, or to some other prince
We have been banished from our own country on the simple pre
text that the tradition of that kingdom demanded such action: for
in our homeland it is the custom that, whenever there occurs a sur
plus population of men, the leaders of the different provinces meet
together and order the young men of the entire realm to gather
before them. They then cast lots and so pick out the most able and
the strongest, who must journey off to foreign lands and seek a
living for themselves. This is done so that the country in which
they have been born may be freed of its surplus manpower. It has
happened recently that in our own country the supply of men has
become too great. Our leaders met to cast lots. They chose these
young men whom you see in your presence and ordered them to
obey the tradition handed down from ancient time. They elected
us two brothers as their leaders, simply because we come from the
ruling family: myself, who bear the name Hengist, and this man
who is called Horsa. We duly obeyed the decrees, whose
authority is sanctioned by their antiquity. We put to sea and with
only Mercury to guide us we journeyed to your kingdom.'

When he heard the name Mercury mentioned, the King looked

them full in the face and asked them what their religion was. 'We worship the gods of our own country,' replied Hengist: 'Saturn, Jove and the others who rule over this world, and more especially Mercury, whom in our language we call Woden. Our ancestors dedicated the fourth day of the week to him, and down to our time that day is called Wednesday from his name. Next after him we worship the goddess who is the most powerful of them all, Freia by name, to whom they dedicated the sixth day, which after her we call Friday.' 'I am greatly grieved,' replied Vortigern, 'by your belief, which, indeed, can better be called unbelief; but all the same I am delighted that you have come, for either God Himself, or someone else, has brought you here to help me at a most convenient moment. My enemies harass me on every side; and if you share with me the hardship of my battles, then I will welcome you in all honour to my kingdom and enrich you with gifts of all sorts and with grants of land.' The barbarians agreed to this without more ado. A treaty was made between them and they took up residence in the palace itself.

Soon afterwards the Picts assembled a huge army, crossed the borders from Albany, and began to ravage the northern parts of the island. As soon as this was announced to Vortigern, he collected his own soldiers together and crossed the Humber to meet the Picts. When the two sides came together, the Britons and their enemies fought bitterly with each other, first on one flank and then on the other. In the end, however, the Britons did not have much battling to do, for the Saxons who were present fought so manfully that the enemy, used until now to being on the winning side, were forced to retreat almost immediately.

Once he had won this victory with the help of the Saxons, [vi.11] Vortigern increased his gifts to them. To their leader Hengist he gave many lands in the neighbourhood of Lindsey, so that he could maintain himself and his fellow-soldiers. Hengist was a clever man and an astute one. When he came to understand the friendship which the King bore him, he went to him and made the following request to him: 'My lord, on every side your enemies are harassing you yourself and also those of your fellow-countrymen who have any love for you. They are all threatening that they will recall Aurelius Ambrosius from the land of Armorica, so that they can depose you and make him King in your place. If you agree, let us send to our own country and invite more soldiers to come from there, so that our own battle-strength may be increased. There is, too, one other boon that I would ask of you in your clemency, if I did not fear to have it refused to me.' 'Send your messengers to Germany,' answered Vortigern, 'and invite as many men as you have thought necessary. Then ask of me what you will, for it will not be refused to you.' Hengist bowed his head and thanked Vortigern. 'You have rewarded me with large houses and broad estates,' he answered, 'but not yet with the honourable position which should have seemed worthy of a nobleman, seeing that my ancestors were of noble blood. Together with so many other things, you ought, indeed, to have given me some city or castle, so that I could be held in greater respect among the princes of your kingdom. The rank of Earl or Prince could well have been offered to me as well, seeing that I come from a race that has held both titles.' 'I am forbidden to make you gifts of that sort,' answered Vortigern, 'for you are pagans and foreigners, and I do not yet know your habits and customs well enough to be able to consider you as the equals of my own countrymen. Even if I could look upon you as fellow-citizens, I could never contemplate giving you something which would be disapproved of by the princes of my realm.' 'I am your servant,' replied Hengist. 'Grant me, then, within the territory which you have assigned to me, as much land as can be encircled by a single thong, so that I can build there a fortress into which I may retreat in time of need. I am your faithful liege. I have been so in the past and I shall remain so in the future. What I propose to do I shall carry out in all fidelity to you.' The King was moved by the words of Hengist. He granted him his request and ordered him to send messengers to Germany, so that the soldiers could be summoned from that country and come quickly to bring help. Hengist immediately sent representatives to Germany. He then took the hide of a bull and cut it into a single leather thong. With this thong he marked out a certain precipitous site which he had chosen with the greatest possible cunning. Inside the space which he had measured he began to build a fortress. Once this was completed, it took its name from the thong, since it had been measured out with one. This place, which we call Castrum Corrigie in Latin, was ever afterwards known as Kaercarrei in the Welsh tongue and as Thanceastre in Saxon.

Meanwhile the messengers returned from Germany, bringing [vi.12] with them eighteen ships full of carefully picked soldiers. They also brought with them the daughter of Hengist, a girl called Renwein, whose beauty seemed second to none.[1] Once they had arrived, Hengist invited King Vortigern to his home to inspect the new building and to review the warriors who had just landed. The King came there incognito. He praised the fortress which had been built so quickly and he took into his service the soldiers whom Hengist had summoned. While he was being entertained at a royal banquet, the girl Renwein came out of an inner room carrying a golden goblet full of wine. She walked up to the King, curtsied low and said: 'Laverd King, was hail!' When he saw the girl's face, Vortigern was greatly struck by her beauty and was filled with desire for her. He asked his interpreter what it was that the girl had said and what he ought to reply to her. 'She called you Lord King,' answered the interpreter, 'and did you honour by drinking your health. What you should reply is "drinc hail".' Vortigern immediately said the words 'drinc hail' and ordered Renwein to drink. Then he took the goblet from her hand, kissed her and drank in his turn. From that day to this the tradition has endured in Britain that the one who drinks first at a banquet says 'was hail' to his partner and he who takes the drink next replies 'drinc hail'.

1. The story of Hengist and his beautiful daughter is taken from Nennius, *Historia Brittonum*, §37.

Vortigern was tipsy from the mixture of drinks which he had consumed. Satan entered his heart, so that he fell in love with Renwein and asked her father to give her to him. I say that Satan entered his heart because, despite the fact that he was a Christian, he was determined to make love with this pagan woman. Hengist, who was a very clever man, immediately noticed the unbalanced nature of the King's personality. He consulted his brother Horsa and the other senior men who were around him as to what he should do about the King's request. They agreed unanimously that the girl should be handed over to the King and that in exchange for her they should demand the province of Kent.

No time was wasted. Renwein was given to Vortigern and the province of Kent to Hengist: this last without the knowledge of Earl Gorangonus who ruled over the territory. The King was married to the pagan woman that very night and she pleased him beyond all measure. By this action he immediately incurred the enmity of his leaders and, indeed, of his own sons – for he was already the father of three boys, whose names were Vortimer, Katigern and Paschent.

[vi.13]   It was at this time that St Germanus, the Bishop of Auxerre, came, and Lupus, Bishop of Troyes, with him, to preach the word of God to the Britons: for their Christian faith had been corrupted not only by the pagans but also by the Pelagian heresy, the poison of which had infected them for many a long day.[1] However, the religion of the true faith was restored to them by the preaching of these saintly men. This they made clear almost daily by frequent miracles, for through their agency God performed many wonders, which Gildas has described with great literary skill in his treatise.

As soon as Renwein had been handed over to the King, as narrated above, Hengist said to him: 'I am now your father-in-law and I have the right to give you advice. You must not spurn what I say, for with the powerful support of my people you will over-

1. Details of the Pelagian heresy and of the coming to Britain of Germanus and Lupus are given by Bede in his *Ecclesiastical History*, Bk I, chs. 10 and 17.

come all your enemies. Let us invite my son Octa to come here, and his younger brother Ebissa, both of them distinguished warriors. Give them the lands which are in the northern parts of Britain, near to the Wall between Deira and Scotland. There they will withstand the onslaught of the barbarians, so that you yourself can live peacefully on this side of the Humber.'

Vortigern did what Hengist said and told the Saxons to invite anyone who they considered was strong enough to help him. Messengers set off. Octa and Ebissa arrived, and a man called Cherdic, too, with three hundred boats filled with a fully-equipped army. Vortigern received them all kindlily and rewarded them with lavish gifts. With their support he conquered his enemies and was victorious in every battle.

Hengist invited more and more ships and increased his strength daily. When the Britons saw this, they were afraid that the Saxons would rebel. They told the King that he should banish the newcomers from the lands over which he ruled, for pagans ought not to be in close communication with Christians, nor to be allowed to infiltrate in this way, for the Christian faith forbade it. What was more, so large a force had now come that the inhabitants were terrified by them. Already no one could tell who was a pagan and who was a Christian, for the pagans were associating with their daughters and their female relations. By making such objections as these they urged the King not to let the Saxons stay any longer, for they feared that their fellow-countrymen would be crushed in some treasonable revolt.

Vortigern was completely opposed to accepting his people's advice, for, because of his wife, he loved the Saxons above all other folk. Once the Britons understood this, they immediately deserted Vortigern. Angered with him as they were, they promoted his son Vortimer to the kingship. Vortimer was completely in agreement with the people and set to work to expel the barbarians, attacking them and making bloody inroads among them. He fought four pitched battles against the Saxons and won every one of them.[1] The first was upstream along the River Derwent and the second above the ford at Epiford, where Horsa and Katigern (the second son of Vortigern) met hand to hand and both died, for each was mortally wounded by the other. The third battle was on the sea-coast and there the Saxons fled, sneaking off like women to their ships and taking refuge in the Isle of Thanet. Vortimer besieged them there and harassed them daily with naval attacks. When they could no longer endure the assault of the Britons, the Saxons sent King Vortigern, who had fought on their side in all the battles, to his own son Vortimer to ask permission for them to withdraw and to depart in safety to Germany. While the parley was being held, the Saxons seized the occasion to embark in their longships and to sail off towards Germany, leaving their women and children behind.

[vi.14]   As soon as he had won this victory, Vortimer started to hand back to the inhabitants of Britain the possessions which had been removed from them. He treated them with affection and honour, and, at the request of St Germanus, restored their churches. A certain evil spirit which had found its way into the heart of his step-mother Renwein immediately became envious of this virtuous behaviour of his and inspired her to plot Vortimer's death. Renwein collected all the information she could about noxious poisons and then, by the hands of one of his servants whom she had first corrupted with innumerable bribes, she gave Vortimer a poison to drink. The moment that famous warrior had swallowed it, he was seized with a sudden debility which left him no hope of survival. He immediately summoned all his soldiers to his presence, told them that he was dying, and shared out among them his gold and

1. The battles on the Derwent, at Epiford, etc., are copied from Nennius, *Historia Brittonum*, §44. Nennius writes: 'Four times did Guorthemer valorously encounter the enemy: the first has been mentioned, the second was upon the River Derwent, the third at the Ford, in their language called Episford, though in ours Set thirgabail, where Horsus fell, and Catigirn, the son of Vortigern; the fourth battle he fought was near the stone on the shore of the Gallic Sea, where the Saxons, being defeated, fled to their ships.'

silver and whatever else his ancestors had accumulated. When the
soldiers wept and wailed, he consoled them by saying that the road
down which he was about to travel was the way of all flesh. He
exhorted these brave young warriors, whose habit it had been to
do battle at his side in his wars, to fight for their country and to do
their utmost to defend it from hostile invasion. Then an extremely
bold idea came to him: he ordered a bronze pyramid to be constructed for him and set up in the port where the Saxons usually
landed.[1] After his death his body was to be buried on top of this,
in the hope that when the barbarians saw his tomb they would
reverse their sails and hurry back to Germany. None of them, he
said, would dare to come near, once they set eyes on his burial-
place. How great was the courage of this man, who was determined to be feared after his death by those whom he had terrified
during his lifetime! However, once he really was dead, the Britons
did quite differently, for they buried his body in the town of
Trinovantum.

Vortigern was restored to the kingship after the death of his [vi.15]
son. At the request of his wife, he sent messengers to Hengist in
Germany to ask him to return to Britain. Hengist was to come
secretly and with a few men only, for Vortigern was afraid that if
he arrived in any other way a quarrel would begin between the
barbarians and the local inhabitants.

As soon as he had heard of the death of Vortimer, Hengist collected together three hundred thousand fully-armed men, fitted
out a fleet and came back to Britain. When the arrival of such an
enormous host was made known to Vortigern and the princes of
the realm, they became greatly incensed. They consulted together
and decided to oppose the Saxons and to drive them away from
their coasts. The daughter of Hengist sent messengers to tell her
father of this decision and he in his turn considered what he could
best do to counteract it.

1. Vortimer's idea of the bronze pyramid is adapted from Nennius,
Historia Brittonum, §44.

Hengist brooded over the various lines of action he could adopt and finally chose one of them: this was to approach the people of Britain as though his intentions were peaceful and then to betray them. With this end in view Hengist sent messengers to the King, ordering them to tell Vortigern that he had not brought this vast horde of men with him so that they could settle in the kingdom with him or so that with their help he could do violence to the country. The reason why he had brought them was that he had thought that Vortimer was still alive. It was Vortimer whom he had intended to resist, should that King have attempted to oppose him. Now that he was quite clear that Vortimer was dead, Hengist placed himself and his men at the disposition of Vortigern. From this vast force the King should retain in his realm as many as he wished; and all those whom he wanted to dismiss should, with the full agreement of Hengist, return to Germany. If all this seemed acceptable to Vortigern, then Hengist asked him to name a day and a place where they might meet together, so that he, Hengist, could arrange everything in accordance with the King's wishes.

When all this was announced to the King, it pleased him immensely, for the last thing he wanted was for Hengist to leave. After long debate, he ordered the Britons and the Saxons to assemble at the Cloister of Ambrius on the first day of May, which was coming soon, so that there these matters might be settled. This was agreed to on both sides.

Hengist then thought out a new method of betrayal. He ordered each of his soldiers to conceal a large dagger inside his boot.[1] At some moment when, in apparent security, the Britons were discussing the subject in hand, Hengist himself would give his men this signal: 'Nimet oure saxes.' Each of them should then be ready to attack boldly the Briton standing beside him: in short, each should draw his dagger and without a moment of hesitation cut his companion's throat. The appointed day soon came. They all

1. The story of the Massacre of Mount Ambrius is taken from Nennius, *Historia Brittonum*, §46, where the word of attack is 'Nimader sexa!'

gathered together in the neighbourhood which had been chosen and the peace conference duly began. When Hengist saw that a suitable moment had come for his act of treachery, he bellowed out: '*Nimet oure saxes!*' He himself immediately seized hold of Vortigern and held him tight by his royal robe. The moment they heard this signal the Saxons drew their daggers, attacked the leaders standing near them and cut the throats of about four hundred and sixty counts and earls, who were thinking of something quite different. Afterwards the holy Eldadus buried the corpses and said the last rites over them according to the custom of the Christian Church: this not far from Kaercaradduc, which is now called Salisbury, in the cemetery beside the Cloister of Ambrius, who had founded it there himself many years before.[1] The Britons had all come there unarmed, thinking of nothing but the peace conference. The result was that the Saxons, who for their part had come there thinking of nothing but treachery, were able to kill them the more easily, unarmed as they were.

However, the pagans did not achieve their objective without loss, for many of them were slain as they tried to kill their enemies. The Britons picked up stones and sticks from the ground and struck down their betrayers in self-defence.

A certain Count of Gloucester, called Eldol, was among those [vi.16] present. The moment he saw this act of treachery, he seized a wooden stake which he had found by chance, and proceeded to defend himself with it. He broke the limbs of anyone within reach whom he could hit with this piece of wood, dispatching him forthwith to Hell. He shattered skulls, arms, shoulder-blades and even legs, causing the greatest possible terror, and before he left the spot he had killed seventy men with the stake which he held. He could not resist so vast a force for long, but got away and sought refuge in his own city.

1. This passage is in the Berne MS. It is interesting to note that it is not in the Harlech MS., nor in the Welsh translation of Jesus College, Oxford, MS. LXI.

Many were killed on both sides, but the Saxons had the upper hand; for the Britons, who had not expected anything of this sort to happen, had come unarmed and had little chance of offering resistance. The Saxons had intended to kill Vortigern, so that they might complete the evil task which they had begun; but instead they bound him tight and threatened him with death, demanding his cities and his fortresses in exchange for his life. Vortigern immediately conceded everything that they demanded, given only that he might be allowed to escape alive. When everything had been promised them on oath, the Saxons freed him from his chains. They went first to London and captured the city. Next they took York, Lincoln and Winchester, ravaging the neighbouring countryside and attacking the peasantry, just as wolves attack sheep which the shepherds have forsaken. When Vortigern saw this horrible devastation, he fled to certain parts of Wales, not knowing what he could do against this accursed people.

[vi.17]   In the end Vortigern summoned his magicians,[1] asked them for their opinion and ordered them to tell him what to do. They all gave him the same advice: that he should build for himself an immensely strong tower, into which he could retreat in safety if he should lose all his other fortresses.[2] He surveyed a great number of places in an attempt to find a site suitable for this, and in the end he came to Mount Erith. There he assembled stonemasons from different parts of the country and ordered them to build a tower for him. The masons gathered and began to lay the foundations of their tower. However much they built one day the earth swallowed up the next, in such a way that they had no idea where their work had vanished to.

When this was announced to Vortigern he consulted his magicians a second time, to give them a chance of explaining the reason

1. Geoffrey is now preparing us for the entry of Merlin. Magicians are mentioned for the first time: 'vocatis denique magis suis. . . .'

2. The story of Vortigern's tower and the discovery of the boy Merlin, called there 'Ambros', is taken from Nennius, Historia Brittonum, §§40–42.

for it. They told him that he should look for a lad without a father, and that, when he had found one, he should kill him, so that the mortar and the stones could be sprinkled with the lad's blood. According to them the result of this would be that the foundations would hold firm.

Messengers were immediately sent out through the different parts of the country to find such a person if they could. They came to a town which was afterwards called Kaermerdin and there they saw some lads playing by the town gate. They went to look at the game. Tired by their journey, they sat down in a circle, still hoping to find what they were seeking. At last, when much of the day had passed, a sudden quarrel broke out between two of the lads, whose names were Merlin and Dinabutius. As they argued, Dinabutius said to Merlin: 'Why do you try to compete with me, fathead? How can we two be equal in skill? I myself am of royal blood on both sides of my family. As for you, nobody knows who you are, for you never had a father!' At this word the messengers looked up. They examined Merlin closely and asked the standers-by who he was. They were told that no one knew who his father had been, but that his mother was daughter of a king of Demetia and that she lived in that same town, in St Peter's Church, along with some nuns.

The messengers lost no time. They hurried off to the governor [vi.18] of the town and ordered him in the King's name to send Merlin and his mother to Vortigern. When the governor knew the object of their errand, he immediately sent Merlin and his mother to Vortigern, so that the King could do what he wanted with them. When they were brought into his presence, the King received the mother with due courtesy, for he knew that she came of a noble family. Then he began to ask her by what man she had conceived the lad. 'By my living soul, Lord King,' she said, 'and by your living soul, too, I did not have relations with any man to make me bear this child. I know only this: that, when I was in our private apartments with my sister nuns, some one used to come to me in the form of a most handsome young man. He would often hold me tightly in his arms and kiss me. When he had been some little time with me he would disappear, so that I could no longer see him. Many times, too, when I was sitting alone, he would talk with me, without becoming visible; and when he came to see me in this way he would often make love with me, as a man would do, and in that way he made me pregnant. You must decide in your wisdom, my Lord, who was the father of this lad, for apart from what I have told, I have never had relations with a man.'

The King was amazed by what he heard. He ordered a certain Maugantius[1] to be summoned to him, so that this man could tell whether or not what the woman said was possible. Maugantius was brought in and listened to the whole story, point by point. 'In the books written by our sages,' he said to Vortigern, 'and in many historical narratives, I have discovered that quite a number of men have been born in this way. As Apuleius asserts in the *De deo Socratis*, between the moon and the earth live spirits which we call incubus demons. These have partly the nature of men and partly that of angels, and when they wish they assume mortal shapes and have intercourse with women. It is possible that one of these appeared to this woman and begot the lad in her.'

[*vi.19*]   When he had listened to all this, Merlin went up to the King and asked: 'Why have my mother and I been brought into your presence?' 'My magicians have advised me,' answered Vortigern, 'that I should look for a fatherless man, so that my building can be sprinkled with his blood and thus stand firm.' 'Tell your magicians to appear in front of me,' answered Merlin, 'and I will prove that they have lied.'

The King was amazed at what Merlin said. He ordered his

1. Maugantius is introduced without explanation: '*iussit Maugantium ad se vocari* . . .' I have softened this by adding 'a certain'. As *Tatlock*, p. 177, says: '. . . a strange appearance *ex vacuo*. . . . This suggests that he [= Geoffrey] found the two rare names [= Maugantius and Dinabutius] in a source.'

magicians to come immediately and sit down in front of Merlin.
'Just because you do not know what is obstructing the foundations
of the tower which these men have begun,' said Merlin to the
magicians, 'you have recommended that my blood should be
sprinkled on the mortar to make the building stand firm. Tell me,
then, what lies hidden under the foundation. There is certainly
something there which is preventing it from holding firm.'

The magicians, who were terrified, said nothing. Merlin, who
was also called Ambrosius,[1] then went on: 'My Lord King, summon your workmen. Order them to dig in the earth, and, underneath, you will find a pool. That is what is preventing the tower
from standing.' This was done. A pool was duly found beneath the
earth, and it was this which made the ground unsteady.

Ambrosius Merlin went up to the magicians a second time and
said: 'Tell me, now, you lying flatterers. What lies beneath the
pool?' They remained silent, unable to utter a single sound.
'Order the pool to be drained,' said Merlin, 'and at the bottom
you will observe two hollow stones. Inside the stones you will see
two Dragons which are sleeping.'

The King believed what Merlin said, for he had told the truth
about the pool. He ordered the pool to be drained. He was more
astounded by Merlin than he had ever been by anything. All those
present were equally amazed at his knowledge, and they realized
that there was something supernatural about him.

1. The words 'qui et Ambrosius dicebatur' have all the air of being a gloss.

Part Five

THE PROPHECIES OF MERLIN

[vii.1] I HAD not yet reached this point in my story when Merlin began to be talked about very much, and from all sorts of places people of my own generation kept urging me to publish his Prophecies. Outstanding among these people was Alexander, Bishop of Lincoln, a man of the greatest religion and wisdom. No one else among the clergy or the people was waited upon by so many noblemen as he was, for his never-failing piety and his open-handed generosity attracted them to his service.

As I was particularly keen to please him, I translated the Prophecies and sent them to him with a letter which ran as follows:

[vii.2] 'Alexander, Bishop of Lincoln, my admiration for your noble behaviour leaves me no other choice but to translate the "Prophecies of Merlin" from the British tongue into Latin, before I have finished the history which I had already begun of the deeds of the kings of the Britons. My intention had been to complete that other work first, and only then to have devoted myself to this present one. With the two tasks to preoccupy me I was afraid that my ability might well prove inadequate for both of them. However, I was assured in advance of the kind indulgence which the sympathetic understanding of your own subtle wit would afford me. I therefore pressed my rustic reed-pipe to my lips and, modulating on it in all humility, I translated into Latin this work written in a language which is unknown to you. All the same, I am greatly surprised that you should have deigned to commit the task to so poor a pen as mine, when your all-powerful wand could command the service of so many men more learned and more splendid than I – men who would soothe the ears of your own wise self with the delight of their sublimer song. Leaving on one side all the wise men of this entire island of Britain, I feel no shame at all in maintaining that it is you and you alone who should, in preference to all the others, declaim it with bold accompaniment, if only the highest honour had not called you away to other preoccupations. However, since it has pleased you that Geoffrey of Monmouth should sound his own pipe in this piece of soothsaying, please do not hesitate to show favour to his music-makings. If he produces any sound which is wrong or unpleasant, force him back into correct harmony with your own Muses' baton.'

While Vortigern, King of the Britons, was still sitting on the [vii.3] bank of the pool which had been drained of its water, there emerged two Dragons, one white, one red. As soon as they were near enough to each other, they fought bitterly, breathing out fire as they panted. The White Dragon began to have the upper hand and to force the Red One back to the edge of the pool. The Red Dragon bewailed the fact that it was being driven out and then turned upon the White One and forced it backwards in its turn. As they struggled on in this way, the King ordered Ambrosius Merlin to explain just what this battle of the Dragons meant. Merlin immediately burst into tears. He went into a prophetic trance and then spoke as follows:

'Alas for the Red Dragon, for its end is near. Its cavernous dens shall be occupied by the White Dragon, which stands for the Saxons whom you have invited over. The Red Dragon represents the people of Britain, who will be overrun by the White One: for Britain's mountains and valleys shall be levelled, and the streams in its valleys shall run with blood.

'The cult of religion shall be destroyed completely and the ruin of the churches shall be clear for all to see.

'The race that is oppressed shall prevail in the end, for it will resist the savagery of the invaders.

'The Boar of Cornwall shall bring relief from these invaders, for it will trample their necks beneath its feet.

'The Islands of the Ocean shall be given into the power of the Boar and it shall lord it over the forests of Gaul.

'The House of Romulus shall dread the Boar's savagery and the end of the Boar will be shrouded in mystery.

'The Boar shall be extolled in the mouths of its peoples, and its deeds will be as meat and drink to those who tell tales.

'Six of the Boar's descendants shall hold the sceptre after it, and next after them will rise up the German Worm. The Sea-wolf shall exalt this Worm and the forests of Africa shall be committed to its care.

'Religion shall be destroyed a second time and the sees of the primates will be moved to other places. London's high dignity shall adorn Durobernia: and the seventh pastor of York will be visited in the realm of Armorica. Menevia shall be dressed in the pall of the City of the Legions, and a preacher from Ireland shall be struck dumb by a child still growing in the womb.

'A shower of blood shall fall and a dire famine shall afflict mankind.

'The Red One will grieve for what has happened, but after an immense effort it will regain its strength.

'Calamity will next pursue the White One and the buildings in its little garden will be torn down.

'Seven who hold the sceptre shall perish, one of them being canonized.

'The bellies of mothers shall be cut open and babies will be born prematurely. Men will suffer most grievously, in order that those born in the country may regain power.

'He who will achieve these things shall appear as the Man of Bronze and for long years he shall guard the gates of London upon a brazen horse.

'Then the Red Dragon will revert to its true habits and struggle to tear itself to pieces.

'Next will come the revenge of the Thunderer and every one of the farmer's fields will be a disappointment to him.

'Death will lay hands on the people and destroy all the nations. Those who are left alive will abandon their native soil and will sow their seeds in other men's fields.

'A king who is blessed will fit out a navy and will be reckoned the twelfth in the court among the saints.

'The realm shall be deserted in the most pitiful way and the harvest threshing-floors shall be overgrown once more by forests rich in fruit.

'Once again the White Dragon shall rise up and will invite over a daughter of Germany. Our little gardens will be stocked again with foreign seed and the Red Dragon will pine away at the far end of the pool.

'After that the German Worm shall be crowned and the Prince of Brass will be buried. A limit was set for him, beyond which he was powerless to pass. For a hundred and fifty years he shall remain in anguish and subjection, and then for three hundred more he shall sit enthroned. The North Wind will rise against him, snatching away the flowers which the West Wind has caused to bloom. There will be gilding in the temples, but the sword's cutting edge will not cease its work.

'The German Dragon will find it hard to escape to its cavernous lairs, for vengeance for its treason will overtake it. In the end it will become strong again just for a short time, but the decimation of Normandy will be a sorry blow.

'There shall come a people dressed in wood and in iron corselets who will take vengeance on it for its wickedness. This people shall give their dwellings back to the earlier inhabitants, and the destruction of foreigners will be clear for all to see.

'The seed of the White Dragon shall be rooted up from our little gardens and what is then left of its progeny shall be decimated. They shall bear the yoke of perpetual slavery and they will wound their own Mother with their spades and plough-shares.

'Two more Dragons shall follow, one of which will be killed

by the sting of envy, but the second will return under the cover of authority.

'The Lion of Justice shall come next, and at its roar the towers of Gaul shall shake and the island Dragons tremble. In the days of this Lion gold shall be squeezed from the lily-flower and the nettle and silver shall flow from the hoofs of lowing cattle.

'Those who have had their hair waved shall dress in woollen stuffs of many colours, and the outer garment shall be a fair index of the thoughts within.

'The feet of those that bark shall be cut off.

'Wild animals shall enjoy peace, but mankind will bewail the way in which it is being punished.

'The balance of trade shall be torn in half; and the half that is left shall be rounded off.

'Kites will lose their ravenous hunger and the teeth of wolves will be blunted.

'The Lion's cubs shall be transformed into salt-water fishes and the Eagle of Mount Aravia shall nest upon its summit.

'Venedotia shall be red with the blood of mothers and the house of Corineus will slaughter six brothers.

'The island will lie sodden with the tears of the night-time, and everyone will be encouraged to try to do everything. Those who are born later shall strive to fly over even the most lofty things; but the favour given to newcomers will be loftier even than that.

'Piety will frown upon the man who has inherited goods from the impious: that is, until he takes his style of dress from his own father. Girded around with a wild boar's teeth, he shall climb over the mountain summits and higher than the shadow of the Helmeted Man.

'Albany will be angry: calling her near neighbours to her, she shall give herself up entirely to bloodshed. Between her jaws there will be found a bit which was forged in the Bay of Armorica. The Eagle of the Broken Covenant shall paint it with gold and will rejoice in her third nesting.

'The cubs shall roar as they keep watch; they will forsake the forest groves and come hunting inside the walls of cities. They will cause great slaughter among any who oppose them, and the tongues of bulls shall they slice off. They shall load with chains the necks of the roaring ones and live again the days of their fore-fathers.

'Thereafter, from the first to the fourth, from the fourth to the third, from the third to the second shall the thumb be rolled in oil.

'The sixth shall throw down the walls of Ireland and transmute its forests into a level plain. This sixth shall unite the different parts into one whole, and he shall be crowned with the head of a lion. His beginning will yield to his own unstable disposition, but his end shall soar up towards those on high. He shall restore the dwel-lings of the saints throughout the lands, and settle the pastors in places which befit them. Two towns shall he cover with funeral palls and to virgins he will present virgin gifts. By doing this he will earn the favour of the Thunderer and he will be placed among the blessed. From him there will emerge a She-lynx, and this will nose its way into all things and strive for the downfall of its own race. Because of the She-lynx Normandy will lose both its isles and be deprived of its former dignity.

'Then the island's inhabitants shall return to it, for a great dissension will arise among the foreigners.

'A hoary old man upon a snow-white horse shall divert the River Periron and above the stream he will measure out a mill with his white rod.

'Cadwallader shall summon Conanus and shall make an alliance with Albany. Then the foreigners shall be slaughtered and the rivers will run with blood.

'The mountains of Armorica shall erupt and Armorica itself shall be crowned with Brutus' diadem. Kambria shall be filled with joy and the Cornish oaks shall flourish. The island shall be called by the name of Brutus and the title given to it by the foreigners shall be done away with.

'From Conanus there shall descend a fierce Boar, which will try the sharpness of its tusks in the forests of Gaul; for it will lop down all the larger oak-trees, taking care, however, to protect the smaller ones.

'The Arabs shall dread this Boar and so shall the Africans, for the impetus of its onslaught will carry it into the remotest parts of Spain.

'Next after the Boar shall come the Ram of the Castle of Venus, with golden horns and a beard of silver. It will breathe such a fog from its nostrils that the entire surface of the island will be over-shadowed by it. In the days of the Ram there shall be peace, and the harvests will be plentiful because of the richness of the soil. Women shall become snake-like in their gait and every step they take will be full of arrogance. The Castle of Venus will be restored and Cupid's arrows will continue to wound.

'The source of the River Amne shall turn into blood; and two kings will fight each other at the Ford of the Staff for the sake of a Lioness.

'All the soil will be fruitful beyond man's need; and human beings will fornicate unceasingly.

'Three generations will witness all that I have mentioned, and then the kings buried in the town of London will be disinterred.

'Famine will return, and death, and citizens will grieve for their townships.

'The Boar of Commerce shall come and call back the scattered flocks to the feeding-ground which they have forsaken. Its breast will be as food to the hungry and its tongue will assuage the thirst of those who are dry. From its mouth shall flow forth rivers which will water the parched gullets of men.

'Then a Tree shall spring up on the top of the Tower of London. It will be content with only three branches and yet it will over-shadow the whole length and breadth of the island with the spread of its leaves. The North Wind will come as the Tree's enemy and with its noxious breath it will tear away the third of the branches.

he two branches which are left will occupy the place of the one
lpped off: this until one of them destroys the other by the very
bundance of its leaves. This last branch will fill the place of the
ther two and it will offer a roosting-place to birds come from
oreign parts. To birds native to the country it will seem harmful,
or through their dread of its shadow they will lose their power of
ree flight.

'The Ass of Wickedness will come next, swift against the gold-
miths, but slow against the wolves' ravenous appetite.

'In these days the oaks shall burn in the forest glades and acorns
hall burgeon on the lime trees' boughs.

'The Severn Sea shall flow forth through seven mouths and the
River Usk shall be boiling hot for seven months. Its fish will die
ecause of the heat and from them serpents will be born.

'The baths shall grow cold at Bath and its health-giving waters
hall breed death.

'London shall mourn the death of twenty thousand and the
Thames will be turned into blood.

'Monks in their cowls shall be forced into marriage and their
amentation will be heard on the mountain-peaks of the Alps.

'Three springs shall burst forth in the town of Winchester and [vii.4]
he streams which run from them will divide the island into three
parts. Whoever will drink from the first will enjoy long life and
will never be afflicted by the onslaught of illness. Whoever will
drink from the second shall perish from insatiable hunger: pallor
and dread will be clear to see on his face. Whoever will drink from
the third shall die a sudden death, and it will not be possible for his
body to be buried. In their effort to avoid so voracious a death-fit,
men will do their best to cover it over with layers of different
materials; but whatever structure is placed on top will immediately
take on the form of some other substance. As soon as they are
placed there, earth will be turned into stones, stones into liquid,
wood into ashes and ash into water.

'However, from a town in Canute's Forest a girl shall be sent to remedy these matters by her healing art. Once she has consulted all the oracles, she shall dry up the noxious springs simply by breathing on them. Next, when she has restored her own strength by some invigorating drink, she shall carry the Forest of Caledon in her right hand and in her left the buttressed forts of the walls of London. Wherever she passes she shall leave sulphurous footprints which will reek with a double flame. The smoke from them will stir up the Ruteni and will provide food for the creatures who live under the sea. Tears of compassion shall flow from her eyes and she will fill the island with her dreadful cries. He that will kill her shall be a stag of ten tines, four of which will bear golden coronets; but the other six will be turned into the horns of oxen and these horns will rouse the three islands of Britain with their accursed bellowing.

'The Daneian Forest shall be wakened from its sleep and, bursting into human speech, it shall shout: "Kambria, come here! Bring Cornwall at your side! Say to Winchester: 'The earth will swallow you up. Move the see of your shepherd to where the ships come in to harbour. Then make sure that the limbs which remain follow the head! The day approaches when your citizens will perish for their crimes of perjury. The whiteness of your wool has done you harm and so, too, has the variety of their dye. Woe to the perjured people, for their famous city shall come toppling down because of them!' "

'The ships shall rejoice at such a great increase and each one of them will be constructed out of the material of two.

'A Hedgehog loaded with apples shall re-build the town and, attracted by the smell of these apples, birds will flock there from many different forests. The Hedgehog shall add a huge palace and then wall it round with six hundred towers.

'London will view this with envy and will increase her own fortifications threefold. The River Thames will surround London on all sides and the report of that engineering feat will cross the Alps.

'The Hedgehog will hide its apples inside Winchester and will onstruct hidden passages under the earth.

'In that time the stones shall speak.

'The sea over which men sail to Gaul shall be contracted into a arrow channel. A man on any one of the two shores will be audible o a man on the other, and the land-mass of the island will grow reater.

'The secrets of the creatures who live under the sea shall be evealed and Gaul will tremble for fear.

'Next a Heron shall emerge from the Forest of Calaterium and y round the island for two whole years. By its cry in the night it ill call all winged creatures together and assemble in its company very genus of bird. They will swoop down on to the fields which en have cultivated and devour every kind of harvest. A famine ill attack the people and an appalling death-rate will follow the mine.

'As soon as this terrible calamity has come to an end, the accursed ird will transfer its attention to the Galabes Valley and raise it up to a lofty mountain. On its highest peak the Heron will plant an k and on the branches of the oak it shall build its nest. Three eggs all be laid in the nest and from them will emerge a Fox, a Wolf d a Bear. The Fox will devour its mother and then put on an ss's head. Once it has assumed this monstrous guise, it will terrify brothers and drive them away to Normandy. In that country ey will in their turn stir up the tusky Boar. Back they will come a boat and in that way they will meet the Fox once more. As it gins the contest, the Fox will pretend that it is dead and will ove the Boar to pity. Soon the Boar will go up to the Fox's rpse, and, standing over it, will breathe into its eyes and face. e Fox, not unmindful of its ancient cunning, will bite the Boar's t hoof and sever it completely from the Boar's body. Then the x will leap at the Boar and tear off its right ear and its tail, and nk off to hide in the mountain caves. The deluded Boar will then k the Wolf and the Bear to restore to it the parts which it has

lost. Once they have agreed to support the Boar, they will promis
it two feet, two ears and a tail, from which they will manufactur
truly porcine members. The Boar will agree to this and will stan
waiting for the promised return of its parts. Meanwhile the Fox wi
come down from the mountains and will metamorphose itsel
into a Wolf. Under the pretence of holding a conference with th
Boar, it will approach that animal craftily and eat it up. Then th
Fox will change itself into a Boar and stand waiting for its brother
pretending that it, too, has lost some of its members. As soon a
they come it will kill them with its tusk without a moment's dela
and then have itself crowned with a Lion's head.

'In the days of the Fox a Snake shall be born and this will brin
death to human beings. It will encircle London with its long ta
and devour all those who pass by.

'A Mountain Ox shall put on a Wolf's head and grind its teet
white in the Severn's workshop. The Ox will collect round itse
the flocks of Albany and those of Wales; and this company wi
drain the Thames dry as it drinks.

'An Ass shall call to itself a long-bearded Goat and then wi
change shapes with it. As a result the Mountain Bull will lose i
temper: it will summon the Wolf and then transfix the Ass and th
Goat with its horn. Once it has indulged its savage rage upon then
it will eat up their flesh and their bones, but the Ox itself wi
be burned up on the summit of Urianus. The ashes of its funer
pyre shall be transmuted into Swans, which will swim awa
upon dry land as though in water. These Swans will eat u
fish inside fish and they will swallow men inside men. Whe
they become old they will take the shape of Sea-wolves ar
continue their treacherous behaviour beneath the sea. The
will sink ships and so gather together quite a treasure-house
silver.

'Then the Thames shall begin to flow again. It will gather t
gether its tributaries and overflow the confines of its bed. It w
submerge near-by towns and overturn the mountains in its cours

It will join to itself the Springs of Galabes, filled as they are to the very brim with wickedness and deceit.

'As a result a number of mutinies will occur, and these will encourage the Venedoti to make war. The oaks of the forest shall band together and come into conflict with the rocks of the Gewissei.

'A Raven will fly down with the Kites and eat up the bodies of the dead.

'An Owl will nest on the walls of Gloucester and in its nest will be hatched an Ass. The Snake of Malvern will nurture this Ass and teach it many deceitful tricks. The Ass will put on a crown and then clamber above all that is most lofty and terrify the people with its hideous braying. In the days of the Ass the Pacaian Mountains shall totter and the country districts shall be deprived of their forest lands: for there shall come a Worm which will puff forth fire and this Worm will burn up the trees with the breath which it exhales. Out of the Worm shall come seven Lions, malformed with goats' heads. With the fetid breath from their nostrils the Lions will corrupt married women and cause wives so far faithful to one husband to become common prostitutes. The father shall not know his own son, for human beings will copulate wantonly as cattle do.

'Then indeed shall come a very Giant of Wickedness, who will terrify everyone with the piercing glance of his eyes. Against him will arise the Dragon of Worcester, which will do its best to destroy him; but when they come to grips the Dragon will be worsted and overwhelmed by its conqueror's wickedness. The Giant will climb on the Dragon, throw off all his clothes and then ride upon it naked. The Dragon will rear the Giant up into the air and lash his naked body with its erected tail; but the Giant will recover his strength and cut the Dragon's throat with his sword. Finally the Dragon will become entangled in its own tail and will die of poison.

'The Boar of Totnes shall succeed the Giant and will oppress the people with grievous tyranny. Gloucester shall send a Lion which will harass the raging Boar in a series of battles. This Lion

will trample the Boar under foot and terrify it with its open maw.
Finally the Lion will be at odds with all in the kingdom and climb
up on the backs of the nobles. A Bull will enter the conflict and
strike the Lion with its right hoof. The Bull will pursue the Lion
through all the narrow by-ways of the kingdom, but in the end it
will break its horns against the walls of Oxford. The Fox of
Caerdubalum will wreak vengeance on the Lion and eat it up with
its teeth. Then the Adder of Lincoln will coil round the Fox and
announce its presence to the assembled Dragons with a terrifying
hiss. The Dragons will attack each other and tear each other to
pieces. A Dragon with wings will overwhelm a Dragon without
wings, driving its venomous claws into the other's muzzle. Two
more Dragons will join the battle and the one will kill the other.
A fifth Dragon will replace the two dead ones and will destroy
the two left alive by various stratagems. It will climb on the back of
one, holding a sword in its claws, and hack its head away from its
body. Then it will cast its slough and climb on the second one and
seize its opponent's tail in its right and left claws. Naked it will overwhelm the other, when fully covered it will achieve nothing. It will
torment other Dragons by climbing on their backs, and drive them
round the kingdom.

'Then a roaring Lion will intervene, terrifying in its monstrous
cruelty. This Lion will reduce fifteen portions to a single entity and
by itself it will hold the people in its power.

'A Giant, snow-white in colour and gleaming bright, will
beget a people which is radiant.

'Soft living will enervate the leaders, and those under their
command will be changed into beasts. In their number will arise
a Lion, fat with human blood. A Man with a Sickle will act as the
Lion's helper in the harvest, but when the man is perplexed in his
mind the Lion will destroy him.

'The Charioteer of York will soothe the people. He will throw
his master out and climb up into the chariot which he is driving. He
will draw his sword and threaten the East, and he will fill with blood

the ruts made by his wheels. Next he will turn himself into a Sea-fish and mate with a Snake which has attracted him by its hissing.

'As a result there shall be born three Bulls, which will glitter like lightning. They will eat up their pasture-lands and then be turned into trees. The first Bull will carry a whip made of vipers; and it will turn its back on the one born second. The second Bull will struggle to snatch the whip from the first, but the whip will be seized by the third. They will avert their gaze from each other until they have thrown away the poison cup.

'A Farmer from Albany shall take their place and down his back a Snake shall hang. He will spend his time ploughing the earth, so that the harvests of his homeland may grow white; but the Snake will busy itself in scattering poison, to prevent the green corn from ever coming to harvest.

'The population shall decrease through some deadly calamity, and the walls of the towns will come tumbling down. The City of Claudius will be proposed as a source of remedy and this city will put forward the Foster-daughter of the Scourger. She shall come bearing a saucer of medicine and in next to no time the island will be restored.

'Two men shall hold the sceptre one after the other and a Horned Dragon will serve them both. The first man will come clad in iron and riding upon a flying Serpent. He will sit astride its back, with his body naked, and he will grasp its tail in his right hand. The seas will be made turbulent by his cry and he will strike terror into the second man. As a result the second man will make an alliance with a Lion, but a quarrel will ensue and they will fight. Each of the two will suffer greatly from the other's blows, but the animal's ferocity will enable it to win.

'A man shall come with a drum and a lute and he will soothe the Lion's savageness. The various peoples in the kingdom will be pacified as a result, and they will encourage the Lion to take the saucer of medicine. As it sits in the dwelling allocated to it, it will examine the dose, but it will stretch out its hands towards Albany.

The regions of the north will be saddened by this and they will throw open the gates of their temples.

'A Wolf will act as standard-bearer and lead the troops, and it will coil its tail round Cornwall. A soldier in a chariot will resist the Wolf and transform the Cornish people into a Boar. As a result the Boar will devastate the provinces, but it will hide its head in the depths of the Severn.

'A man shall wrestle with a drunken Lion, and the gleam of gold will blind the eyes of the onlookers. Silver will shine white in the open space around, causing trouble to a number of wine-presses. Men will become drunk with the wine which is offered to them: they will turn their backs on Heaven and fix their eyes on the earth. The stars will avert their gaze from these men and alter their accustomed course. The harvests will dry up through the stars' anger and all moisture from the sky will cease.

'Roots and branches shall change their places and the oddness of this will pass for a miracle.

'Before the amber glow of Mercury the bright light of the Sun shall grow dim and this will strike horror into those who witness it. The planet Mercury, born in Arcady, shall change its shield; and the Helmet of Mars shall call to Venus. The Helmet of Mars shall cast a shadow and in its rage Mercury shall over-run its orbit. Iron Orion shall bare its sword. The watery Sun shall torment the clouds. Jupiter shall abandon its pre-ordained paths and Venus desert its appointed circuits. The malice of the planet Saturn will pour down like rain, killing mortal men as though with a curved sickle. The twelve mansions of the stars will weep to see their inmates transgress so. The Gemini will cease their wonted embraces and will dispatch Aquarius to the fountains. The scales of Libra will hang awry, until Aries props them up with its curving horns. The tail of Scorpio shall generate lightning and Cancer will fight with the Sun. Virgo shall climb on the back of Sagittarius and so let droop its maiden blossoms. The Moon's chariot shall run amok in the Zodiac and the Pleiades will burst into tears. None of

these will return to the duty expected of it. Ariadne will shut its
door and be hidden within its enclosing cloudbanks.

'In the twinkling of an eye the seas shall rise up and the arena of
the winds shall be opened once again. The winds shall do battle
together with a blast of ill-omen, making their din reverberate
from one constellation to another.'

Part Six

THE HOUSE OF CONSTANTINE
(CONTINUED)

[viii.1] WHEN Merlin had made these prophecies, and others too, he filled all those present with amazement by the equivocal meaning of his words. Vortigern, who was even more astonished than the others, himself spoke highly of the young man's wit and his oracular pronouncements, for that particular period in history had produced no one who was ready to speak his mind in this way in front of the King.

Vortigern wanted particularly to learn what his own end would be, and he asked the young man to tell him what he knew about it. Merlin gave the following answer: 'Run from the fiery vengeance of the sons of Constantine, that is if you have the power to escape it. At this very moment they are fitting out their ships. Even as I speak they are leaving the coasts of Armorica and spreading their sails to cross the sea. They will make for the island of Britain, attack the Saxon people and conquer the race which they detest. The first thing they will do will be to burn you alive, shut up inside your tower! You made a fatal mistake when you betrayed their father and invited the Saxons to your island. You summoned them as your protectors, but in effect their coming ensured your own violent death. Two different ways of dying threaten you and it is not easy to see which of the two you will avoid. On the one hand the Saxons are ravaging your kingdom and will try to kill you. On the other hand the two brothers Aurelius and Uther are landing, and they will do their utmost to take vengeance on you for their father's death. Look for some refuge if you can: for tomorrow they will steer for the shore at Totnes. The Saxons' faces will be smeared with red blood; and when Hengist is killed Aurelius Ambrosius will be crowned King. He will restore peace to the people and build

up the Church again; but he himself will die of poison. His brother
Utherpendragon will succeed him, but his days too will be cut
short by poison. Your own descendants will play a part in this
dastardly act, but the Boar of Cornwall will eat them up.'

When the next day dawned, with no time lost, Aurelius Ambrosius came ashore.

As soon as the news of his coming reached them, the Britons, [viii.2]
who had been scattered with such great slaughter, gathered together again from all sides, reassured as they were and made more
optimistic than they had been before by the coming of their fellow-
countrymen. The clergy were convened. They anointed Aurelius
as King and did homage to him in the usual way. The Britons coun-
selled an immediate attack on the Saxons, but the King persuaded
them against it, for he wanted to hunt down Vortigern first.
Aurelius Ambrosius had been so grieved by the betrayal of his
father that he felt no other action of any sort could be contemplated
until he avenged him. In order to carry out his design, he marched
his army into Kambria and made for the castle of Genoreu, for it
was there that Vortigern had fled in his search for a safe refuge. This
castle, which belonged to Erging country, was beside the River
Wye, on a hill called Cloartius.[1]

As soon as he reached the place, Ambrosius, who could think of
nothing but the betrayal of his father and brother, said to Eldol, the
Duke of Gloucester: 'See now, my Lord Duke, if the fortifications
and the walls of this place can protect Vortigern, and stop me
burying the point of my sword in his entrails! He has earned a
violent death, and I imagine that you yourself must be fully aware

1. Vortigern had built his tower of refuge on Mount Erith [= Snowdon],
p. 166. MS. 1706 reads simply 'venit tandem ad montem Erith'. Jesus elaborates
this to: 'he found a spot suited for a castle in the place called at this hour
dinas Emrys, in the Yrri [= Snowdon]'. The Arthurian Society met on
Dinas Emreis on 18 August 1957. Now we are told that the castle is called
Genoreu, and that it is on a hill called Cloartius, in Erging country, beside
the River Wye. Cp. Lloyd, Art., pp. 460–61, where Cloartius is Little Doward
in Monmouthshire.

of how much he has deserved it. Of all men he is surely the most villainous! How much he deserves to die of unmentionable tortures! First of all he betrayed my father Constantine, who had freed him and his country from the invading Picts. Then he betrayed my brother Constans, whom he had caused to be made King so that he, Vortigern, could destroy him. Finally, when he had himself seized the crown by using his own crafty wits, he imported pagans to mix with the local population, so that he could destroy the men who remained loyal to me. By God's will, he has himself now fallen unwarily into the very snare which he prepared for my faithful adherents; for when the Saxons discovered how evil he was, they drove him out of the kingdom, a deed which ought to grieve no one. However, in my opinion, there is one aspect of all this which everyone must regret: that this evil man, through the heathen whom he invited over, has exiled the nobility, laid waste a fertile country, destroyed the holy churches and virtually obliterated Christianity from one sea to the other. Act, then, like true men, my fellow-countrymen, and take your first vengeance upon him by whose agency all these things have come about. After that we must turn our arms against the enemies who beset us, and free our homeland from their hungry maw!'

They lost no time, but moved into position with their siege-machines and did their utmost to break down the walls. When everything else had failed, they tried fire; and this, once it took hold, went on blazing until it burned up the tower and Vortigern with it.

[viii.3]   When news of this reached Hengist and his Saxons, he was greatly frightened, for he dreaded the courage of Aurelius. The man was so brave and hardy that while he was living in various places in Gaul no one had dared to meet him in single combat. Whenever he had fought such a duel, he either dashed his opponent from his horse or else broke his own spear into splinters. What is more, he was liberal in his gifts, regular in his attendance at divine services, modest in all his behaviour and unwilling ever to tell a lie.

He fought well on foot and even better when mounted; and he was most skilled in commanding an army.

While Aurelius was still in Armorican Britain, rumour, which never halts its daily round, had brought reports of his accomplishments into the island. As a result the Saxons dreaded him and they now retreated across the Humber. They fortified the towns and castles in those parts, for the region had always been a refuge towards which they could retreat. The nearness of Scotland afforded them protection, for that country had never missed an opportunity of making matters worse whenever the Britons were in distress. It was a land frightful to live in, more or less uninhabited, and it offered a safe lurking-place to foreigners. Indeed, by its geographical position, it lay open to the Picts, the Scots, the Danes, the Norwegians and anyone else who came ashore to ravage the island.

Assured as they thus were of the sympathy of the country, the Saxons retreated in that direction, so that if need arose they could take refuge there, just as if they were in their own stronghold. As soon as this was reported to Aurelius, his courage rose, for he now had every hope of victory. He assembled his fellow-countrymen as quickly as he could, reinforced his army and marched northwards. As he passed through the different regions, he grieved to see how desolate they were, but most of all to find the churches razed to the ground. He swore that he would restore them, if only he were victorious.

Hengist took courage once more when he learned of the approach of Aurelius. He assembled a hand-picked army and gave encouragement to every single soldier, exhorting them all to fight like men and not be afraid to join battle with Aurelius. Hengist alleged that Aurelius had few Armorican Britons with him, for their number hardly exceeded ten thousand. What is more, he expressed the lowest possible opinion of the island Britons, seeing that he had defeated them so often in battle. He promised his own men victory, and personal safety, too, in view of their greater number, for there were about two hundred thousand armed men present. [viii.4]

Once he had emboldened all his men in this way, Hengist marched to meet Aurelius in a field called Maisbeli, through which the latter was about to pass. Hengist planned to make a sudden surprise attack and to fall upon the Britons when they were least expecting it. However, this move could not be kept hidden from Aurelius. He did not avoid passing through the field because of this, but hurried on all the more quickly. The moment he came in sight of the enemy, he drew up his troops. He ordered three thousand men from among the Armoricans to take up position with their horses. Those Armoricans who were left he disposed in line of battle here and there among the islanders. He stationed the Demetians on the hills and the Venedotians in the encircling woods. His reason for this was to ensure that, should the Saxons flee in either of those directions, men should be there to block their way.

[viii.5]   Meanwhile Eldol, Duke of Gloucester, went to the King and said: 'I would consider this one day a sufficient recompense for all the remaining days of my life, if only God would grant that I might fight hand-to-hand with Hengist: for one of us two would die as we attacked each other with our swords. I remember the occasion on which we met, ready as we were on our side to make peace. While an agreement was being sought, Hengist betrayed every man present and had a knife stuck into each one of them, except me alone, for I discovered a wooden pole and so escaped. On that day there died four hundred and eighty great leaders and men of high rank, all of whom had come there unarmed. In that moment of great peril, God placed a wooden pole in my hand. With it I defended myself and so escaped.' These were the things which Eldol said. Aurelius then exhorted his comrades to place all their hope in the Son of God, to attack their enemies boldly and to fight as one man for their homeland.

On his side Hengist was marshalling his troops and as he placed them in position he gave them instructions for the battle. He walked round among the ranks to give his orders, so that he could inspire everyone with a concerted zeal for the fight. Finally, when on both sides the companies had been posted in position, the two lines of battle joined combat, matching each other's blows and shedding a great amount of blood. Britons on this side and Saxons on that died of the wounds which they had received. Aurelius urged on the Christians, and Hengist encouraged the pagans. As long as they continued with this battle, Eldol never once stopped his attempts to find an opportunity for fighting hand-to-hand with Hengist, but he was not successful; for when Hengist saw that his men were beaten and that by God's grace the Britons were victorious, he fled immediately, making his way to the castle of Kaerconan, which is now called Cunungeburg. Aurelius pursued him and killed or forced into slavery every man whom he overtook on the way.

When Hengist saw that Aurelius was following him, he decided not to occupy the castle. He once more drew up his people in their companies, arranging them so that they were ready to join battle again; for he knew well that the castle could never withstand Aurelius and that the only defence left to him lay in sword and spear. When Aurelius finally caught up with Hengist, he stationed his own soldiers in their companies and attacked with the utmost ferocity. However, the Saxons resisted as one man, and on both sides troops were wounded mortally. Wherever one looked there was blood flowing and the screams of the dying roused to fury those who were still alive.

The Saxons would have won in the end, if a cavalry detachment of Armorican Britons had not come on the scene. Aurelius had posted this squadron in exactly the same way as he had done in the first battle. When the cavalry arrived the Saxons gave ground before it and once they had moved from their positions they were not able to re-form. At this the Britons attacked even more fiercely, rushing at the enemy as one man. All the time Aurelius was issuing orders to his own men, wounding such of the enemy as came his way, pursuing those who had turned in flight, and so bringing comfort to his own army. In the same way Eldol rushed hither and thither, dealing deadly wounds to those who stood up to him; but whatever else occupied him, his heart was still set on the possibility of fighting hand-to-hand with Hengist.

[viii.6]   As the various companies of troops moved forward in this direction and in that, by chance Eldol and Hengist were brought together, with no advantage to either of them, and they began to rain blows on each other. What men they were, and how much more war-like than the others! As each in turn slashed at the other with his sword, the sparks flew from his blows as if he were at once a source of thunder-claps and of lightning-flashes. For a long time it was not clear on which side lay the greater strength. At one moment Eldol pressed forward and Hengist yielded; and then Eldol drew back and Hengist advanced.

As they fought on in this way Gorlois, Duke of Cornwall, moved up towards them with the squadron which he commanded, harassing the enemy's companies as he came. When he set eyes on Gorlois, Eldol gained a new assurance. He seized hold of Hengist by the nasal of his metal helmet and by exerting all his strength dragged him in among his own men. A great flood-tide of joy boiled up within him and he shouted at the top of his voice: 'God has granted my prayer! Now, men, down with what is left of the Ambrones! Victory is in your hand! Now that Hengist is beaten, you have beaten them all!'

While these things were happening, the Britons redoubled their attacks on the pagans, charging them again and again, and as they retreated attacking them once more with ever-increasing courage. They gave them no respite until finally victory was won. The pagans turned in flight, each man for himself. Some fled to the towns, some to the thickly-wooded mountains, and others again to their own ships. Hengist's son Octa retreated to York with the biggest band; and his kinsman Eosa garrisoned that town with a great force of armed men.

[viii.7]   Once Aurelius had won the victory in this way, he seized the town of Conan which I have already mentioned earlier on, and there he halted for three days. During this time he ordered the dead to be buried, the wounded to receive medical attention, the weary to take rest and all of them to refresh themselves with such consolations as they could find. Next he called his leaders together and ordered them to decide what should be done with Hengist. Among those present was Eldadus, Bishop of Gloucester, the brother of Eldol and a man of the greatest wisdom and piety. When Eldadus saw Hengist standing before the King, he ordered the others to be silent and spoke as follows: 'Even if you all were doing your level best to have this man set free, I would hack him in pieces myself. In this I would be following the prophet Samuel, who, when he held in his power Agag, King of Amalek,[1] hewed him in pieces, saying: "As thy sword hath made women childless, so shall thy mother be childless among women." Do, therefore, the same with this man, who is clearly a second Agag.' Thereupon Eldol took his sword, led Hengist outside the city, and packed him off to Hell by cutting off his head. Aurelius, who was moderate in all that he did, ordered Hengist to be buried and a barrow of earth to be raised over his body, that being the pagan custom.

Then Aurelius led his army to York in order to besiege Octa, the [viii.8] son of Hengist. When Aurelius started investing the city, Octa had doubts as to whether or not he should resist and defend it against such a huge army. He took the advice of his men and then emerged with the more noble of those who were with him, carrying a chain in his hand and having coarse gravel on his head. He presented himself before the King and made the following speech: 'My own gods are vanquished. I do not doubt for a moment that it is your God who reigns supreme, for He has compelled so many noble men to appear before you in this manner. Accept, then, both our persons and this length of chain. If you are not prepared to grant us mercy, then have us bound, for of our own free will we are ready for whatever punishment you propose to inflict.'

Aurelius was filled with compassion; and he ordered a decision to be made on what should be done with the Saxons. When the

1. 1 Samuel xv.33.

others had expressed conflicting opinions, Bishop Eldadus rose to his feet again and gave his own advice in the following words: 'The Gibeonites came of their own free will to seek mercy of the Children of Israel, and they received that mercy. Shall we Christians be harder than the Jews, and refuse mercy to these men? It is mercy they are asking for: let them have mercy, I say. The island of Britain is big enough; and in many parts there are no inhabitants at all. Let them occupy those places, then, and be our subjects for all time.' The King agreed to what Eldadus advised and took pity on the Saxons. Following Octa's example, Eosa, too, came in, and the others who had fled with him, and they received pardon. Aurelius granted them the region near Scotland and signed a treaty with them.

[viii.9]   With his enemies beaten, Aurelius summoned to York his leading men and the princes of his realm, and ordered them to restore the churches which the Saxon people had destroyed. He himself began to re-build the metropolitan cathedral of that city and the other episcopal churches in the see. When fifteen days had passed and he had put the various craftsmen to work in the places concerned, he set off for the town of London, which the fury of the enemy had certainly not spared. Grieved as he was by the destruction of the town, he collected together from every quarter such citizens as were left alive, and began the task of re-building it.

It was from that city that he ruled his kingdom, bringing new life to laws which had been allowed to fall into disuse and restoring to their rightful heirs the scattered possessions of long-dead folk. Any estates which, in this major disaster, had no one left alive to inherit them, were shared among those who had fought at his side. The entire energy of Aurelius was devoted to restoring the realm, re-building the churches, renewing peace and the rule of law, and administering justice.

Next he went to Winchester, to restore that town as he had restored others like it. As soon as he had repaired everything that needed such attention if the town was to be restored at all, he took

the advice of Bishop Eldadus and visited the monastery near
Kaercaradduc, which is now called Salisbury. It was there that
were buried the leaders and princes whom the infamous Hengist
had betrayed. A monastery of three hundred brethren stood there,
on Mount Ambrius,[1] for it was Ambrius, so they say, who had
founded the monastery years before. As Aurelius inspected the
place in which the dead lay, he was moved to compassion and burst
into tears. In the end he turned his mind to other considerations,
asking himself what he could do to ensure that the spot should be
remembered; for it was his opinion that the greensward covering
so many noble men who had died for their fatherland was certainly
worthy of some memorial.

Aurelius collected carpenters and stone-masons together from [viii.10]
every region and ordered them to use their skill to contrive some
novel building which would stand for ever in memory of such
distinguished men. The whole band racked their brains and then
confessed themselves beaten. Then Tremorinus, Archbishop of the
City of the Legions, went to the King and said: 'If there is anyone
anywhere who has the ability to execute your plan, then Merlin,
the prophet of Vortigern, is the man to do it. In my opinion, there
is no one else in your kingdon who has greater skill, either in the
foretelling of the future or in mechanical contrivances. Order
Merlin to come and use his ability, so that the monument for
which you are asking can be put up.'

Aurelius asked many questions about Merlin; then he sent a
number of messengers through the various regions of the country
to find him and fetch him. They travelled through the provinces
and finally located Merlin in the territory of the Gewissei, at the

---

1. There is a curious confusion here. By *Mount Ambrius*, the *Cloister of
Ambrius*, etc., Geoffrey may be thinking of Avebury and muddling it with
Amesbury. When Merlin brings the stones of the Giant's Ring from Mount
Killaraus in Ireland, he re-erects them as Stonehenge. Geoffrey repeatedly
treats Stonehenge and Avebury/Amesbury as if they were one place. Cp.
my index for individual references.

Galabes Springs, where he often went. They explained to him what they wanted of him and then conducted him to the King. The King received Merlin gaily and ordered him to prophesy the future, for he wanted to hear some marvels from him. 'Mysteries of that sort cannot be revealed,' answered Merlin, 'except where there is the most urgent need for them. If I were to utter them as an entertainment, or where there was no need at all, then the spirit which controls me would forsake me in the moment of need.'

He gave the same refusal to everyone present. The King had no wish to press him about the future, but he spoke to him about the monument which he was planning. 'If you want to grace the burial-place of these men with some lasting monument,' replied Merlin, 'send for the Giants' Ring which is on Mount Killaraus in Ireland. In that place there is a stone construction which no man of this period could ever erect, unless he combined great skill and artistry. The stones are enormous and there is no one alive strong enough to move them. If they are placed in position round this site, in the way in which they are erected over there, they will stand for ever.'

[viii.11]   At these words of Merlin's Aurelius burst out laughing. 'How can such large stones be moved from so far-distant a country?' he asked. 'It is hardly as if Britain itself is lacking in stones big enough for the job!' 'Try not to laugh in a foolish way, your Majesty,' answered Merlin. 'What I am suggesting has nothing ludicrous about it. These stones are connected with certain secret religious rites and they have various properties which are medicinally important. Many years ago the Giants transported them from the remotest confines of Africa and set them up in Ireland at a time when they inhabited that country. Their plan was that, whenever they felt ill, baths should be prepared at the foot of the stones; for they used to pour water over them and to run this water into baths in which their sick were cured. What is more, they mixed the water with herbal concoctions and so healed their wounds. There is not a single stone among them which hasn't some medicinal virtue.'

When the Britons heard all this, they made up their minds to send for the stones and to make war on the people of Ireland if they tried to hold them back. In the end the King's brother, Utherpendragon, and fifteen thousand men, were chosen to carry out the task. Merlin, too, was co-opted, so that all the problems which had to be met could have the benefit of his knowledge and advice. They made ready their ships and they put to sea. The winds were favourable and they arrived in Ireland.

At that time there reigned in Ireland a young man of remarkable [viii.12] valour called Gillomanius. As soon as he heard that the Britons had landed in the country, he collected a huge army together and hurried to meet them. When he learned the reason of their coming, Gillomanius laughed out loud at those standing round him. 'I am not surprised that a race of cowards has been able to devastate the island of the Britons,' said he, 'for the Britons are dolts and fools. Who ever heard of such folly? Surely the stones of Ireland aren't so much better than those of Britain that our realm has to be invaded for their sake! Arm yourselves, men, and defend your fatherland, for as long as life remains in my body they shall not steal from us the minutest fragment of the Ring.'

When he saw that the Irish were spoiling for a fight, Uther hurriedly drew up his own line of battle and charged at them. The Britons were successful almost immediately. The Irish were either mangled or killed outright, and Gillomanius was forced to flee. Having won the day, the Britons made their way to Mount Killaraus. When they came to the stone structure, they were filled with joy and wonder. Merlin came up to them as they stood round in a group. 'Try your strength, young men,' said he, 'and see whether skill can do more than brute strength, or strength more than skill, when it comes to dismantling these stones!'

At his bidding they all set to with every conceivable kind of mechanism and strove their hardest to take the Ring down. They rigged up hawsers and ropes and they propped up scaling-ladders, each preparing what he thought most useful, but none of these things advanced them an inch. When he saw what a mess they were making of it, Merlin burst out laughing. He placed in position all the gear which he considered necessary and dismantled the stones more easily than you could ever believe. Once he had pulled them down, he had them carried to the ships and stored on board, and they all set sail once more for Britain with joy in their hearts.

The winds were fair. They came to the shore and then set off with the stones for the spot where the heroes had been buried. The moment that this was reported to him, Aurelius dispatched messengers to all the different regions of Britain, ordering the clergy and the people to assemble and, as they gathered, to converge on Mount Ambrius, where they were with due ceremony and rejoicing to re-dedicate the burial-place which I have described. At the summons from Aurelius the bishops and abbots duly assembled with men from every rank and file under the King's command. All came together on the appointed day. Aurelius placed the crown on his head and celebrated the feast of Whitsun in right royal fashion, devoting the next three days to one long festival. As part of this, he bestowed lands on those who had no holdings of their own, thus rewarding them for the efforts they had made to serve him. The two metropolitan sees of York and the City of the Legions were without incumbents. With the general consent of his people, whom he wished to consult in this matter, Aurelius gave York to Samson, a most distinguished man who was famous for his great piety. The City of the Legions he bestowed upon Dubricius, whom divine providence had already singled out as one suitable for promotion there.

Once he had settled these matters, and others of a similar nature, Aurelius ordered Merlin to erect round the burial-place the stones which he had brought from Ireland. Merlin obeyed the King's orders and put the stones up in a circle round the sepulchre, in exactly the same way as they had been arranged on Mount Killaraus in Ireland, thus proving that his artistry was worth more than any brute strength.[1]

1. See p. 19 and n.28.

At this same time Paschent, the son of Vortigern, who had fled [viii.13] to Germany, was stirring up every armed soldier in that kingdom against Aurelius Ambrosius. His great desire was to avenge his father. He promised the Germans limitless money in gold and silver, if only he could subdue Britain with their help. In the end, when he had suborned all the young men with his promises, he fitted out the greatest possible fleet, landed in the northern regions of the island and began to lay waste to them. This was reported to the King. He summoned his own army, hastened to meet Paschent and challenged the raging enemy to combat. They in their turn came out to fight and joined battle with the local inhabitants. By the grace of God they were deprived of victory and were forced to take flight.

Once he had been compelled to run away, Paschent did not dare [viii.14] to return to Germany. Shifting his sails, he went off to Gillomanius in Ireland and was well received by him. Gillomanius took pity on Paschent when the latter explained his misfortune. He promised Paschent help and himself complained of the injury which Uther, the brother of Aurelius, had done him, too, by coming to seek the Giant's Ring. A treaty was agreed upon between them. They fitted out ships, went on board and then landed near the town of Menevia. As soon as this was known, a force of armed men was assembled and Utherpendragon set off for Kambria to fight them. His brother Aurelius was lying ill at the time in Winchester and was unable to be present. When this was made known to Paschent, Gillomanius and the Saxons who were with them, they were delighted, for they thought that with Aurelius ill the kingdom could easily be conquered.

While the people were discussing what had happened, one of the Saxons, called Eopa, came to Paschent. 'How much will you give the man who kills Aurelius Ambrosius for you?' he asked. 'If only I could find a man who was prepared to do that,' answered Paschent, 'I would give him a thousand pounds of silver and my own friendship as long as I lived. If by good fortune I win the crown of this island, I will make him a captain in my army, and that I will promise on oath.' 'I have learned the British language,' said Eopa, 'I am familiar with the habits of the people, and I have some knowledge of medical practice. If only you will fulfil what you promise, then I will disguise myself as a Christian and a Briton, I will gain admittance to the King's presence by pretending to be a doctor, and I will mix for him a potion which will kill him. To enable me to gain an audience more readily I will pretend that I am a monk, as devout as can be and learned in all dogma.' As soon as he had made this suggestion, Paschent came to an agreement with him, confirming on oath what he had already promised.

Eopa thereupon shaved off his beard, had his head tonsured, took the habit of a monk and set off for Winchester with a load of pots which he had filled with medicines. As soon as he arrived in the town, he offered his service to the King's retainers, who received him warmly. No one could have been more welcome than a doctor. Eopa was told to come in and they led him to the King. He promised that he would restore the King to health, if only the latter would swallow his medicines. Eopa was ordered to prepare a draught immediately. He mixed a poison and gave it to the King. Aurelius took it and drained it at a gulp; then he was told by the accursed Ambro to snuggle down under the bed-covering and to go to sleep: this so that the noisome poison could work the more efficaciously. The King immediately obeyed the advice of the man who had betrayed him, and dropped off to sleep, imagining that he was about to recover his health. The poison ran quickly through his veins and the pores of his body; and thus death, which has the trick of sparing no man, came to him while he slept. Meanwhile the accursed traitor slipped away in the crowd and was nowhere to be found in the court.

While these things were happening at Winchester, there appeared a star of great magnitude and brilliance, with a single beam shining from it. At the end of this beam was a ball of fire, spread out in the shape of a dragon. From the dragon's mouth stretched forth two rays of light, one of which seemed to extend its length beyond the latitude of Gaul, while the second turned towards the Irish Sea and split up into seven smaller shafts of light.

This star appeared three times, and all who saw it were struck [viii.15] with fear and wonder. Uther, the King's brother, who was hunting for the enemy army, was just as terrified as the others. He summoned his wise men, so that they might tell him what the star portended. He ordered Merlin to be fetched with the others, for Merlin had come with the army so that the campaign could have the benefit of his advice. As he stood in the presence of his leader and was given the order to explain the significance of the star, he burst into tears, summoned up his familiar spirit, and prophesied aloud. 'Our loss is irreparable,' he said. 'The people of Britain is orphaned. Our most illustrious King has passed away. Aurelius Ambrosius, the famous King of the Britons, has died. By his death we shall all die, unless God brings us help. Hasten forward, most noble leader! Hasten forward, Uther, and do not put off for a moment making contact with the enemy. Victory shall be yours and you will be King of all Britain. The star signifies you in person, and so does the fiery dragon beneath the star. The beam of light, which stretches towards the shore of Gaul, signifies your son, who will be a most powerful man. His dominion shall extend over all the kingdoms which the beam covers. The second ray signifies your daughter, whose sons and grandsons shall hold one after the other the kingship of Britain.'

Although he remained in some doubt whether or not what [viii.16] Merlin had prophesied was true, Uther nevertheless continued to advance against the enemy as he had begun. He had now come within half a day's march of Menevia. As soon as his approach was announced to Gillomanius, Paschent and the Saxons who were there, they marched out to meet him and do battle with him. The moment the armies came in sight of each other, they drew up their lines of battle on either side, marched forward to make contact, and so began the fight. As usually happens in such a combat, soldiers were slain on both sides as they fought. In the end, when much of the day had passed, Uther proved the stronger and won the victory, killing Gillomanius and Paschent in the process. The barbarians turned in flight and ran to their ships, and in their retreat they were cut down by the islanders who pursued them.

By the grace of Christ victory thus came to our leader. After this great undertaking, Uther set out for Winchester with all possible speed. Messengers who came to meet him told him of the King's death, saying that Aurelius was soon to be buried by the bishops of the country near the monastery of Ambrius and inside the Giants' Ring, the construction of which he had himself ordered during his lifetime. When they heard of his death, the bishops, abbots and all the clergy of that diocese had assembled in the town of Winchester. They arranged his funeral in a way becoming to so great a King. Since, while still alive, he had ordained that he should be put to rest in the cemetery which he had himself prepared, they bore his body thither and buried him there with royal pomp.

[viii.17]   Uther, the brother of Aurelius, convened the clergy and the people of his kingdom and took into his safe-keeping the crown of the island. With the agreement of everyone present he was appointed King. Mindful of the explanation given by Merlin of the star about which I have told you, he ordered two Dragons to be fashioned in gold, in the likeness of the one which he had seen in the ray which shone from that star. As soon as the Dragons had been completed – this with the most marvellous craftsmanship – he made a present of one of them to the congregation of the cathedral church of the see of Winchester. The second one he kept for himself, so that he could carry it round to his wars. From that moment onwards he was called Utherpendragon, which in the British language means 'a dragon's head'. He had been given this title because it was by means of a Dragon that Merlin had prophesied that he would become King.

[viii.18]   Meanwhile Octa the son of Hengist, and his kinsman Eosa, considering themselves freed from the treaty which they had made

with Aurelius Ambrosius, did everything they could to harass the
King and to over-run his dominions. They started by allying to
themselves those Saxons whom Paschent had brought over, and
then they sent their messengers to Germany to summon the rest
of them. Octa put himself in the centre of this huge army and invaded the northern provinces. He went on satiating his lust for
cruelty until he had destroyed all the towns and strong-points
from Albany as far as York. Finally, just as he had begun to besiege
that town, Utherpendragon arrived with the entire strength of his
kingdom and met Octa in a pitched battle. The Saxons resisted
manfully. They remained unbroken in the face of the assaults by
the Britons and in the end they drove their enemy back in flight.
Having once gained the victory, they pursued the Britons as far
as Mount Damen, continuing as long as the sun gave light to see by.

   This hill was a steep one. On its summit it had a hazel wood, and
half-way up there were jagged rocks well suited to be the lairs of
wild animals. The Britons occupied the hill and spent the night
among these rocks and hazel-bushes. Then, as the Plough began
to revolve its pole, Uther ordered his leaders and princes to be
summoned to him, so that with their advice he might decide how
they could attack the enemy. They all came together in the King's
presence; and he ordered them to say what they advised. He asked
Gorlois, the Duke of Cornwall, a man of great experience and
mature years, to give his opinion first. 'This is no moment,' said
Gorlois, 'for chattering or empty beating about the bush. While
we see that some of the night still remains, we must act boldly and
bravely – that is, if we expect any longer to enjoy either life or
liberty. The numerical strength of the pagans is very great and they
are spoiling for a fight. We, on the other hand, have far fewer
men. If we once wait for day to dawn, I see no point in our attacking
them at all. Let us move, then, while the darkness lasts. We must
clamber down in close formation and surprise them in their camp
by the very unexpectedness of our attack. Without any shadow of
doubt we shall triumph over them, if only we attack them all

together in the boldest possible fashion, for they will not have foreseen anything of this sort, nor will they have expected us to attack in this way.'

The advice of Gorlois pleased the King and all the others, too, and they carried out his suggestions. As soon as they were armed and drawn up in companies, they set out for the enemy's camp, with the intention of mounting a mass assault; but as they moved forward the sentinels observed their coming and awakened their comrades, who were sound asleep, by blowing on their cornets. The enemy were surprised and thrown into confusion. Some of them rushed to arm themselves and others were so terrified that they ran off in whatever direction the impulse of the moment suggested to them. The Britons moved forward in close formation and soon came to the camp itself. They charged forward with drawn swords, located the gateway and rushed in among the enemy. Engaged as they were at a moment when they least expected it, the enemy offered no effectual resistance. Our own men, on the other hand, became more and more bold as they saw their plans succeeding. The Britons made every effort to press forward eagerly. They butchered the pagans with might and main, killing off some thousands of them. In the end Octa and Eosa were captured and the Saxons were completely routed.

[viii.19]   After this victory Uther went to the town called Alclud, and while there he settled the affairs of that region and restored peace everywhere. Then he visited all the lands of the Scots and reclaimed that rebellious people from their state of savagery; for he administered justice throughout the regions in a way that none of his predecessors had been able to do. In his time those who had committed any crime were greatly terrified, for they were punished mercilessly. When he had finally pacified the northern provinces, he moved to London. He ordered Octa and Eosa to be kept in prison there.

The next Eastertide Uther told the nobles of his kingdom to assemble in that same town of London, so that he could wear his

rown and celebrate so important a feast-day with proper ceremony. They all obeyed, travelling in from their various cities and
assembling on the eve of the feast. The King was thus able to
celebrate the feast as he had intended and to enjoy himself in the
company of his leaders. They, too, were all happy, seeing that he
had received them with such affability. A great many nobles had
gathered there, men worthy of taking part in such a gay festivity,
together with their wives and daughters.

Among the others there was present Gorlois, Duke of Cornwall,
with his wife Ygerna, who was the most beautiful woman in
Britain. When the King saw her there among the other women,
he was immediately filled with desire for her, with the result that
he took no notice of anything else, but devoted all his attention to
her. To her and to no one else he kept ordering plates of food to
be passed and to her, too, he kept sending his own personal attendants with golden goblets of wine. He kept smiling at her and
engaging her in sprightly conversation. When Ygerna's husband
saw what was happening, he was so annoyed that he withdrew
from the court without taking leave. No one present could persuade him to return, for he was afraid of losing the one object that
he loved better than anything else. Uther lost his temper and ordered Gorlois to come back to court, so that he, the King, could
seek satisfaction for the way in which he had been insulted. Gorlois
refused to obey. The King was furious and swore an oath that he
would ravage Gorlois' lands, unless the latter gave him immediate
satisfaction.

Without more ado, while the bad blood remained between the
two of them, the King collected a huge army together and hurried
off to the Duchy of Cornwall, where he set fire to towns and castles.
Gorlois' army was the smaller of the two and he did not dare to
meet the King in battle. He preferred instead to garrison his castles
and to bide his time until he could receive help from Ireland. As
he was more worried about his wife than he was about himself,
he left her in the castle of Tintagel, on the sea-coast, which he

thought was the safest place under his control. He himself too
refuge in a fortified camp called Dimilioc,[1] so that, if disaste
overtook them, they should not both be endangered togethe
When the King heard of this, he went to the encampment wher
Gorlois was, besieged it and cut off every line of approach.

Finally, after a week had gone by, the King's passion for Ygern
became more than he could bear. He called to him Ulfin of Rid
caradoch, one of his soldiers and a familiar friend, and told hin
what was on his mind. 'I am desperately in love with Ygerna,' sai
Uther, 'and if I cannot have her I am convinced that I shall suffe
a physical breakdown. You must tell me how I can satisfy m
desire for her, for otherwise I shall die of the passion which
consuming me.' 'Who can possibly give you useful advice
answered Ulfin, 'when no power on earth can enable us to com
to her where she is inside the fortress of Tintagel? The castle
built high above the sea, which surrounds it on all sides, and ther
is no other way in except that offered by a narrow isthmus of rock
Three armed soldiers could hold it against you, even if you stoo
there with the whole kingdom of Britain at your side. If only th
prophet Merlin would give his mind to the problem, then with hi
help I think you might be able to obtain what you want.' Th
King believed Ulfin and ordered Merlin to be sent for, for he, too
had come to the siege.

Merlin was summoned immediately. When he appeared in th
King's presence, he was ordered to suggest how the King coul
have his way with Ygerna. When Merlin saw the torment whic
the King was suffering because of this woman, he was amazed a
the strength of his passion. 'If you are to have your wish,' he sai
'you must make use of methods which are quite new and unt
now unheard-of in your day. By my drugs I know how to giv

1. Near the village of Pendoggett, some 5½ miles south-west of Tintage
lies a great encampment of three concentric ramparts and ditches, some 44
yards in overall diameter, which bears the name of Tregeare Rounds an
is known locally as Castle Dameliock.

you the precise appearance of Gorlois, so that you will resemble him in every respect. If you do what I say, I will make you exactly like him, and Ulfin exactly like Gorlois' companion, Jordan of Tintagel. I will change my own appearance, too, and come with you. In this way you will be able to go safely to Ygerna in her castle and be admitted.'

The King agreed and listened carefully to what he had to do. In the end he handed the siege over to his subordinates, took Merlin's drugs, and was changed into the likeness of Gorlois. Ulfin was changed into Jordan and Merlin into a man called Britaelis, so that no one could tell what they had previously looked like. They then set off for Tintagel and came to the Castle in the twilight. The moment the guard was told that his leader was approaching, he opened the gates and the men were let in. Who, indeed, could possibly have suspected anything, once it was thought that Gorlois himself had come? The King spent that night with Ygerna and satisfied his desire by making love with her. He had deceived her by the disguise which he had taken. He had deceived her, too, by the lying things that he said to her, things which he planned with great skill. He said that he had come out secretly from his besieged encampment so that he might make sure that all was well with her, whom he loved so dearly, and with his castle, too. She naturally believed all that he said and refused him nothing that he asked. That night she conceived Arthur, the most famous of men, who subsequently won great renown by his outstanding bravery.

Meanwhile, when it was discovered at the siege of Dimilioc [viii. 20] that the King was no longer present, his army, acting without his instructions, tried to breach the walls and challenge the beleaguered Duke to battle. The Duke, equally ill-advisedly, sallied forth with his men, imagining apparently that he could resist such a host of armed men with his own tiny band. As the struggle between them swayed this way and that, Gorlois was among the first to be killed. His men were scattered and the besieged camp was captured.

The treasure which had been deposited there was shared out in the most inequitable way, for each man seized in his greedy fist whatever good luck and his own brute strength threw in his way.

Not until the outrages which followed this daring act had finally subsided did messengers come to Ygerna to announce the death of the Duke and the end of the siege. When they saw the King sitting beside Ygerna in the likeness of their leader, they blushed red with astonishment to see that the man whom they had left behind dead in the siege had in effect arrived there safely before them. Of course, they did not know of the drugs prepared by Merlin. The King put his arms round the Duchess and laughed aloud to hear these reports. 'I am not dead,' he said. 'Indeed, as you see, I am very much alive! However, the destruction of my camp saddens me very much and so does the slaughter of my comrades. What is more, there is great danger that the King may come this way and capture us in this castle. I will go out to meet him and make peace with him, lest even worse should befall us.'

The King set out and made his way towards his own army, abandoning his disguise as Gorlois and becoming Utherpendragon once more. When he learned all that had happened, he mourned for the death of Gorlois; but he was happy, all the same, that Ygerna was freed from her marital obligations. He returned to Tintagel Castle, captured it and seized Ygerna at the same time, she being what he really wanted. From that day on they lived together as equals, united by their great love for each other; and they had a son and a daughter. The boy was called Arthur and the girl Anna.

[viii.21]   As the days passed and lengthened into years, the King fell ill with a malady which affected him for a long time. Meanwhile the prison warders who guarded Octa and Eosa, as I have explained above, led a weary life. In the end they escaped with their prisoner to Germany and in doing so terrified the kingdom: for rumour had it that they had already stirred up Germany, and had fitted out a huge fleet in order to return to the island and destroy it. This, indeed

actually happened. They came back with an immense fleet and
more men than could ever be counted. They invaded certain parts
of Albany and busied themselves in burning the cities there and
the citizens inside them. The British army was put under the
command of Loth of Lodonesia, with orders that he should keep
the enemy at a distance. This man was one of the leaders, a valiant
soldier, mature both in wisdom and age. As a reward for his prowess,
the King had given him his daughter Anna and put him in charge
of the kingdom while he himself was ill. When Loth moved
forward against the enemy he was frequently driven back again
by them, so that he had to take refuge inside the cities. On other
occasions he routed and dispersed them, forcing them to fly
either into the forests or to their ships. Between the two sides
the outcome of each battle was always in doubt, it being hard to
tell which of them was victorious. Their own arrogance was a
handicap to the Britons, for they were unwilling to obey the
orders of their leaders. This undermined their strength and they
were unable to beat the enemy in the field.

Almost all the island was laid waste. When this was made known [viii.22]
to the King, he fell into a greater rage than he could really bear in
his weakened state. He told all his leaders to appear before him,
so that he could rebuke them for their overweening pride and
their feebleness. As soon as he saw them all assembled in his presence,
he reproached them bitterly and swore that he himself would lead
them against the enemy. He ordered a litter to be built, so that he
could be carried in it; for his weakness made any other form of
progress impossible. Then he instructed them all to be in a state of
preparedness, so that they could advance against the enemy as soon
as the opportunity offered. The litter was constructed immediately,
the men were made ready to start and the opportunity duly came.

They put the King in his litter and set out for St Albans, where [viii.23]
the Saxons I have told you about were maltreating all the local
population. When Octa and Eosa were informed of the Britons'
arrival and of the fact that their King had been brought along in a

litter, they were too proud to fight him, on the grounds that he had had to be carried there. According to them Uther was already half-dead and it was not decent for such great men as themselves to fight with a person in that state. They thereupon retired into the town, leaving the gates wide open to show that they were not afraid of him. When this was reported to Uther, he immediately ordered the city to be besieged and an assault to be made on the walls from every side. The Britons obeyed him, investing the city and attacking its walls. They slaughtered some few of the Saxons, breached the walls and would have entered if the Saxons had not finally begun to resist.

The Britons were now having the best of it, so that the Saxons repented of their former arrogance and decided to defend themselves wherever they could. They climbed to the top of the walls and drove the Britons back with every weapon they could lay hands on. As the two sides fought each other, night came on, inviting them all to lay down their arms and rest. Many needed this repose, but the majority preferred some plan by which they could destroy their enemies.

When the Saxons realized what harm their arrogance had done them (for the Britons had been on the point of winning a victory) they determined to sally forth at daybreak and challenge their enemies to a pitched battle in the open field. That, indeed, is what they did. As soon as the rising sun heralded the day, they marched out, company by company, thus putting their plan into operation. As soon as the Britons saw this they divided their own men into companies and made the first attack. The Britons advanced and the Saxons stood their ground. Great slaughter was done on both sides. In the end, when the day was far advanced, the King of the Britons was victorious, Octa and Eosa were killed, and the Saxons turned tail. So overjoyed was the King at what had happened that, although he had previously been unable to lift himself up without the support of someone else, he now sat up straight in his litter after a little effort and suddenly seemed to recover his health.

The Ambrones used to call me the half-dead King,' he said, and burst out laughing as he spoke. 'That was because I lay flat in my litter, greatly reduced as I was by my illness. Half-dead, indeed, I really was; but I would rather be half-dead and beat them than safe and sound, with a full expectation of life, and be beaten by them. Death with honour means more to me than living on in disgrace!'

Once the Saxons had been defeated, as I have explained above, [viii.24] they did not for that reason abandon their evil behaviour. On the contrary, they went off to the northern provinces and preyed relentlessly upon the people there. King Uther was keen to pursue them, as he had proposed, but his princes dissuaded him from it, for after his victory his illness had taken an even more serious turn. As a result the enemy became bolder still in their enterprises, striving by every means in their power to take complete control of the realm. Having recourse, as usual, to treachery, they plotted to see how they could destroy the King by cunning. When every other approach failed, they made up their minds to kill him with poison. This they did: for while Uther lay ill in the town of St Albans, they sent spies disguised as beggars, who were to discover how things stood at court. When the spies had obtained all the information that they wanted, they discovered one additional fact which they chose to use as a means of betraying Uther. Near the royal residence there was a spring of very limpid water which the King used to drink when he could not keep down any other liquids because of his illness. These evil traitors went to the spring and polluted it completely with poison, so that all the water which welled up was infected. When the King drank some of it, he died immediately. Some hundred men died after him, until the villainy was finally discovered. Then they filled the well in with earth. As soon as the death of the King was made known, the bishops of the land came with their clergy and bore his body to the monastery of Ambrius and buried it with royal honours at the side of Aurelius Ambrosius, inside the Giants' Ring.

Part Seven

ARTHUR OF BRITAIN

[ix.1] AFTER the death of Utherpendragon, the leaders of the Britons assembled from their various provinces in the town of Silchester and there suggested to Dubricius, the Archbishop of the City of the Legions, that as their King he should crown Arthur, the son of Uther. Necessity urged them on, for as soon as the Saxons heard of the death of King Uther, they invited their own countrymen over from Germany, appointed Colgrin as their leader and began to do their utmost to exterminate the Britons. They had already over-run all that section of the island which stretches from the River Humber to the sea named Caithness.

Dubricius lamented the sad state of his country. He called the other bishops to him and bestowed the crown of the kingdom upon Arthur. Arthur was a young man only fifteen years old; but he was of outstanding courage and generosity, and his inborn goodness gave him such grace that he was loved by almost all the people. Once he had been invested with the royal insignia, he observed the normal custom of giving gifts freely to everyone. Such a great crowd of soldiers flocked to him that he came to an end of what he had to distribute. However, the man to whom open-handedness and bravery both come naturally may indeed find himself momentarily in need, but poverty will never harass him for long. In Arthur courage was closely linked with generosity, and he made up his mind to harry the Saxons, so that with their wealth he might reward the retainers who served his own household. The justness of his cause encouraged him, for he had a claim by rightful inheritance to the kingship of the whole island. He therefore called together all the young men whom I have just mentioned and marched on York.

As soon as this was announced to Colgrin, he assembled the

Saxons, Scots and Picts, and came to meet Arthur with a vast multitude. Once contact was made between the two armies, beside the River Douglas, both sides stood in grave danger for their lives. Arthur, however, was victorious. Colgrin fled, and Arthur pursued him; then Colgrin entered York and Arthur besieged him there.

As soon as Baldulf, the brother of Colgrin, heard of the latter's flight, he came to the siege with six thousand troops, in the hope of freeing the beleaguered man. At the time when his brother had gone into battle, Baldulf himself had been on the sea-coast, where he was awaiting the arrival of Duke Cheldric, who was on his way from Germany to bring them support. When he was some ten miles distant from the city of York, Baldulf decided to take the advantage of a night march, so that he could launch an unexpected attack. Arthur heard of this and ordered Cador, Duke of Cornwall, to march to meet Baldulf that same night, with six hundred cavalry and three thousand foot. Cador surrounded the road along which the enemy was marching and attacked the Saxons unexpectedly, so that they were cut to pieces and killed, and those who remained alive were forced to flee. As a result Baldulf became extremely worried at the fact that he could not bring help to his brother. He debated with himself how he could manage to talk with Colgrin; for he was convinced that by consulting together it would be possible for them to hit upon a safe solution – that is, if only he could make his way into his brother's presence.

Once Baldulf had come to the conclusion that no other means of access was open to him, he cut short his hair and his beard and dressed himself up as a minstrel with a harp. He strode up and down in the camp, pretending to be a harpist by playing melodies on his instrument. No one suspected him and he moved nearer and nearer to the city walls, keeping up the same pretence all the time. In the end he was observed by the besieged, dragged up over the top of the walls on ropes and taken to his brother. When Colgrin set eyes on Baldulf he had the solace of embracing him and kissing him to his heart's desire, as though Baldulf had been restored to him from the dead. Finally, when, after exhaustive discussions, they had abandoned all hope of ever escaping, messengers returned from Germany to say that they had brought with them to Albany six hundred ships which were commanded by Cheldric and loaded with brave soldiery. When Arthur's advisers learned this, they dissuaded him from continuing the siege any longer, for if so large an enemy force were to come upon them they would all be committed to a most dangerous engagement.

[ix.2]   Arthur accepted the advice of his retainers and withdrew into the town of London. There he convened the bishops and the clergy of the entire realm and asked their suggestion as to what it would be best and safest for him to do, in the face of this invasion by the pagans. Eventually a common policy was agreed on and messengers were dispatched to King Hoel in Brittany to explain to him the disaster which had befallen Great Britain. This Hoel was the son of Arthur's sister; and his father was Budicius, the King of the Armorican Britons.[1] As a result, as soon as he heard of the terrifying way in which his uncle was being treated, Hoel ordered his fleet to be made ready. Fifteen thousand armed warriors were assembled and at the next fair wind Hoel landed at Southampton. Arthur received him with all the honour due to him, and each man embraced the other repeatedly.

[ix.3]   They let a few days pass and then they marched to the town of Kaerluideoit, which was besieged by the pagans about whom I have already told you. This town is situated upon a hill between two rivers, in the province of Lindsey: it is also called by another

1. Arthur's sister Anna is first mentioned on p. 208. On p. 209 she is married to Loth of Lodonesia. She later had two sons, Gawain and Mordred, who were thus Arthur's nephews. There is some confusion here. For 'Arthur's sister' we must read 'the sister of Aurelius Ambrosius', making Hoel I Arthur's first cousin. Cp. Madeleine Blaess, 'Arthur's sisters', in *Bulletin Bibliographique de la Société Internationale Arthurienne*, Vol. VIII (1956), pp. 69–77.

name, Lincoln. As soon as they had arrived there with their entire
force, keen as they were to fight with the Saxons, they inflicted
unheard-of slaughter upon them; for on one day six thousand of
the Saxons were killed, some being drowned in the rivers and the
others being hit by weapons. As a result, the remainder were
demoralized. The Saxons abandoned the siege and took to flight.

Arthur pursued the Saxons relentlessly until they reached Caledon
Wood. There they re-formed after their flight and made an effort
to resist Arthur. The Saxons joined battle once more and killed a
number of the Britons, for the former defended themselves manfully. They used the shelter of the trees to protect themselves from
the Britons' weapons. As soon as Arthur saw this, he ordered the
trees round that part of the wood to be cut down and their trunks
to be placed in a circle, so that every way out was barred to the
enemy. Arthur's plan was to hem them in and then besiege them,
so that in the end they should die of hunger. When this had been
done, he ordered his squadrons to surround the wood and there
he remained for three days. The Saxons had nothing at all to eat.
To prevent themselves dying of sheer hunger, they asked permission to come out, on the understanding that, if they left behind
all their gold and silver, they might be permitted to return to
Germany with nothing but their boats. What is more, they
promised that they would send Arthur tribute from Germany and
that hostages should be handed over. Arthur took counsel and
then agreed to their petition. He retained all their treasure, and
took hostages to ensure that the tribute should be paid. All that
he conceded to the Saxons was permission to leave.

As the Saxons sailed away across the sea on their way home, they
repented of the bargain which they had made. They reversed their
sails, turned back to Britain and landed on the coast near Totnes.
They took possession of the land, and depopulated the countryside
as far as the Severn Sea, killing off a great number of the peasantry.
Then they proceeded by a forced march to the neighbourhood of
Bath and besieged the town. When this was announced to King

Arthur, he was greatly astonished at their extraordinary duplicity. He ordered summary justice to be inflicted upon their hostages, who were all hanged without more ado. He put off the foray with which he had begun to harass the Scots and the Picts, and he hastened to break up the siege. Arthur was labouring under very considerable difficulties, for he had left behind in the city of Alclud his cousin Hoel,[1] who was seriously ill. He finally reached the county of Somerset and approached the siege. 'Although the Saxons, whose very name is an insult to heaven and detested by all men, have not kept faith with me,' he said, 'I myself will keep faith with my God. This very day I will do my utmost to take vengeance on them for the blood of my fellow-countrymen. Arm yourselves, men, and attack these traitors with all your strength! With Christ's help we shall conquer them, without any possible doubt!'

[ix.4]   As Arthur said this, the saintly Dubricius, Archbishop of the City of the Legions, climbed to the top of a hill and cried out in a loud voice: 'You who have been marked with the cross of the Christian faith, be mindful of the loyalty you owe to your fatherland and to your fellow-countrymen! If they are slaughtered as a result of this treacherous behaviour by the pagans, they will be an everlasting reproach to you, unless in the meanwhile you do your utmost to defend them! Fight for your fatherland, and if you are killed suffer death willingly for your country's sake. That in itself is victory and a cleansing of the soul. Whoever suffers death for the sake of his brothers offers himself as a living sacrifice to God and follows with firm footsteps behind Christ Himself, who did not disdain to lay down His life for His brothers. It follows that if any one of you shall suffer death in this war, that death shall be to him as a penance and an absolution for all his sins, given always that he goes to meet it unflinchingly.'

Without a moment's delay each man present, inspired by the benediction given by this holy man, rushed off to put on his armour

1. Geoffrey sometimes calls Hoel I Arthur's 'nephew' when he means 'cousin'. Cp. p. 214, n.1.

and to obey Dubricius' orders. Arthur himself put on a leather jerkin worthy of so great a king. On his head he placed a golden helmet, with a crest carved in the shape of a dragon; and across his shoulders a circular shield called Pridwen, on which there was painted a likeness of the Blessed Mary, Mother of God, which forced him to be thinking perpetually of her. He girded on his peerless sword, called Caliburn, which was forged in the Isle of Avalon. A spear called Ron graced his right hand: long, broad in the blade and thirsty for slaughter. Arthur drew up his men in companies and then bravely attacked the Saxons, who as usual were arrayed in wedges. All that day they resisted the Britons bravely, although the latter launched attack upon attack. Finally, towards sunset, the Saxons occupied a neighbouring hill, on which they proposed to camp. Relying on their vast numbers, they considered that the hill in itself offered sufficient protection. However, when the next day dawned, Arthur climbed to the top of the peak with his army, losing many of his men on the way. Naturally enough, the Saxons, rushing down from their high position, could inflict wounds more easily, for the impetus of their descent gave them more speed than the others, who were toiling up. For all that, the Britons reached the summit by a superlative effort and immediately engaged the enemy in hand-to-hand conflict. The Saxons stood shoulder to shoulder and strove their utmost to resist.

When the greater part of the day had passed in this way, Arthur went berserk, for he realized that things were still going well for the enemy and that victory for his own side was not yet in sight. He drew his sword Caliburn, called upon the name of the Blessed Virgin, and rushed forward at full speed into the thickest ranks of the enemy. Every man whom he struck, calling upon God as he did so, he killed at a single blow. He did not slacken his onslaught until he had dispatched four hundred and seventy men with his sword Caliburn. When the Britons saw this, they poured after him in close formation, dealing death on every side. In this battle fell Colgrin, with his brother Baldulf and many thousands of others with them. Cheldric, on the contrary, when he saw the danger threatening his men, immediately turned away in flight with what troops were left to him.

[ix.5]   As soon as King Arthur had gained the upper hand, he ordered Cador, the Duke of Cornwall, to pursue the Saxons, while he himself hurried off in the direction of Albany. It had reached his ears that the Scots and the Picts had besieged his nephew Hoel in the town of Alclud, where, as I have explained already, Arthur had left him because of his poor health. Arthur therefore hastened to his nephew's assistance, for he was afraid that Hoel might be captured by the barbarians.

Meanwhile the Duke of Cornwall, accompanied by ten thousand men, instead of pursuing the fleeing Saxons, rushed off to their boats, with the intention of preventing them from going on board. Once he had seized their boats, he manned them with the best of his own soldiers and gave those men orders that they were to prevent the pagans from going aboard, if these last came running to the boats. Then he hurried off to pursue the enemy and to cut them to pieces without pity once he had found them: this in obedience to Arthur's command.

The Saxons, who only a short time before used to attack like lightning in the most ferocious way imaginable, now ran away with fear in their hearts. Some of them fled to secret hiding-places in the woods, others sought the mountains, and caves in the hills, in an attempt to add some little breathing-space to their lives. In the end they discovered safety nowhere; and so they came to the Isle of Thanet, with their line of battle cut to pieces. The Duke of Cornwall pursued them thither and renewed the slaughter. Cador drew back in the end, but only after he had killed Cheldric, taken hostages, and forced what remained of the Saxons to surrender.

[ix.6]   Once peace was restored in this way, Cador set out for Alclud. Arthur had already freed the town from the harassing attentions of the barbarians. He now led his army to Moray, where the Scots and the Picts were under siege. They had fought three times against the King and his nephew, suffering defeat at Arthur's hands and then seeking refuge in this particular district. When they reached Loch Lomond, they took possession of the islands in the lake, hoping to find a safe refuge on them. This lake contains sixty[1] islands and has sixty streams to feed it, yet only one of these streams flows down to the sea. On these islands one can make out sixty crags, which between them support exactly the same number of eagles' nests. The eagles used to flock together each year and foretell any prodigious event which was about to occur in the kingdom: this by a shrill-pitched scream which they emitted in concert. It was to these islands, then, that the enemies of whom I have told you fled, hoping to be protected by the lake, although in effect they gained little help from it. Arthur collected together a fleet of boats and sailed round the rivers. By besieging his enemies for fifteen days he reduced them to such a state of famine that they died in their thousands.

While Arthur was killing off the Scots and the Picts in this way, Gilmaurius, the King of Ireland, arrived with a fleet and a huge horde of pagans, in an effort to bring help to those who were besieged. Arthur raised the siege and began to turn his armed strength against the Irish. He cut them to pieces mercilessly and forced them to return home. Once he had conquered the Irish, he was at liberty once more to wipe out the Scots and the Picts. He treated them with unparalleled severity, sparing no one who fell into his hands. As a result all the bishops of this pitiful country, with all the clergy under their command, their feet bare and in their hands the relics of their saints and the treasures of their churches, assembled to beg pity of the King for the relief of their people. The moment they came into the King's presence, they fell on their knees and besought him to have mercy on their sorrowing people. He had inflicted sufficient suffering on them, said the bishops, and there was no need for him to wipe out to the last man those few who had survived so far. He should allow them to have some small tract

1. The text says 'forty', but this is clearly an error.

of land of their own, seeing that they were in any case going to bear the yoke of servitude. When they had petitioned the King in this way, their patriotism moved him to tears. Arthur gave in to the prayers presented by these men of religion and granted a pardon to their people.

[ix.7]   When all this had been accomplished, Hoel took a good look round the side of the loch which I have described to you. He was surprised to see so many rivers, islands, rocks and eagles' nests, and, what is more, to find exactly the same number of each. While he was meditating upon this remarkable circumstance, Arthur came up to him and told him that in the same neighbourhood there was another pool which was even more extraordinary. It was not very far away from where they were standing. It was twenty feet wide and the same distance long, and its depth was just five feet. Whether it had been shaped into a square by the artistry of man, or by nature, it remained true that, while it produced four different kinds of fish in its four corners, the fish of any one corner were never found in any of the others.

Arthur also told Hoel that there was a third pool in the parts of Wales which are near the Severn. The local people call it Lin Ligua. When the sea flows into this pool, it is swallowed up as though in a bottomless pit; and, as the pool swallows the waters, it is never filled in such a way as to overflow the edges of its banks. When the tide ebbs away, however, the pool belches forth the waters which it has swallowed, as high in the air as a mountain, and with them it then splashes and floods its banks. Meanwhile, if the people of all that region should come near, with their faces turned towards it, thus letting the spray of the waters fall upon their clothing, it is only with difficulty, if, indeed, at all, that they have the strength to avoid being swallowed up by the pool. If, however, they turn their backs, their being sprinkled has no danger for them, even if they stand on the very brink.

[ix.8]   Once he had pardoned the Scottish people, the King moved to York, where he proposed to celebrate the coming feast of the

Nativity of our Lord. As he rode into the city, Arthur grieved to see the desolate state of the holy churches. Samson, the saintly Archbishop, had been driven out, and with him all men of the Christian faith. The half-burnt churches no longer celebrated God's holy office. The fury of the pagans had been so great that it had brought everything to an end. Arthur therefore summoned the clergy and the people, and appointed his own chaplain, Piramus, as Metropolitan of that see. He re-built the churches, which had been razed to the ground, and he graced them with religious communities of men and women. He restored to their family honours the nobles who had been driven out by the Saxon invasions.

There were in York three brothers sprung from the royal line, [ix.9] Loth, Urian and Auguselus, who had been Princes in those parts before the Saxon victories. Arthur was determined to do for them what he had done for the others: that is, to grant them back their hereditary rights. He returned the kingship of the Scots to Auguselus; to Urian, the brother of Auguselus, he gave back the honour of ruling over the men of Moray; and Loth, who in the days of Aurelius Ambrosius had married that King's own sister and had had two sons by her, Gawain and Mordred, he restored to the dukedom of Lothian and other near-by territories which formed part of it.

Finally, when he had restored the whole country to its earlier dignity, he himself married a woman called Guinevere. She was descended from a noble Roman family and had been brought up in the household of Duke Cador. She was the most beautiful woman in the entire island.

As soon as the next summer came round, Arthur fitted out a [ix.10] fleet and sailed off to the island of Ireland, which he was determined to subject to his own authority. The moment he landed, King Gilmaurius, about whom I have told you before, came to meet him with a numberless horde of his peoples ready to fight against him. However, when Arthur began the battle, Gilmaurius' army, which was naked and unarmed, was miserably cut to pieces where it stood, and ran away to any place where it could find refuge. Gilmaurius himself was captured immediately and forced to submit. The remaining princes of the country, thunderstruck by what had happened, followed their King's example and surrendered. The whole of Ireland was thus conquered.

Arthur then steered his fleet to Iceland, defeated the people there and subdued the island. A rumour spread through all the other islands that no country could resist Arthur. Doldavius, King of Gotland, and Gunhpar, King of the Orkneys, came of their own free will to promise tribute and to do homage.

The winter passed and Arthur returned to Britain. He established the whole of his kingdom in a state of lasting peace and then remained there for the next twelve years.

[ix.11] Arthur then began to increase his personal entourage by inviting very distinguished men from far-distant kingdoms to join it. In this way he developed such a code of courtliness in his household that he inspired peoples living far away to imitate him. The result was that even the man of noblest birth, once he was roused to rivalry, thought nothing at all of himself unless he wore his arms and dressed in the same way as Arthur's knights. At last the fame of Arthur's generosity and bravery spread to the very ends of the earth; and the kings of countries far across the sea trembled at the thought that they might be attacked and invaded by him, and so lose control of the lands under their dominion. They were so harassed by these tormenting anxieties that they re-built their towns and the towers in their towns, and then went so far as to construct castles on carefully-chosen sites, so that, if invasion should bring Arthur against them, they might have a refuge in their time of need.

All this was reported to Arthur. The fact that he was dreaded by all encouraged him to conceive the idea of conquering the whole of Europe. He fitted out his fleets and sailed first of all to Norway, for he wished to give the kingship of that country to Loth, who was his brother-in-law.[1] Loth was the nephew of Sichelm the King of Norway, who had just died and left him the kingship in his will. However, the Norwegians had refused to accept Loth and had raised a certain Riculf to the royal power, for they considered that they could resist Arthur now that their towns were garrisoned. The son of this Loth, called Gawain, was at that time a boy twelve years old. He had been sent by Arthur's brother-in-law to serve in the household of Pope Sulpicius, who had dubbed him a knight. As soon as Arthur landed on the coast of Norway, as I had begun to explain to you, King Riculf marched to meet him with the entire population of the country and then joined battle with him. Much blood was shed on either side, but in the end the Britons were victorious. They surged forward and killed Riculf and a number of his men. Once they were sure of victory, they invested the cities of Norway and set fire to them everywhere. They scattered the rural population and continued to give full licence to their savagery until they had forced all Norway and all Denmark, too, to accept Arthur's rule.

As soon as he had subdued these countries and raised Loth to the kingship of Norway, Arthur sailed off to Gaul. He drew his troops up in companies and began to lay waste the countryside in all directions. The province of Gaul was at that time under the jurisdiction of the Tribune Frollo, who ruled it in the name of the Emperor Leo. The moment Frollo heard of the coming of Arthur, he marched out supported by the entire armed force which he had under command. He was determined to fight against Arthur, but in effect he could offer little resistance. The young men of all the islands which Arthur had subdued were there to fight at his side, and he was reported to have so powerful a force that it could hardly have been conquered by anyone. What is more, the better part of the army of the Gauls was already in Arthur's service, for he had bought them over by the gifts which he had given them. As

1. Geoffrey is in his usual confused state about Loth and Gawain. Cp. p. 214, n.1 and p. 216, n.1. In the text Loth is called Arthur's 'uncle by marriage'.

soon as Frollo saw that he was having the worst of the fight, he quitted the battle-field without more ado and fled to Paris with the few men left to him.

There Frollo reassembled his scattered people, garrisoned the town and made up his mind to meet Arthur in the field a second time. Just as Frollo was considering how to strengthen his army by calling upon neighbouring peoples, Arthur arrived unexpectedly and besieged him inside the city. A whole month passed. Frollo grieved to see his people dying of hunger, and sent a message to Arthur to say that they should meet in single combat and that whichever was victorious should take the kingdom of the other. Being a man of immense stature, courage and strength, Frollo relied upon these advantages when he sent his message, hoping in this way to find a solution to his problem. When the news of Frollo's plan reached Arthur, he was immensely pleased; and he sent word back that he would be willing to hold the meeting that had been suggested. An agreement was come to on both sides and the two met on an island outside the city, the populace gathering to see what would happen to them.

Arthur and Frollo were both fully armed and seated on horses which were wonderfully fleet of foot. It was not easy to foretell which would win. For a moment they stood facing each other with their lances held straight in the air: then they suddenly set spurs to their horses and struck each other two mighty blows. Arthur aimed his lance with more care and hit Frollo high up on his chest. He avoided Frollo's weapon, and hurled his enemy to the ground with all his might. Arthur then drew his sword from the scabbard and was just hurrying forward to strike Frollo when the latter leapt quickly to his feet, ran forward with his lance levelled and with a deadly thrust stabbed Arthur's horse in the chest, thus bringing down both horse and rider. When the Britons saw their King thrown to the ground, they were afraid that he was dead and it was only with great self-control that they restrained themselves from breaking the truce and hurling themselves as one man upon the

Gauls. Just as they were planning to invade the lists, Arthur sprang quickly to his feet, covered himself with his shield, and rushed forward to meet Frollo. They stood up to each other hand to hand, giving blow for blow, and each doing his utmost to kill the other. In the end Frollo found an opening and struck Arthur on the forehead. It was only the fact that he blunted the edge of his sword-blade at the point where it made contact with Arthur's metal helmet that prevented Frollo from dealing a mortal blow. When Arthur saw his leather cuirass and his round shield grow red, he was roused to even fiercer anger. He raised Caliburn in the air with all his strength and brought it down through Frollo's helmet and so on to his head, which he cut into two halves. At this blow Frollo fell to the ground, drummed the earth with his heels and breathed his soul into the winds. The moment this was made known throughout the army, the townsfolk ran forward, threw open their gates and surrendered their city to Arthur.

As soon as Arthur had won his victory, he divided his army into two and put one half under the command of Hoel, ordering him to go off to attack Guitard, the leader of the Poitevins. With the other half Arthur busied himself in subduing the remaining provinces which were still hostile to him. Hoel soon reached Aquitania, seized the towns of that region, and, after harassing Guitard in a number of battles, forced him to surrender. He also ravaged Gascony with fire and sword, and forced its leaders to submit.

Nine years passed. Once Arthur had subjected all the regions of Gaul to his power, he returned once more to Paris and held a court there. He called an assembly of the clergy and the people, and settled the government of the realm peacefully and legally. It was then that he gave Neustria, now called Normandy, to his Cup-bearer Bedevere, and the province of Anjou to his Seneschal Kay. He gave a number of other provinces to the noblemen who had served him. Once he had pacified all these cities and peoples he returned to Britain just as spring was coming on.

When the feast of Whitsuntide began to draw near, Arthur, [ix.12] who was quite overjoyed by his great success, made up his mind to hold a plenary court[1] at that season and place the crown of the kingdom on his head.[2] He decided, too, to summon to this feast the leaders who owed him homage, so that he could celebrate Whitsun with greater reverence and renew the closest possible pacts of peace with his chieftains. He explained to the members of his court what he was proposing to do and accepted their advice that he should carry out his plan in the City of the Legions.

Situated as it is in Glamorganshire,[3] on the River Usk, not far from the Severn Sea, in a most pleasant position, and being richer in material wealth than other townships, this city was eminently suitable for such a ceremony. The river which I have named flowed by it on one side, and up this the kings and princes who were to come from across the sea could be carried in a fleet of ships. On the other side, which was flanked by meadows and wooded groves, they had adorned the city with royal palaces, and by the gold-painted gables of its roofs it was a match for Rome. What is more, it was famous for its two churches. One of these, built in honour of the martyr Julius, was graced by a choir of most lovely virgins dedicated to God. The second, founded in the name of the blessed Aaron, the companion of Julius, was served by a monastery of canons, and counted as the third metropolitan see of Britain. The city also contained a college of two hundred learned men, who were

1. This plenary court held at Caerleon reminds one of many other plenary courts described in the French Arthurian romances and of the pageantry of similar scenes in the *romans d'aventure*. The field sports which follow the feast make one think of the opening lines of Marie de France's *Lanval*.

2. . . . . *and place the crown of the kingdom on his head.* Arthur had been crowned at Silchester by Dubricius, Archbishop of the City of the Legions, p. 212. Here he holds plenary court at the City of the Legions and wears his crown in state. Similarly, on p. 198, Aurelius Ambrosius wears his crown in state at a Whitsun assembly at Mount Ambrius. Cp., for example, 'The Conqueror wore his crown in state in Winchester every Easter, as he wore it at Westminster at Whitsuntide and at Gloucester at Christmas', *Enc. Brit.*, XXIII, p. 647, *sub titulo* Winchester.

3. Now Monmouthshire.

skilled in astronomy and the other arts, and who watched with great attention the courses of the stars and so by their careful computations prophesied for King Arthur any prodigies due at that time.

It was this city, therefore, famous for such a wealth of pleasant things, which was made ready for the feast. Messengers were sent to the different kingdoms and invitations were delivered to all those who were due to come to the court from the various parts of Gaul and from the near-by Islands in the Sea. The following people came: Auguselus, King of Albany, which is now known as Scotland; Urian, King of the men of Moray; Cadwallo Laurh, King of the Venedoti, who are now called the North Welsh; Stater, King of the Demetae, now the South Welsh; and Cador, King of Cornwall. There came, too, the Archbishops of the three metropolitan sees: London, York, and Dubricius from the City of the Legions. The last named, who was the Primate of Britain and legate of the Papal See, was so remarkably pious that by merely praying he could cure anyone who was ill. The leading men from the principal cities were there: Morvid, Earl of Gloucester; Mauron, Earl of Worcester; Anarauth, Earl of Salisbury; Artgualchar, Earl of Guerensis, which is now called Warwick; Jugein from Leicester; Cursalem from Caistor; Kynniarc, Duke of Durobernia; Urbgennius from Bath; Jonathel of Dorchester; and Boso of Rydychen: that is, Oxford.

In addition to these great leaders there came other famous men of equal importance: Donaut map Papo, Cheneus map Coil, Peredur map Peridur, Grifud map Nogord, Regin map Claut, Eddeliui map Oledauc, Kynar map Bangan, Kynmaroc, Gorbonian map Goit, Worloit, Run map Neton, Kymbelin, Edelnauth map Trunat, Cathleus map Kathel, Kynlit map Tieton and many others whose names it is too tedious to tell. Gilmaurius, King of Ireland, came from the neighbouring islands, with Malvasius, King of Iceland, Doldavius, King of Gotland, Gunhpar, King of the Orkneys, Loth, King of Norway, and Aschil, King of the Danes. From lands across the sea came Holdin, the leader of

the Ruteni; Leodegarius, Earl of Hoiland; Bedevere the Cup-
bearer, who was Duke of Normandy; Borellus of Cenomania;
Kay the Seneschal, who was Duke of Anjou; Guitard of Poitou;
the Twelve Peers from the various regions of Gaul, led by Gerin
of Chartres; and then Hoel, leader of the Armorican Britons, with
the princes who did him homage.

All these marched with a train of accoutrements, mules and
horses such as I find it hard to describe. Once they are listed,
there remained no prince of any distinction this side of Spain
who did not come when he received his invitation. There was
nothing remarkable in this: for Arthur's generosity was known
throughout the whole world and this made all men love him.

[ix.13]   Finally, when they had all assembled in the town and the time
of the feast had come, the Archbishops were led forward to the
palace, so that they could place the royal crown upon the King's
head. Since the plenary court was being held in his own diocese,
Dubricius made ready to sing mass in celebration of the moment
when the King should place the crown upon his head. As soon as
the King was enrobed, he was conducted with due pomp to the
church of the metropolitan see. On his right side and on his left
there were two archbishops to support him. Four Kings, of Albany,
Cornwall, Demetia and Venedotia, preceded him, as was their right,
bearing before him four golden swords. A company of clerics of
every rank advanced before him, chanting in exquisite harmony.

From another direction the archbishops and bishops led the
Queen, adorned with her own regalia, to the church of the dedicated Virgins. Before her walked the four consorts of the Kings
already mentioned, carrying four white doves according to the
custom. All the married women present followed behind her with
great rejoicing.

Afterwards, when the procession was over, so much organ
music was played in the two churches and the choirs sang so sweetly
that, because of the high standard of the music offered, the knights
who were there hardly knew which of the churches to enter first.

They flocked in crowds, first to this one, then to the other, so that if the whole day had been spent in celebration they would not have been bored. Finally, high mass was celebrated in both churches.

The King and the Queen then took off their crowns and put on lighter regalia. The King went off with the men to feast in his own palace and the Queen retired with the married women to feast in hers; for the Britons still observed the ancient custom of Troy, the men celebrating festive occasions with their fellow-men and the women eating separately with the other women. When they were all seated as the rank of each decreed, Kay the Seneschal, robed in ermine and assisted by a thousand noblemen who were all clad in ermine too, bore in the food. The same number of men, clad this time in minever, followed Bedevere the Cup-bearer from another entrance, helping him to pass drinks of all sorts in goblets of every conceivable shape. Meanwhile, in the Queen's palace, innumerable servants, dressed in varying liveries, were performing their duties, each according to his office.

If I were to describe everything, I should make this story far too long. Indeed, by this time, Britain had reached such a standard of sophistication that it excelled all other kingdoms in its general affluence, the richness of its decorations, and the courteous behaviour of its inhabitants. Every knight in the country who was in any way famed for his bravery wore livery and arms showing his own distinctive colour; and women of fashion often displayed the same colours.[1] They scorned to give their love to any man who had not proved himself three times in battle. In this way the womenfolk became chaste and more virtuous and for their love the knights were ever more daring.

Invigorated by the food and drink which they had consumed, [ix.14] they went out into the meadows outside the city and split up into

1. An interesting study could be made of the references to livery and armorial devices in the romances and other works of fiction of the eleventh and twelfth centuries, with an appendix on the behaviour of the 'women of fashion'.

groups ready to play various games. The knights planned an imita-
tion battle and competed together on horseback, while their
womenfolk watched from the top of the city walls and aroused
them to passionate excitement by their flirtatious behaviour. The
others passed what remained of the day in shooting with bows and
arrows, hurling the lance, tossing heavy stones and rocks, playing
dice and an immense variety of other games: this without the
slightest show of ill-feeling. Whoever won his particular game
was then rewarded by Arthur with an immense prize. The next
three days were passed in this way. On the fourth day all those who
in the office which they held had done Arthur any service were
called together and each rewarded with a personal grant of cities,
castles, archbishoprics, bishoprics and other landed possessions.

[ix.15]   Then the saintly Dubricius, who for a long time had wanted to
live as a hermit, resigned from his position as Archbishop. David,
the King's uncle, whose way of life had afforded an example of
unblemished virtue to those whom he had instructed in the faith,
was consecrated in his place. At the same time Tebaus, the celebrated priest of Llandaff, was appointed in the place of the holy
Samson, Archbishop of Dol: this with the approval of Hoel,
King of the Armorican Britons, to whom Tebaus' life and saintly
habits had commended him. The bishopric of Silchester was given
to Maugannius, that of Winchester to Diwanius and that of Alclud
to Eledenius.

While Arthur was distributing these benefices among his clergy,
twelve men of mature years and respectable appearance came
marching in at a slow pace. In their right hands they carried olive
branches, to show that they were envoys. They saluted Arthur and
handed to him a communication from Lucius Hiberius. This letter
read as follows:

'Lucius, Procurator of the Republic, wishes that Arthur, King
of Britain, may receive such treatment as he has deserved. I am
amazed at the insolent way in which you continue your tyrannical

behaviour. I am even more amazed at the damage which you have done to Rome. When I think about it, I am outraged that you should have so far forgotten yourself as not to realize this and not to appreciate immediately what it means that by your criminal behaviour you should have insulted the Senate, to which the entire world owes submission, as you very well know. You have had the presumption to disobey this mighty Empire by holding back the tribute of Britain, which tribute the Senate has ordered you to pay, seeing that Gaius Julius Caesar and other men of high place in the Roman State had received it for many years. You have torn Gaul away from that Empire, you have seized the province of the Allobroges and you have laid hands on all the Islands of the Ocean, the Kings of which paid tribute to my ancestors from the first moment when the might of Rome prevailed in those regions. As a result the Senate has decreed that punishment should be exacted for this long series of wrongs which you have done. I therefore order you to appear in Rome, so that you may submit yourself to your overlords and suffer the penalty of whatever sentence they may pass; and I appoint the middle of next August as the time for your coming. If you fail to arrive, I shall invade your territory myself and do my best to restore to the Roman State all that you have taken from it by your insane behaviour.'

This letter was read aloud in the presence of the kings and the leaders. Arthur then withdrew with them to a gigantic tower near the entrance to the palace, to consider what ought to be done in the face of such a message. As they began to climb the stairs, Cador, Duke of Cornwall, who was a merry man, burst out laughing.

'Until now,' he said to the King, 'I have been afraid that the life of ease which the Britons have been leading might make cowards of them and soften them up during this long spell of peace. Their reputation for bravery on the battle-field, for which they are more famous than any other people, might well have been completely lost to them. Indeed, when it is obvious that men are no longer using their weapons, but are instead playing at dice, burning up their strength with women and indulging in other gratifications of that sort, then without any doubt their bravery, honour, courage and good name all become tainted with cowardice. For the past five years or thereabouts we have thought of nothing but these follies, and we have had no battle experience. It is precisely to free us from this sloth that God has stirred up the resentment of the Romans, so that they may restore our courage to what it used to be in the old days.'

As Cador was saying this to them, and much more in the same strain, they reached their seats. When they had all sat down, Arthur made the following speech:

[ix.16] 'You who have been my companions in good times and in bad, you of whose fortitude both in giving advice and in waging war I have had ample proof in the past, give me now your closest attention, every one of you, and in your wisdom tell me what you consider we should do on receiving such a letter as this. Anything which has been planned with great care by man in his wisdom is realized the more easily when the time for action arrives. It follows that we shall be able to bear this attack of Lucius with great equanimity if we have first of all worked out with one accord how we are best to resist him. For myself, I do not consider that we ought to fear his coming very much, seeing with what a trumped-up case he is demanding the tribute which he wants to exact from Britain. He says that he ought to be given it because it used to be paid to Julius Caesar and those who succeeded him. When these men landed with their armed band and conquered our fatherland by force and violence at a time when it was weakened by civil dissensions, they had been encouraged to come here by the disunity of our ancestors. Seeing that they seized the country in this way, it was wrong of them to exact tribute from it. Nothing that is acquired by force and violence can ever be held legally by anyone.[1] In so far as the

1. In view of Arthur's recent activities in Europe, this is a very bland statement.

Roman has done us violence, he pleads an unreasonable case when he maintains that we are his tributaries in the eyes of the law. Since he presumes to exact something illegal from us, let us by a similar argument seek from him the tribute of Rome! Let him who comes out on top carry off what he has made up his mind to take! If the Roman decrees that tribute ought to be paid him by Britain simply because Julius Caesar and other Roman leaders conquered this country years ago, then I decree in the same way that Rome ought to give me tribute, in that my ancestors once captured that city. Belinus, that most glorious of the Kings of the Britons, with the help of his brother Brennius, the Duke of the Allobroges, hanged twenty of the noblest Romans in the middle of their own forum, captured the city and, when they had occupied it, held it for a long time. Similarly, Constantine, the son of Helen, and Maximianus, too, both of them close relations of mine, wearing the crown of Britain one after the other, each gained the throne of imperial Rome. Do you not agree, then, that it is we who should demand tribute of Rome? As for Gaul and the neighbouring Islands of the Ocean, we need send no answer, for when we snatched those lands from their empire they made no effort to defend them.'

As soon as Arthur had finished his address, Hoel, King of the Armorican Britons, was told to speak first in reply.

'Even if every one of us,' said he, 'were to take the trouble to [ix.17] turn all these things over in his mind and to reconsider each point deep within himself, it is my opinion that no one could find better advice to give than what has just emerged from your own experienced and highly-skilled wisdom. Your speech, adorned as it was with Ciceronian eloquence, has anticipated exactly what we all think. We should have nothing but unstinting praise for the opinion expressed by so steadfast a man as you, for the strength of so wise a mind, the benefit of such excellent counsel. If you are prepared to set out for Rome in such a cause as this, then I have no doubt at all about our being victorious. We shall be defending our liberty when in all justice we demand from our enemies what they have sought from us in the first place. Whoever tries to steal from another the things which are that other's may justly lose to the other whom he is attacking the things which belong to him personally. Since the Romans propose to remove from us that which is our own, without any doubt at all we on the contrary shall take from them what is theirs: that is, if we once have a chance of meeting them in battle. Such a confrontation is longed for by all Britons. Do not the Sybilline Prophecies testify in verse that for the third time someone born of British blood shall seize the Empire of Rome? As far as the first two are concerned, the Prophecies are already fulfilled, for it is well known, as you yourself have said, that those famous Princes Belinus and Constantine once won the imperial crown of Rome. Now we have you as the third man to whom the supreme dignity of such an honour is promised. Make haste, then, to take in your hand what God is only too willing to bestow! Hasten to conquer that which in itself is ripe for the conquering! Hasten to exalt us all, for we shall not shrink from being wounded or even losing our lives if it leads to your being exalted! In order that you may accomplish this, I shall stand at your side with ten thousand armed men.'

[ix.18]   When Hoel had finished speaking, Auguselus, the King of Albany, began in the following words to declare what he thought about this.

'From the moment when I realized that my lord really meant what he has said, such joy entered my heart as I cannot describe in his presence. If the Romans and the Germans remain unscathed and we fail to take vengeance on them like true men for the slaughter they have in the past inflicted upon our fellow-countrymen, then we seem to have achieved nothing at all in the past campaigns which we have waged against so many mighty kings. Now that the opportunity is promised us of meeting them in battle, I am overwhelmed with joy and only too eager for the day on which we shall come together. I thirst for their blood, as I would thirst for a spring if I had been prevented from drinking for three whole days. If only I may live to see that day! How sweet will be the wounds which I shall give and receive, once we come together hand to hand! Death itself will be sweet, if only I may suffer it in avenging our ancestors, safeguarding our liberty and exalting our King! Let us attack these emasculated creatures! Let us attack again and again, so that, when we have crushed them, we may seize all their possessions and rejoice in our victory. For my part I will augment our army to the tune of two thousand armed knights, not counting the infantry that go with them.'

It remained only for the others to say what still needed to be said. [ix.19] One after the other they promised Arthur as many men as they owed him as their feudal service. In addition to those whom the Armorican leader had promised, sixty thousand armed men were mustered from the island of Britain alone. The kings of the other islands, who had not yet developed the habit of using cavalry, promised as many foot-soldiers as each man owed, so that from the six islands of Ireland, Iceland, Gotland, the Orkneys, Norway and Denmark one hundred and twenty thousand men were counted. From the various duchies of Gaul, those of the Ruteni, the Portivenses, the Normans, the Cenomanni, the Angevins and the Poitevins, came eighty thousand; and from the twelve independent territories of those who accompanied Gerin of Chartres came another twelve hundred. The total number of the entire army, not including the foot-soldiers, who were not at all easy to count, was therefore one hundred and eighty-three thousand, three hundred.[1]

1. Hoel promised 10,000 armed men from Brittany; Auguselus promised 2,000 knights and an unspecified number of foot from Albany; Britain was to produce 60,000 armed men; the six Islands of the Sea promised 120,000 foot; 80,000 men were to come from the duchies of Gaul; and the Twelve Peers were to provide 1,200. This adds up to 273,200. We are then told that the total strength, not including the foot, was 183,300. In the manuscripts the figures were Roman ones; and the scribes, as they copied each other, made more and more mistakes. It would probably be easy to see what had gone wrong here if one collated a number of manuscripts. In any case, 120,000 foot is a most improbable figure for the Islands, and these men are expressly omitted from Geoffrey's total, as they were difficult to count. This

[ix.20]   When King Arthur saw that they were all ready to enter hi service, he accepted their offer and ordered them to return home immediately and assemble the troops which they had promised He also instructed them to rendezvous at the port of Barfleur and then to be ready to march with him to the lands of the Allobroges where they would meet the Romans. Finally, he sent word to the Emperors by their own messengers to say that he had no intention whatsoever of paying them tribute and that he was certainly not coming to Rome in order to receive their legal decision in this matter. He was coming, on the contrary, to exact from them what they had decreed in their own judicial sentence that they would demand from him. The messengers set out. At the same time the kings and princes left for home, determined to waste no time in carrying out what they had been ordered to do.

[x.1]   As soon as the contents of this reply were made known, Lucius Hiberius was ordered by the Senate to send a proclamation to the Kings of the Orient to instruct them to prepare an army and to set out in his company to conquer Britain. As quickly as possible there duly assembled Epistrofus, the King of the Greeks; Mustensar, the King of the Africans; Ali Fatima, the King of Spain; Hirtacius, the King of the Parthians; Boccus of the Medes; Sertorius of Libya Serses, King of the Iturei; Pandrasus, King of Egypt; Micipsa, King of Babylon; Politetes, Duke of Bithynia; Teucer, Duke of Phrygia Evander of Syria; Echion of Boethia; Ypolitus of Crete; and all the leaders and princes who owed them homage. From among the members of the Senate there came Marius Lepidus, Gaius Metellu Cocta, Quintus Milvius Catullus, Quintus Carucius and enough more to bring the total up to four hundred thousand, one hundred and sixty when they were all counted.

x.2   They made all the preparations which they considered necessary and then set out for Britain towards the beginning of August.

---

reduces our total to 153,200. Maybe Geoffrey's original total was 183,200 Our total is then 30,000 short. 30,000 knights from Albany would be a nice round figure.

When Arthur learned of their coming, he handed over the task of defending Britain to his nephew Mordred and to his Queen, Guinevere. He himself set off with his army for Southampton, and embarked there with a following wind.

Round about midnight, as he sailed briskly on through the deep sea, surrounded by ships too numerous to count, and following his course closely with joy in his heart, Arthur fell into a very deep slumber. As he lay lulled in sleep he saw a bear flying through the air. At the growling of the bear every shore quaked. Arthur also saw a terrifying dragon flying in from the west and lighting up the countryside with the glare of its eyes. When these two met, they began a remarkable fight. The dragon which I have described attacked the bear time and time again, burning it with its fiery breath and finally hurling its scorched body down to the ground. Arthur woke up at this point and described what he had dreamed to those who were standing round. They interpreted it for him, telling him that the dragon was himself and the bear some giant or other with which he was to fight. The battle between the two animals meant the struggle which would take place between him and the giant, and the victory of the dragon was that which Arthur himself would win. Arthur, however, was sure that it all meant something different, for he considered that this dream had come about because of himself and the Emperor.

Once the night had passed and the dawn began to glow red in the sky, they landed in the port of Barfleur. There they quickly pitched their tents and prepared to await the coming of the Kings of the Islands and the leaders of the neighbouring provinces.

Meanwhile the news was brought to Arthur that a giant of [x.3] monstrous size had emerged from certain regions in Spain. This giant had snatched Helena, the niece of Duke Hoel, from the hands of her guardians and had fled with her to the top of what is now called the Mont-Saint-Michel. The knights of that district had pursued the giant, but they had been able to do nothing against him. It made no difference whether they attacked him by sea or by land, for he either sank their ships with huge rocks or else killed them with a variety of weapons. Those whom he captured, and they were quite a few, he ate while they were still half alive.

The next night, at two o'clock, Arthur came out from the tents without telling his companions, roused his Seneschal Kay and his Cup-bearer Bedevere and set out for the Mount. Being a man of such outstanding courage, he had no need to lead a whole army against monsters of this sort. Not only was he himself strong enough to destroy them, but by doing so he wanted to inspire his men.

When they came near to the Mount, they saw a fire gleaming on the top and a second fire ablaze on a smaller peak. Bedevere the Cup-bearer was ordered by the King to make his way to this second fire by boat. He could not have reached it in any other way, for the hill rose straight up from the sea. As Bedevere began to climb up to the summit, he heard a woman's scream come from above him. This terrified him at first, for he was afraid that the monster was there. His courage soon returned, however, and he drew his sword from its scabbard and climbed up the hillside. On the top he could see nothing at all, except the great fire which he had observed before. Then he made out a newly-made tumulus nearby, and at its side an old woman who was weeping and wailing. The moment she saw him the old woman stopped weeping and began to speak to him instead. 'Unhappy man!' said she. 'What ill fortune has brought you to this spot? I pity you, for you are about to suffer death by the most unspeakable tortures. This very night a foul monster will destroy the flower of your youth. The most odious of all giants will come here. Cursed be his name! It is he who carried the Duke's niece off to this mountain. I have just buried her in this very spot. With her he brought me, her nurse. Without a moment's hesitation he will destroy you, too, by some unheard-of form of death. How hideous the fate of my fairest nurseling was! When this foul being took her in his arms, fear flooded her tender breast and so she ended a life which was worthy of a longer span. Since he was unable to befoul with his filthy lust this child who was my sister soul, my second self, the joy and happiness of my life, in the madness of his bestial desire he raped me, against my will, as I swear by God and my own old age. Flee, my dear sir! Flee! If he comes, as he usually does, to have intercourse with me, he will find you here and tear you to pieces and destroy you miserably!'

Bedevere was as much moved as it is possible for a human being to be. He soothed the old woman with kind words, comforted her with the promise of speedy help and returned to Arthur to tell him all that he had discovered. Arthur grieved for the fate of the girl and ordered the other two to leave him to attack the monster alone. Should the need arise, they were to come to his assistance as smartly as they knew how and attack the giant in their turn. They then made their way to the taller of the two peaks. There they handed their horses over to their squires and began to clamber to the top, Arthur going on ahead.

At that moment the inhuman monster was standing by his fire. His face was smeared with the clotted blood of a number of pigs at which he had been gnawing. He had swallowed bits of them while he was roasting the rest over the live embers on the spits to which he had fixed them. The moment he saw the newcomers, nothing then being farther from his thoughts, he rushed to snatch up his club, which two young men would have found difficulty in lifting off the ground. The King drew his sword from its scabbard, held his shield in front of him and rushed forward at full speed to prevent the giant from seizing his club. The giant was quite aware of the advantage Arthur was hoping to gain. He took up his club and dealt the King such a mighty blow on his shield that he filled the shore in either direction with the reverberation of the impact and deafened Arthur's ears completely. The King grew white-hot in the fierceness of his rage. He struck the giant on the forehead with his sword and gave him such a blow that, although it was not mortal, all the same the blood ran down his face and into his eyes and prevented him from seeing. The giant had warded off the blow with his club and in this way had protected his forehead from a mortal wound. Blinded as he was by the blood which was gushing out, he rushed forward all the more fiercely. Just as a boar hurls itself at the huntsman, despite the latter's boar-spear, so the giant rushed against the King's sword. He seized Arthur round the middle and forced him to the ground on his knees. Arthur gathered his strength and quickly slipped out of the giant's clutches. Moving like lightning, he struck the giant repeatedly with his sword, first in this place and then in that, giving him no respite until he had dealt him a lethal blow by driving the whole length of the blade into his head just where his brain was protected by his skull. At this the evil creature gave one great shriek and toppled to the ground with a mighty crash, like some oak torn from its roots by the fury of the winds. The King laughed with relief. He ordered Bedevere to saw off the giant's head and to hand it over to one of their squires, so that it might be carried to the camp for all to go and stare at.

Arthur said that he had not come into contact with anyone so strong since the time he killed the giant Retho on Mount Arvaius, after the latter had challenged him to single combat. Retho had made himself a fur cloak from the beards of the kings whom he had slain. He sent a message to Arthur, telling him to rip his own beard off his face and when it was torn off send it to him. Since Arthur was more distinguished than any of the other kings, Retho promised in his honour to sew his beard higher up the cloak than the others. If Arthur would not do this, then Retho challenged him to a duel, saying that whoever proved the stronger should have the fur cloak as a trophy and also the beard of the man he had beaten. Soon after the battle began, Arthur was victorious. He took the giant's beard and the trophy too. From that day on, as he had just said, he had met nobody stronger than Retho.

When they had won their victory, as I have told you, the three returned to their tents with the head, just as dawn was succeeding to night. All their men crowded round them to gape at it and praise the man who had freed the country from such a voracious

onster. Hoel, however, grieved over the fate of his niece. He
rdered a chapel to be built above her grave on the mountain-top
where she had been buried. The peak took its name from the girl's
urial-place, and to this very day it is called Helena's Tomb.[1]

As soon as all those whom Arthur was awaiting had finally [x.4]
ssembled, he marched from there to Autun, where he expected
at the Emperor would be. However, by the time he reached the
iver Aube he was informed that the Emperor had pitched his
amp not far away and was advancing with such an enormous army
at it was being said that no one could possibly resist him. Arthur
as not dismayed, for he had no intention whatsoever of abandon-
g the plans which he had made. Instead, he pitched his own camp
n the river-bank, in a spot from which he could easily move his
amp forward, or, if the need arose, withdraw under cover.

Arthur sent two of his leaders, Boso of Oxford and Gerin of
Chartres, together with his own nephew Gawain, to Lucius
iberius, to tell him either to withdraw altogether from Gallic
rritory or else to march out the next day to see which of them
ad more right to Gaul. The young men of Arthur's court were
verjoyed at the prospect before them. They began to egg Gawain
n to foment some incident in the Emperor's camp, to give them
a opportunity of fighting with the Romans. They made their
vay into the presence of Lucius and duly ordered him either to
vithdraw from Gaul or to come out to fight the very next day. As
ucius was replying that he had not come there in order to with-
caw, but rather that he might govern the country, his nephew
aius Quintillanus who was present was heard to mutter that the
ritons were better at boasting and making threats than they were
: proving their courage and prowess on the battle-field. Gawain
as immediately incensed at this. He drew his sword from the
abbard which was hanging at his belt, rushed at Gaius and cut
ff his head. He and his fellow-envoys then retreated to their

1. See Lewis Thorpe, 'Le Mont-Saint-Michel et Geoffroi de Monmouth'
Millénaire Monastique du Mont-Saint-Michel, Vol. II, 1967, pp. 377-82.

horses. The Romans pursued them, some on foot and some o
horseback, hoping to avenge the loss of their fellow-countryma
upon the messengers, who were making off at full speed. Gerin o
Chartres suddenly turned round, just as one of the Romans wa
straining to hit him, couched his lance, pierced the enemy throug
his protective armour and the middle of his body, and hurled hir
to the ground with all his might. Boso of Oxford, envious of th
mighty deed done by the man from Chartres, wheeled his ow
horse round and stuck his spear into the throat of the first man h
met, mortally wounding him and dashing him from the nag o
which he was careering along. In the meantime Marcellus Muti
was making every effort to avenge Quintillianus. He was alread
threatening Gawain from the rear, and was on the point of layin
hold of him, when Gawain swung round and with the sword whic
he brandished clove him through helm and head to his chest, bic
ding him, when he got to hell, to tell Quintillianus, whor
Gawain had just cut down in the camp, that this was why th
Britons were so good at boasting and making threats.

Gawain drew his troops up in some order and ordered them t
wheel round in formation, each doing his utmost to unhorse one c
the enemy. They agreed to what he proposed. They all turned bac
and each of them killed his man. All the same, the Romans conti
ued the pursuit, hitting out at the Britons with their swords an
spears, but not succeeding in capturing or unhorsing any of them.

Just as they were riding up to a certain wood, so the story goe
there suddenly emerged from the trees about six thousand Briton
who had heard of the retreat of their leaders and had conceale
themselves there in order to bring them help. Out they cam
sticking spurs into their horses and filling the air with their shou
With their rounded shields hung in front of their chests, the
attacked the Romans out of the blue and immediately drove the
back in flight. The Britons chased after the Romans as one ma
hurling some of them from their horses with their spears, capturir
others and killing quite a few.

When this was made known to the Senator Petreius, he hurried to the assistance of his comrades, accompanied by ten thousand men. He forced the Britons to withdraw to the wood from which they had emerged, but not before he had lost some of his own men in the process. As they fled the Britons turned at bay in the narrow woodland paths and inflicted great slaughter on their pursuers. Meanwhile Hyderus, the son of Nu, was hurrying forward to support them as they retreated in this way. The Britons then made a stand, showing their chests now to the same Romans to whom they had previously presented their backs, and doing their level best to deal mighty blows in the most manly way possible.

The Romans, too, stood their ground, in some sectors managing to kill the Britons, but elsewhere being killed by them. The Britons wanted a fight with all their heart and soul, but once they had begun it they did not care much whether they won or lost. The Romans, on the other hand, who were given careful instructions as to when they should move forward and when retreat by Petreius Cocta, like the good captain he was, behaved with more circumspection, so that Petreius was able to inflict great damage on his opponents. As soon as Boso noticed this, he called aside from the others a number of the Britons whom he knew to be among the bravest, and delivered the following speech to them: 'Seeing that we began this skirmish without informing Arthur, we must take great care, now that our men are fully engaged, that we do not have the worst of it. If that does happen, then we shall suffer a great loss of man-power and at the same time have the King cursing us. You must all pluck up your courage and follow me through the ranks of the Romans, so that, if fortune favours us, we can either kill or else capture Petreius.'

They all set spurs to their horses, and, keeping close together, forced their way through the wedge-shaped ranks of the enemy. They reached the spot where Petreius was giving orders to his men. Boso rushed headlong at him, seized him round the neck and fell to the ground with him as he had planned. The Romans came running up to rescue Petreius from his assailants. At the same time the Britons moved forward to give every help to Boso. There followed a tremendous slaughter between the two sides, with much din and confusion, as the Romans tried to free their leader and the Britons strove to hold him captive. Men were wounded on both sides as they dealt deadly blows and received them. In this contest it was made quite clear who was the better man with spear, sword and javelin. In the end the Britons advanced with closed ranks, withheld the onslaught of the Romans and made their way, with Petreius in their midst, to the safety of their own lines. Without a moment's respite they then made a counter-attack upon the Romans, who were now for the most part weakened, dispirited, and ready to show their backs, for they had lost their commander. The Britons pressed on against them, striking at them from the rear. They unhorsed them with their blows, plundered them where they lay, and rode on over their looted bodies in pursuit of the others. A few they took prisoner for they wanted some to hand over to the King.

In the end, when they had done all the damage they could to the Romans, the Britons withdrew to their camp with their spoil and prisoners. They explained what had happened to them and with the joy of victory in their hearts handed Petreius Cocta and the rest of their captives over to Arthur. He congratulated them and promised them honours and yet more honours in that they had behaved so gallantly although he was not there to lead them. He decided to throw the captives into prison. He summoned to his presence the men who were to lead them off to Paris the following day and hand them over to the town gaolers for safe-keeping against the time when he should decide what else should be done with them. He ordered Duke Cador, Bedevere the Cup-bearer and Borellus and Richerius, two of his leading men, with their personal bodyguards, to lead the party, until they reached a spot beyond which they need not really fear a rescue-attempt by the Romans.

[x.5]   It so happened that the Romans got wind of what the Britons

had planned. At their Emperor's command they chose fifteen
thousand of their troops, who, that very same night, were to
hurry on ahead of the Britons, along their projected line of march,
and then to attack them and do their utmost to free their fellow-
countrymen. The Romans put two Senators, Vulteius Catellus
and Quintus Carucius, in charge of their troops, together with
Evander the King of Syria, and Sertorius the King of Libya. That
very night they set out with the force which I have described,
intending to follow the line of march as instructed. They chose a
place suitable for an ambush and hid in a spot through which they
thought their enemies would pass.

After morning came, the Britons duly set out with their captives.
They soon came near to the place in question, not realizing what a
trap their cunning enemies had prepared for them. As the Britons
moved forward in their march, the Romans suddenly broke cover.
They attacked the Britons, who were expecting nothing of the
sort, and broke their line. Although they were attacked unexpectedly, and scattered, the Britons re-formed their lines and resisted bravely. They stationed some of their troops in a circle round
the prisoners. The remainder they drew up into companies, which
then engaged the enemy. The Britons put Richerius and Bedevere
in charge of the force which they set to guard the prisoners. Cador,
Duke of Cornwall, and Borellus were given command of the
others. The entire Roman detachment had rushed out in a dis-
orderly fashion, without troubling to draw their men up into
companies. They attacked with all their might, aiming to slaughter
the Britons while the latter were still drawing up their own battle-
lines and making plans to defend themselves. The Britons suffered
great losses, and would have endured the shame of losing the
captives whom they were convoying, if good fortune had not
quickly brought the reinforcements of which they were in such
need. Guitard, the Duke of the Poitevins, came to hear of the
ambush which I have described, and he marched in with three
thousand men. Now that they were able to rely upon this help,

the Britons won in the end and so managed to take revenge upon their imprudent ambushers for all the slaughter they had caused. However, they lost many of their troops in the first stage of the battle. Indeed, they lost Borellus, the famous leader of the Cenomanni, who was pierced through the throat by his opponent's spear while he was fighting with Evander the King of Syria, and so vomited forth his life with his blood. At the same time they lost four noble princes: Hyrelgas of Periron; Maurice Cador of Cahors; Aliduc of Tintagel; and Her, the son of Hider. It would not have been easy to find braver men than these. However, the Britons did not lose their courage, nor did they despair. They made every effort to press forward, doing their utmost to guard their prisoners and at the same time to destroy their enemies. In the end the Romans were unable to stand the attack which the Britons launched, and they quickly retreated from the battle-field and began to make for their own camp. The Britons pursued them relentlessly, killing them as they went and taking many captives. They allowed them no respite until they had killed Vulteius Catellus and Evander the King of Syria, and scattered the others completely.

Once they were sure of victory the Britons sent on to Paris the prisoners they were convoying. They themselves turned back to their King with those whom they had just captured, promising him hope of a decisive victory in that they who were so few had triumphed over this immense enemy which had been dispatched against them.

[x.6]   Lucius Hiberius bore all these disasters ill. Harassed as he was by a variety of anxieties, he swayed first this way and then that, for he could not make up his mind whether to engage in a full-scale battle with Arthur or to withdraw inside Autun and there await reinforcements from the Emperor Leo. In the end he let his misgiving take the upper hand. The next night he marched his troops into Langres, on his way to the city of Autun. This move was reported to Arthur. He made up his mind to outmarch Lucius along this route. That same night he by-passed the city of Langres on his

eft hand, and entered a valley called Saussy,[1] through which
Lucius would have to pass.

Arthur decided to draw up his troops in battle-formation. He
ordered one legion, the command of which he entrusted to Earl
Morvid, to stay constantly in reserve, so that, if need arose, he
would know where he could withdraw, re-fit his companies, and
plan new attacks on the enemy. He drew up the remainder of his
troops in seven divisions,[2] to each of which he allocated five
thousand, five hundred and fifty-five fully-equipped men. One
part of each of the divisions which he drew up consisted of cavalry
and the second part of foot-soldiers. They were given the following standing-orders: whenever the infantry showed signs of advancing to the attack, the cavalry of that division, moving forward
obliquely with closed ranks, should do its utmost to break the
force of the enemy. According to the British custom, the infantry
battalions were drawn up in a square, with a right and left wing.

Auguselus, the King of Albany, was put in charge of the right
wing, and Cador, Duke of Cornwall, of the left wing of the first
division. Two famous leaders, Gerin of Chartres and Boso of
Rydychen, called Oxford in the Saxon language, were put in
command of a second division, with Aschil, King of the Danes,

1. The text has 'quandem vallem . . . que Siesia vocabatur'. The spelling of
Siesia varies considerably in the different MSS. and Jesus has 'the glen of
Assnessia'. I had decided upon Saussy from a study of the campaign and the
map before I read Tatlock's note on his pp. 102–3: 'There is an obscure place
thirty-five miles southwest of Langres named Saussy, on the way to Autun,
in high land with lower land at the side; the best guess, but too far in distance
and name to fit Geoffrey's words well.' Tatlock is being too difficult. Many
of Geoffrey's accredited places are obscure and his sense of distance is noto-
ously vague. Cannae, Waterloo and Alamein were fought in obscure
places. For two up-to-date views, see William Matthews, 'Where was Siesia-
essoyne?' in Speculum, Vol. XLIX (1974), pp. 680–86; and H. E. Keller,
'Two toponymical problems in Geoffrey of Monmouth and Wace:
strusia and Siesia' in Speculum, Vol. XLIX (1974), pp. 687–98.

2. The arithmetic is faulty, but scribes play havoc with numbers. The text
has 'per catervas septenas', not including the reserve division of Morvid. In
effect there are four front-line divisions, four support divisions and the two
reserve divisions under Morvid and Arthur, making ten in all.

and Loth, King of the Norwegians, in charge of a third. Hoel
King of the Bretons, and Gawain, the King's nephew, commande
a fourth. In support of these, four other divisions were placed i
the rear. Kay the Seneschal was put in charge of one, along wit
Bedevere the Cup-bearer. Holdin, the leader of the Ruteni, an
Guitard, Duke of the Poitevins, commanded the second. Jugein o
Leicester, Jonathel of Dorchester, and Cursalem of Caistor too
charge of the third, and Urbgennius of Bath of the fourth.[1]

Behind all these the King chose a position for himself and for
single legion which he had appointed to remain under his order
There he set up the Golden Dragon which he had as his persona
standard. To this point the wounded and exhausted could withdraw
in case of necessity, as if to a fortified camp. In the legion which h
held back under his own command there were six thousand, si
hundred and sixty-six men.

[x.7]   When all his troops were placed in position, Arthur gave them
the following order of the day: 'My countrymen, you who hav
made Britain mistress of thirty kingdoms, I commend you fo
your courage, which, far from lessening, seems to me to increas
in strength every day, despite the fact that you have waged n
war for five long years, during which time you have devoted
yourselves to the enjoyment of a life of ease rather than to th
practice of war. Nevertheless, you do not seem to have degenerate
in the least from your inborn valour. On the contrary, you hav
retained your courage to the full, for you have just put the Roman
to flight, at a moment when, encouraged by the pride which cam
so naturally to them, they were doing their utmost to deprive yo
of your freedom. Moving forward with the advantage of numbe
on their side, it was they who attacked you, but they were no
strong enough to resist your advance and they had to withdraw i
shame to that city over there. In a short time they will march o

---

1. The text is clear, but there is obviously an error here. Presumabl
Geoffrey meant Jugein and Jonathel to command the third support division
and Cursalem and Urbgennius to command the fourth.

gain and come through this valley on their way to Autun. You will be able to attack them when they least expect it and slaughter them like so many sheep. No doubt they imagined, when they planned to make your country pay them tribute and to enslave you yourselves, that they would discover in you the cowardice of Eastern peoples. Perhaps they have not heard of the wars you waged against the Danes and Norwegians and the leaders of the Gauls, when you delivered those peoples from their shameful allegiance to the Romans and forced them to submit to my own overlordship. We who had the strength to win a mightier battle will without any doubt at all be successful in this more trifling affair, if only we make up our minds with the same determination to crush these feeble creatures. What rewards you will win, if only you obey my will and my orders, as loyal soldiers ought to do! Once we have beaten the Romans in the field, we can immediately set off for Rome itself. As soon as we march upon Rome, we shall capture it. When we have captured it, you shall occupy it. And yours shall be its gold, silver, palaces, towers, castles, cities and all the other riches of the vanquished!'

As Arthur spoke, they all joined in one great shout of approval, for, as long as he was still alive, they were ready to die rather than leave the battle-field.

Lucius Hiberius found out about the trap which was laid for him. [x.8] His first inclination was to run away, but he changed his mind. His courage returned to him and he decided to march out to meet the Britons through this same valley. He called his generals together, and delivered the following speech to them.

'My noble leaders,' he said, 'you to whose sovereignty the kingdoms both of the East and of the West owe obedience, remember now the deeds of your ancestors. They did not hesitate to shed their blood in their efforts to conquer the enemies of the Republic. They left an example of bravery and soldierly courage to those who were to come after them, for they fought as if God had decreed that none of them should ever die in battle. They

nearly always won, avoiding death in their victory, for they held
that no death could come to any man other than that ordained by
the will of God. In that way the Republic increased in power as
their own prowess became greater. All the integrity, honour and
munificence which distinguished men of noble birth flourished
in them down the years. This lifted them and their descendants to
the overlordship of the whole world. I now want to rouse this
same spirit in you. I beg you to remember the bravery of your forefathers. Strong in this courage, you must now march forth to meet
your enemies in the valley where they lie in ambush for you. Do
your utmost to exact from them what is rightly yours. Do not
imagine for a moment that I sought refuge in this city because I
feared them, or was afraid of meeting them in battle. On the contrary, I imagined that they would come after us in their senseless
bravado and that, as they rushed forward, we might suddenly turn
upon them. I thought that we might slaughter them as they tailed
out in pursuit. Now, however, since they have behaved in a different way from what we anticipated, we in our turn must make
new plans. We must go out to meet them and attack them as
bravely as we possibly can. If they have the first advantage, then
we must withstand them without letting our lines be broken, and
bear the brunt of their initial attack. In this way we shall win without any shadow of doubt. In many a battle the side that stands firm
in the first assault achieves victory in the end.'

As soon as Lucius had said these things and added a few other
similar remarks, his men agreed with one accord. With heads erect
and hands raised they swore an oath, and then armed themselves
as quickly as they could. Once they were equipped, they marched
out from Langres and made their way to the valley I have described, where Arthur had drawn up his own forces. In their turn
they drew up twelve wedge-shaped legions, all of them infantry.
They were arranged in wedges, in the Roman fashion, each single
legion containing six thousand, six hundred and sixty-six men.
Separate commanders were appointed to each of the legions, and

according to the orders of these generals so they were to advance
to the assault or stand firm when they themselves were attacked.

The Romans placed Lucius Catellus and Ali Fatima, the King of
Spain, in command of the first legion; Hirtacius, King of the
Parthians, and the Senator Marius Lepidus in command of the
second; and Boccus, King of the Medes, with the Senator Gaius
Metellus, in command of the third. They gave the command of
the fourth legion to Sertorius, the King of Libya, and to the Senator
Quintus Milvius. These four legions were placed in the first line.
Behind them and in their rear were another four. They placed
Serses, King of the Iturei, in charge of the first; Pandrasus, King of
Egypt, in charge of the second; Politetes, Duke of Bithynia, in
charge of the third; and Teucer, Duke of Phrygia, in charge of the
fourth. Behind these again came yet another four legions: to the
first of them they appointed the Senator Quintus Carucius; to
the second Lelius Hostiensis; to the third Sulpicius Subuculus; and
to the fourth Mauricius Silvanus.

Lucius himself moved about among them, now here, now there,
making suggestions and telling them how to proceed. He commanded that a golden eagle, which he had brought with him as a
standard, should be set up firmly in the centre. He gave orders that
anyone whom the tide of battle had cut off from the others should
do his utmost to force his way back to this eagle.

Now at last they stood face to face with javelins raised, the [x.9]
Britons on this side and the Romans on that. As soon as they heard
the sound of the battle-trumpets, the legion commanded by the
King of Spain and Lucius Catellus charged boldly at the division
led by the King of Scotland and the Duke of Cornwall, but the
latter stood firm, shoulder to shoulder, and the Roman force was not
able to breach it. As the Roman legion persisted in its fierce attack,
the division commanded by Gerin and Boso moved up at the
double. The Roman legion fought bravely, as has already been
said, but this fresh division attacked it with a sudden cavalry charge,
broke through and came into contact with the legion which the

King of the Parthians was directing against the division of Aschil, King of the Danes. Without a moment's delay the two forces met all along the line in a general mêlée, piercing each other's ranks and engaging each other in deadly combat. There ensued the most pitiable slaughter on both sides, with a bedlam of shouting and with men tumbling head foremost or feet first to the ground all over the place and vomiting forth their life with their heart's blood.

At first the Britons had the worst of it, for Bedevere the Cup-bearer was killed and Kay the Seneschal was mortally wounded. When Bedevere met Boccus, the King of the Medes, he was run through by the latter's lance and fell dead inside the enemy lines. Kay the Seneschal did his utmost to avenge Bedevere, but he was surrounded by battalions of Medes and received a mortal wound. Nevertheless, brave soldier as he was, he cut a way through with the force which he was commanding, scattered the Medes and would have retreated to his own support-group with his line of battle unbroken, had he not come up against the legion of the King of Libya, whose counter-attack completely scattered the troops under Kay's command. Even then he fell back with a few men still alive and made his way to the Golden Dragon with the corpse of Bedevere. How the Neustrians grieved when they saw the body of their leader Bedevere slashed with so many wounds! The Angevins, too, bewailed as they treated the wounds of their leader Kay in every manner they could think of.

This, however, was no moment for weeping and wailing, with the battle-lines meeting on both sides in a bath of blood and giving them little respite for lamentations of this sort before they were compelled to look to their own defence. Hyrelgas, the nephew of Bedevere, was greatly moved by his uncle's death. He gathered round him three hundred of his own men, made a sudden cavalry charge and rushed through the enemy lines to the spot where he had seen the standard of the King of the Medes, for all the world like a wild boar through a pack of hounds, thinking little of what might happen to himself, if only he could avenge his uncle. When

he came to the place where he had seen the King, he killed him,
carried off his dead body to his own lines, put it down beside the
corpse of the Cup-bearer and hacked it completely to pieces.
With a great bellow, Hyrelgas roused his fellow-countrymen's
battalions to fury, exhorting them to charge at the enemy and to
harass them with wave after wave of assault, for now a new-found
rage boiled up within them and the hearts of their frightened opponents were sinking. They were drawn up, he shouted, in better
order in their battalions than their enemies, fighting hand-to-hand
as they were, and they were in a position to attack repeatedly and to
inflict more serious losses. The Britons were roused by this encouragement. They attacked their enemy all along the line, and
terrible losses were sustained in both armies.

Vast numbers fell on the side of the Romans, including Ali
Fatima the King of Spain, Micipsa the Babylonian, and the
Senators Quintus Milvius and Marius Lepidus. On the side of the
Britons there died Holdin the Duke of the Ruteni, Leodegarius of
Boulogne, and the three British leaders Cursalem of Caistor,
Guallauc of Salisbury, and Urbgennius of Bath. The troops these
men had commanded were greatly weakened and they drew back
until they reached the battle-line of the Armorican Britons, which
was commanded by Hoel and Gawain. However, this force burst
into flame, as it were, rallied those who had been retreating, and
compelled the enemy, who, a moment before, had been in pursuit,
to withdraw in its turn. The Britons pressed on hard, hurling the
fugitives to the ground and killing them. They did not pause
in their slaughter until they reached the Emperor's own bodyguard. When he saw what disaster had overtaken his men, the
Emperor hurried forward to give them support.

When the battle began again, the Britons were sadly mauled. [x.10]
Chinmarchocus, the Duke of Tréguier, fell dead, and with him
there died two thousand men. Three other famous leaders were
killed: Riddomarcus, Bloctonius, and Iaginvius of Bodloan. Had
these men been rulers of kingdoms, succeeding ages would have

celebrated their fame, for their courage was immense. In the attack which they launched with Hoel and Gawain, and which I have described to you, no enemy with whom they came to grips escaped alive from their swords and lances. Eventually they reached the bodyguard of Lucius himself. There they were cut off by the Romans and met their end at the same time as their leader Chinmarchocus and his comrades whom I have mentioned.

No better knights than Hoel and Gawain have ever been born down the ages. When they learned of the death of their followers, they pressed on even more fiercely. They spurred on this way and that, first in one direction, then in another, in their relentless attack on the Emperor's bodyguard. Gawain, fearless in his courage, did his utmost to come up with Lucius himself in the fight. He made every effort to push forward, for he was the bravest of all the knights. He decimated the enemy by his onslaught and as he killed them he moved ever forward. Hoel was in no way less brave. He was raging like a thunderbolt in another sector, encouraging his own men and bringing death to his enemies. He parried their attacks with the utmost courage, giving and receiving blows, but not drawing back for a second. It would be difficult to say which of these two was the braver.

[x.11] By dint of forcing his way through the enemy troops, as I have said above, Gawain finally found the opening for which he was longing. He rushed straight at the Roman general and fought with him hand to hand. Lucius was in the prime of his youth. He was a man of great courage, strength and prowess, and there was nothing that he wanted more than to join battle with a knight who would force him to prove his worth as a soldier. He accepted Gawain's challenge and fought with him. He was very keen to begin and rejoiced that his opponent was so famous a man. The contest between these two lasted for a long time. They dealt each other mighty blows, holding out their shields to their opponent's onslaught and each planning how he could kill the other.

As Gawain and Lucius fought bitterly in this way, the Romans

suddenly recovered. They attacked the Bretons and so brought
help to their general. They repulsed Hoel, Gawain and their
troops, and began to cut their way into them. It was at this juncture
that the Romans suddenly came face to face with Arthur and his
division. He had heard a moment before of this slaughter which
was being inflicted on his men. He moved up with his own division,
drew his wonderful sword Caliburn and encouraged his fellow-
soldiers by shouting loudly at them. 'What the Devil are you
doing, men?' he demanded. 'Are you letting these effeminate
creatures slip away unhurt? Not one must escape alive! Think of
your own right hands, which have played their part in so many
battles and subjected thirty kingdoms to my sovereignty! Remember your ancestors, whom the Romans, then at the height of their
power, made tributaries. Remember your liberty, which these
halflings, who haven't anything like your strength, plan to take
away from you! Not one must escape alive! Not one must escape,
I say!'

As he shouted these insults, and many others, too, Arthur dashed
straight at the enemy. He flung them to the ground and cut them to
pieces. Whoever came his way was either killed himself or had his
horse killed under him at a single blow. They ran away from him
as sheep run from a fierce lion whom raging hunger compels to
devour all that chance throws in his way. Their armour offered
them no protection capable of preventing Caliburn, when wielded
in the right hand of this mighty King, from forcing them to vomit
forth their souls with their life-blood. Ill luck brought two Kings,
Sertorius of Libya and Politetes of Bithynia, in Arthur's way. He
hacked off their heads and bundled them off to hell.

When the Britons saw their King fighting in this way, they
became more bold. They charged as one man at the Romans,
attacking them in close formation. While the infantry was assail-
ing them in this way in one sector, the cavalry strove to beat
them down and run them through in another. The Romans
fought back bitterly. Urged on by Lucius, they strove to take

vengeance on the Britons for the slaughter inflicted by their noble King. The fight continued with as much violence on both sides as if they had only just at that moment come to blows with one another. On our side Arthur dealt blow after blow at his enemies (as I have told you already), shouting to the Britons to press on with the slaughter. On their side Lucius Hiberius urged his men on, repeatedly leading them himself in daring counter-attacks. He fought on with his own hand, going the round of his troops in each sector and killing every enemy who came his way, either with his lance or his sword. The most fearful slaughter was done on both sides. At times the Britons would have the upper hand, then the Romans would gain it.

In the end, as the battle continued between them, Morvid, the Earl of Gloucester, moved up at the double with his division, which, as I have told you, had been posted higher up in the hills. He attacked the enemy in the rear, when they were expecting nothing of the kind. His assault broke through their lines. As he moved forward he scattered them with tremendous slaughter. Many thousands of the Romans were killed. In the end, Lucius himself, their general, was brought to bay in the midst of his troops. He fell dead, pierced through by an unknown hand. The Britons followed up their advantage and finally won the day, but only after a supreme effort.

[x.12]   The Romans were scattered. In their terror some fled to out-of-the-way spots and forest groves, others made their way to cities and towns, and all of them sought refuge in the places which seemed safest to them. The Britons pursued them as fast as they could go, putting them to death miserably, taking them prisoner and plundering them: this the more easily as most of them voluntarily held out their hands to be bound, like so many women, in the hope of prolonging their lives a little. All this was ordained by divine providence. Just as in times gone by the ancestors of the Romans had harassed the forefathers of the Britons with their unjust oppressions, so now did the Britons make every effort to pro-

tect their own freedom, which the Romans were trying to take
away from them, by refusing the tribute which was wrongly demanded of them.

As soon as victory was assured, Arthur ordered the bodies of [x.13]
his leaders to be separated from the carcasses of the enemy. Once
they were gathered together, he had these bodies prepared for
burial with royal pomp and then they were carried to the abbeys
of their own native districts and interred there with great honour.
Bedevere the Cup-bearer was borne, with loud lamentations, by
the Neustrians to Bayeux, his own city, which his grandfather
Bedevere I had founded. There he was laid to rest with all honour,
beside a wall in a certain cemetery in the southern quarter of the
city. Kay, who was mortally wounded, was carried away to Chinon,
the town which he himself had built. Not long afterwards he died
from his wound. As was fitting for a Duke of the Angevins, he
was buried in a certain wood belonging to a convent of hermits not
far from that town. Holdin, the Duke of the Ruteni, was carried to
Flanders and laid to rest in his own city of Thérouanne. At Arthur's
command, the rest of the leaders and princes were borne to abbeys
in the vicinity. He took pity on his enemies and told the local inhabitants to bury them. He ordered the body of Lucius to be
carried to the Senate, with a message that no other tribute could be
expected from Britain.

Arthur spent the following winter in this same locality and
found time to subdue the cities of the Allobroges. When summer
came, he made ready to set out for Rome, and was already beginning to make his way through the mountains when the news was
brought to him that his nephew Mordred, in whose care he had
left Britain, had placed the crown upon his own head. What is
more, this treacherous tyrant was living adulterously and out of
wedlock with Queen Guinevere, who had broken the vows of her
earlier marriage.

About this particular matter, most noble Duke, Geoffrey of [xi.1]
Monmouth prefers to say nothing. He will, however, in his own

poor style and without wasting words, describe the battle which our most famous King fought against his nephew, once he had returned to Britain after his victory; for that he found in the British treatise already referred to. He heard it, too, from Walter of Oxford, a man most learned in all branches of history.

As soon as the bad news of this flagrant crime had reached his ears, Arthur immediately cancelled the attack which he had planned to make on Leo, the Emperor of the Romans. He sent Hoel, the leader of the Bretons, with an army of Gauls, to restore peace in those parts; and then without more ado he himself set off for Britain, accompanied only by the island kings and their troops. That most infamous traitor Mordred, about whom I have told you, had sent Chelric, the leader of the Saxons, to Germany, to conscript as many troops as possible there, and to return as quickly as he could with those whom he was to persuade to join him. Mordred had made an agreement with Chelric that he would give him that part of the island which stretched from the River Humber to Scotland and all that Hengist and Horsa had held in Kent in Vortigern's day. In obedience to Mordred's command, Chelric landed with eight hundred ships filled with armed pagans. A treaty was agreed to and Chelric pledged his obedience to the traitor Mordred as if to the King. Mordred had brought the Scots, Picts and Irish into his alliance, with anyone else whom he knew to be filled with hatred for his uncle. In all, the insurgents were about eighty thousand in number, some of them pagans and some Christians.

Surrounded by this enormous army, in which he placed his hope, Mordred marched to meet Arthur as soon as the latter landed at Richborough. In the battle which ensued Mordred inflicted great slaughter on those who were trying to land. Auguselus, the King of Albany, and Gawain, the King's nephew, died that day, together with many others too numerous to describe. Ywain, the son of Auguselus' brother Urian, succeeded him in the kingship; and in the wars which followed he became famous because of the many brave deeds which he accomplished. In the end, but only with enormous difficulty, Arthur's men occupied the sea-shore. They drove Mordred and his army before them in flight and inflicted great slaughter on them in their turn. Profiting from their long experience in warfare, they drew up their troops most skilfully. They mixed their infantry with the cavalry and fought in such a way that when the line of foot-soldiers moved up to the attack, or was merely holding its position, the horse charged at an angle and did all that they could to break through the enemy lines and to force them to run away.

However, the Perjurer re-formed his army and so marched into Winchester on the following night. When this was announced to Queen Guinevere, she gave way to despair. She fled from York to the City of the Legions and there, in the church of Julius the Martyr, she took her vows among the nuns, promising to lead a chaste life.

Now that he had lost so many hundreds of his fellow-soldiers, [xi.2] Arthur was more angry than ever. He buried his dead and then marched on the third day to the city of Winchester and laid siege to his nephew who had taken refuge there. Mordred showed no sign of abandoning his plans. He gave his adherents every encouragement he could think of, and then marched out with his troops and drew them up ready for a pitched battle with his uncle. The fight began and immense slaughter was done on both sides. The losses were greater in Mordred's army and they forced him to fly once more in shame from the battle-field. He made no arrangements whatsoever for the burial of his dead, but fled as fast as ship could carry him, and made his way towards Cornwall.

Arthur was filled with great mental anguish by the fact that Mordred had escaped him so often. Without losing a moment, he followed him to that same locality, reaching the River Camblam,[1]

---

1. On 4 August 1960 I visited Camelford and walked along the River Camel as far as Slaughter Bridge. According to local legend the battle between Arthur and Mordred took place in the near-by water-meadow. On the bank of the Camel, where the stream had cut for itself a steep bluff overhung with hazel bushes, in a spot most difficult of access, I found an ancient

where Mordred was awaiting his arrival. Mordred was indeed the boldest of men and always the first to launch an attack. He immediately drew his troops up in battle order, determined as he was either to win or to die, rather than run away again as he had done in the past. From his total force of troops, about which I have told you, there still remained sixty thousand men under his command. From these he mustered six divisions, in each of which he placed six thousand, six hundred and sixty-six armed men. From those who were left over he formed one single division, and, when he had assigned leaders to each of the others, he placed this last division under his own command. As soon as they were all drawn up, he went round to encourage each of them in turn, promising them the possessions of their enemies if only they stood firm and were successful in battle.

On the other side, Arthur, too, was marshalling his army. He divided his men into nine divisions of infantry, each drawn up in a square, with a right and left wing. To each he appointed a commander. Then he exhorted them to kill these perjured villains and robbers who, at the request of one who had committed treason against him, the King, had been brought into the island from foreign parts to steal their lands from them. He told them, too, that this miscellaneous collection of barbarians, come from a variety of countries – raw recruits who were totally inexperienced in war – would be quite incapable of resisting valiant men like themselves, who were the veterans of many battles, provided

-----

stone, 2′ 1½″ × 9′ 5 ″, with some partly-defaced lettering in mixed classical and rustic capitals. The stone was uneven and broken, and the letters were straggling and irregular, but the following fragment of an inscription was clearly to be deciphered: LATIN . . . IIC IACIT FILIVS M . . . AR . . .= possibly 'Latinus hic iacet filius Merlini Arturus'. In Corpus Inscriptionum Insularum Celticarum, R. A. S. Macalister, 1945, Vol. I, pp. 447–9, it is transcribed as LATINI IC IACIT FILIVS MAGARI, with an Ogham inscription LA[TI]NI at the top end.

always that they made up their minds to attack boldly and to fight like men.

While the two commanders were encouraging their men in this way in both the armies, the lines of battle suddenly met, combat was joined, and they all strove with might and main to deal each other as many blows as possible. It is heartrending to describe what slaughter was inflicted on both sides, how the dying groaned, and how great was the fury of those attacking. Everywhere men were receiving wounds themselves or inflicting them, dying or dealing out death. In the end, when they had passed much of the day in this way, Arthur, with a single division in which he had posted six thousand, six hundred and sixty-six men, charged at the squadron where he knew Mordred was. They hacked a way through with their swords and Arthur continued to advance, inflicting terrible slaughter as he went. It was at this point that the accursed traitor was killed and many thousands of his men with him.

However, the others did not take to flight simply because Mordred was dead. They massed together from all over the battle-field and did their utmost to stand their ground with all the courage at their command. The battle which was now joined between them was fiercer than ever, for almost all the leaders on both sides were present and rushed into the fight at the head of their troops. On Mordred's side there fell Chelric, Elaf, Egbrict and Bruning, all of them Saxons; the Irishmen Gillapatric, Gillasel and Gillarvus; and the Scots and Picts, with nearly everyone in command of them. On Arthur's side there died Odbrict, King of Norway; Aschil, King of Denmark; Cador Limenich; and Cassivelaunus, with many thousands of the King's troops, some of them Britons, others from the various peoples he had brought with him. Arthur himself, our renowned King, was mortally wounded and was carried off to the Isle of Avalon, so that his wounds might be attended to. He handed the crown of Britain over to his cousin Constantine, the son of Cador Duke of Cornwall: this in the year 542 after our Lord's Incarnation.

Part Eight

THE SAXON DOMINATION

[xi.3] As soon as Constantine had been crowned, the Saxons and the two sons of Mordred promptly rose against him. They failed in their attempt to overthrow him; and, after a long series of battles, they fled. One of them made his way into London and the other to Winchester, and they took command of those two cities.

It was at this time that the saintly Daniel died, the most devout Bishop of the church of Bangor. The Bishop of Gloucester was promoted to be Archbishop of London. It was then, too, that David, the most holy Archbishop of the City of the Legions, died in the town of Menevia, inside his own abbey, which he loved more than all the other monasteries of his diocese, for St Patrick, who prophesied David's own birth, had founded it. He was seized by some sudden illness and died while on a visit to his friars there. He was buried in that same church, on the order of Mabgo, King of the Venedotians. Kinoc, the priest of the church of Llanbadarn, was promoted to this higher rank and replaced him in the metropolitan see.

[xi.4] Constantine continued to harass the sons of Mordred. First he forced the Saxons to submit to his authority; and then he captured the two cities which I have mentioned. He killed one of the young men in front of the altar in the church of St Amphibalus, where he was taking refuge. The second hid himself in the monastery of certain friars in London. Constantine discovered him and slew him without mercy, beside the altar there. Four years later he was himself struck down by the vengeance of God. They buried him by the side of Utherpendragon, within the circle of stones called Stonehenge in the English language, which had been built with such wonderful skill not far from Salisbury.

[xi.5] Constantine's nephew succeeded him, a young man of extraordinary bravery called Aurelius Conanus. He ruled over the whole island and would indeed have been worthy of such a crown if he had not taken such delight in civil war. He gained the king-ship only by attacking his own uncle (who ought to have reigned after Constantine), throwing him into prison and killing his two sons. Aurelius Conanus died in the third year of his reign.

Vortiporius came after Conanus. The Saxons rose against him [xi.6] and brought over their fellow-countrymen from Germany in a huge fleet. Vortiporius fought a battle against them, beat them and so gained control of the entire kingdom. After this he governed the people frugally and peacefully.

Malgo came next. He was the most handsome of almost all the [xi.7] leaders of Britain and he strove hard to do away with those who ruled the people harshly. He was a man brave in battle, more generous than his predecessors and greatly renowned for his courage. Unfortunately he made himself hateful to God, for he was given to the vice of homosexuality. He became ruler of the entire island; and then in a series of bloodthirsty wars he subjected to his authority the six neighbouring Islands of the Ocean: that is, Ireland, Iceland, Gotland, the Orkneys, Norway and Denmark.

After Malgo came Keredic, a fomenter of civil discords, hateful [xi.8] to God and to the Britons also. When the Saxons came to under-stand his fickleness, they sent to Ireland for Gormund the King of the Africans, who had gone there with an enormous fleet and conquered the people of that country. As a result of this treachery by the Saxons, Gormund, accompanied by a hundred and sixty thousand Africans, came over to Britain, which, between them, the Saxons and the local inhabitants were completely devastating: the former by breaking their oath of fealty, the latter by continually waging civil wars among themselves. Gormund made a treaty with the Saxons and then attacked King Keredic. After a long series of battles, he drove the King from city to city and then forced him to take refuge in Cirencester, where he besieged him. Isembard, the nephew of Louis King of the Franks, went to join him there and made a treaty of friendship with him. The terms of the treaty were that, as a token of his friendship for Gormund, Isembard should renounce his Christian faith: this on the understanding that with the latter's help he could wrest the kingdom of Gaul from his uncle, by whom, so he alleged, he had been forcibly and unjustly expelled.

The city I have mentioned was captured and burnt. Gormund then fought Keredic and chased him over the Severn into Wales. Next he ravaged the fields, set fire to all the neighbouring cities, and gave free vent to his fury until he had burnt almost all the land in the island, from one sea to another. All the settlements were smashed to the ground with a great force of battering-rams. All the inhabitants were destroyed by flashing swords and crackling flames, and the priests of their church along with them. Those left alive fled, shattered by these dreadful disasters; but wherever they went, no havens of safety remained open to them in their flight.

[xi.9]   You foolish people, weighed down by the sheer burden of your own monstrous crimes, never happy but when you are fighting one another, why have you so far weakened yourselves in domestic upsets that you, who need to submit far-distant kingdoms to your own authority, are now like some fruitful vineyard which has gone sour and you cannot protect your own country, wives and children from your enemies? Keep on with your civil squabbling and forget what the Gospel says: 'Every kingdom divided against itself shall be brought to desolation, and a house divided against itself shall fall.' Because your kingdom was divided against itself, because the lunacy of civil war and the smoke-cloud of jealousy obscured your mind, because your pride did not permit you to obey a single king, that is why you see your fatherland ravaged by the most impious heathens and your homesteads overturned one upon the other, all of which things those who come after you will lament in the future. They will see the cubs of the wild lioness occupy their castles, cities and other possessions. In their misery they will be

driven forth from all of these, and only with the greatest difficulty
will they ever recover the glory of their former estate, that is if
they recover it at all!

Once this inhuman tyrant Gormund, with his countless thousands [xi.10]
of Africans, had destroyed almost all the island, as I have described
already, he handed over a considerable part of it, called Loegria,
to the Saxons, whose treason had been the cause of his landing.
Such Britons as remained sought refuge in the western parts of the
kingdom: that is, in Cornwall and Wales. From there they continued to make fierce attacks upon their enemies. When the two
Archbishops, Theonus of London and Tadioceus of York, saw
that all the churches under their jurisdiction were razed to the
ground, they fled with such priests as remained alive after such a
calamity to the shelter of the forests of Wales. They took with
them the relics of their saints, for they were afraid that all these holy
bones of the men of ancient times would be destroyed by the barbarian invasion, if they allowed themselves to be martyred where
they stood and so abandoned the bones to the fate which threatened
them. Many priests fled in a great fleet to Armorican Brittany,
with the result that the whole church of the two provinces of
Loegria and Northumbria lost its monasteries. I shall describe
these happenings elsewhere when I come to translate their *Book of
Exile*.

For many years after this the Britons were deprived of the right [xi.11]
to govern their own kingdom and were without sovereign power
over their own island. They made no attempt to recover their
former greatness. On the contrary, they continued to ravage with
civil war the part of their fatherland which still remained theirs,
this part being ruled by three tyrants instead of by a single king.
In the same way the Saxons, too, did not establish a single kingship
in the island. They also owed allegiance to three kings and divided
their energy between attacking their own side and assaulting the
Britons.

It was at this time that Augustine was sent to Britain by Pope [xi.12]

Gregory of blessed memory.[1] This Augustine was to preach th
word of God to the Angles, who, blinded by their pagan super
stition, had done away with Christianity entirely in the part of th
island which they controlled. Christianity still flourished in the par
belonging to the Britons; it had been accepted from the time o
Pope Eleutherius and had never lost its influence among them.

When Augustine arrived he found seven bishoprics and a
archbishopric in the Britons' territory, all of them occupied by
most devout prelates. There were also seven abbeys, and in then
God's flock observed a seemly rule. Among the rest, there was i
the city of Bangor an abbey so noble, and the number of monks i
it was so great, that when the monastic body was divided into seve
sections, each with its prior duly appointed, none of the section
had less than three hundred monks, all of them living by the labou
of their hands. Their Abbot was called Dinoot[2] and he was a ma
remarkably learned in the liberal arts. When Augustine asked th
bishops of the Britons to submit to his orders and to share in com
mon with him the task of preaching the gospel to the Angles, it wa
Dinoot who proved to him on a whole series of grounds that they
owed him no allegiance at all and that they would not dream o
wasting their preaching on their enemies. They had their own
Archbishop and what is more these Saxons were the very peopl
who persisted in depriving them of their own fatherland. That wa
why they hated the Saxons so. They had no interest whatsoever i
the Saxons' faith or their religion, and they had about as much i
common with the Angles as they had with dogs!

[xi.13]   When Ethelbert, the King of the men of Kent, saw that th
Britons were refusing to accept the authority of Augustine an
were scorning his preaching, he bore it very ill. He stirred u
Ethelfrid, King of the Northumbrians, and a number of othe

1. Augustine's coming is described in much greater detail in Bede'
Ecclesiastical History, Bk I, ch. 32, *et seq*.
2. This is the Abbot Dinoot who presided over the monastery o
Bancornaburg in Bk II, ch. 2, of Bede's *Ecclesiastical History*.

petty kings of the Saxons. A huge army was assembled and ordered to march to the city of Bangor and destroy Abbot Dinoot and the other churchmen who had scorned Augustine. They accepted Ethelbert's orders, collected an enormous army together and set out for the land of the Britons. They came to Chester, where Brochmail, who was in command of that city, awaited their coming. A great number of monks and hermits from all the different territories of the Britons, and especially from the city of Bangor, had sought refuge in Chester, so that they could pray there for the people's safety.

Armies were drawn up on both sides, and Ethelfrid, King of the Northumbrians, joined battle with Brochmail. Brochmail stood firm against him, although his force was smaller. In the end, however, Brochmail abandoned the city and fled, but only after inflicting enormous losses on the enemy.

When Ethelfrid occupied the city and discovered the reason why these monks whom I have mentioned had come there, he immediately let his soldiery loose against them. That same day twelve hundred monks won the crown of martydom and assured themselves of a seat in heaven.

After this the Saxon tyrant marched to the town of Bangor. When they heard of his mad frenzy, the leaders of the Britons came from all directions to oppose him: Blederic, Duke of Cornwall; Margadud, King of the Demetae, and Cadvan of the Venedoti. Battle was joined. They wounded Ethelfrid and forced him to flee. They killed so many of his army that some ten thousand and sixty-six died that day. On the side of the Britons there died Blederic, Duke of Cornwall, who commanded the others in these wars.

All the princes of the Britons then assembled in the city of [xii.1] Chester and agreed unanimously that they should make Cadvan their King and that under his command they should cross the Humber in pursuit of Ethelfrid. Once Cadvan had been crowned King of the realm, these princes gathered from all sides and crossed the Humber. The moment that this news reached Ethelfrid, he

came to an understanding with all the kings of the Saxons and
then marched out to meet Cadvan. Just as they were in the act of
drawing up their battle-squadrons on both sides, their friends
arrived and made peace between them. The agreement they came
to was that Ethelfrid should hold the part of Britain which lay
beyond the Humber, and Cadvan the part on this side. They
exchanged hostages and confirmed their treaty by an oath. Later
on, however, such a friendship developed between them that
they started holding everything in common.

In the meantime it happened that Ethelfrid abandoned his wife and
took another woman. He conceived such a hatred for the wife he
had dismissed that he banished her from the kingdom of the
Northumbrians. This woman, who was bearing a child in her
womb at the time, went to King Cadvan and begged him to
intervene with her husband so that she could go back to him.
Cadvan was unable to persuade Ethelfrid to agree. The woman
therefore remained in the household of Cadvan until the day of
her delivery came, the day which brought into the world the child
she had conceived.

Some short time afterwards a son was born to King Cadvan by
his own Queen, for she had become pregnant at the same moment.
The boys were brought up in a way suited to their royal blood.
The son of Cadvan was named Cadwallo and the other boy Edwin.
Later on, as the passage of the years brought them to adolescence,
their parents sent them to Salomon, King of the Armorican Britons,
so that they could learn the lessons of knighthood in his household
and familiarize themselves with other courtly customs. Salomon
received them warmly and they soon became very friendly with
him, so that in the end there was no one else of their age who could
chat more intimately with the King, or indeed more gaily. Later
on they often fought with his enemies in battle while he was
actually present, and by the gallantry of their deeds they brought
their bravery to everyone's attention.

[xii.2]   Years later, when their parents were dead, these two returned to

Britain and inherited the government of that country, renewing
with each other the friendship which their fathers had enjoyed
earlier on.

Two years passed. Edwin then asked Cadwallo if he could
have a crown of his own, so that, according to ancient custom,
he could celebrate traditional ceremonials in the lands of the
Northumbrians, in the way Cadwallo himself was in the habit of
doing south of the Humber. As a result they started to hold a conference beside the River Douglas and the wiser among their counsellors conferred together as to what could best be done. Over on
the other side of the river Cadwallo lay with his head on the lap
of a certain nephew of his, whom they called Brian. Messengers came
to announce the arguments which had been put forward on this
side and that. At this Brian burst out weeping, and the tears which
flowed from his eyes dripped down in such a way that they besprink-
led the King's face and beard. The King thought that it had come on
to rain. He raised his face, saw that the young man was bathed in
tears, and asked the cause of this sudden grief.

'I have every reason to keep on crying,' answered Brian, 'and
so has the British people, too, for, since the time of Malgo, they
have been harassed by a barbarian invasion and they have never
known a prince who could restore them to their former dignity.
Now the minute fragment of honour which yet remained to them
is being made still smaller, and this with your approval, since
these Saxon adventurers, who have taken every opportunity of
betraying our country, are now beginning to be crowned, so that
they may have a share in your kingship. Once they are raised to
the rank of king, will not their fame spread even wider through the
land from which they originally came, and will they not be even
quicker to invite over their fellow-countrymen and so press on with
the extermination of our race? Trickery has always been second
nature to them and they have never kept faith with anyone. In my
opinion we should keep them under, instead of doing them honour.
When King Vortigern first took them into his service, they made a

show of remaining at peace with us, pretending that they would
fight for our country. The moment they were in a position to
reveal their wickedness and to return evil for good, they betrayed
him and massacred the people of this kingdom with great savagery.
After that they betrayed Aurelius Ambrosius, giving him poison
to drink as he sat eating with them, and this after the most awe-
inspiring oaths of fealty. Next they betrayed Arthur, for they
conveniently forgot the oath by which they were bound to him,
and fought against him on the side of his nephew Mordred. More
recently still these liars broke their oath to Keredic, and brought over
Gormund, King of the Africans, to attack him. By this invasion,
our fatherland was snatched away from our fellow countrymen,
and the King I have named was driven into shameful exile.'

[xii.3]   Once Brian had said this, Cadwallo regretted the fact that they
had begun to plan an agreement. He sent a message to Edwin
to say that he had not been able to gain permission from his
counsellors to grant the Saxon's request. Their decision was that
it was contrary to law and to the customs of their ancestors that
an island with one crown should be placed under the sway of
two crowned heads. Edwin then lost his temper. He dismissed the
conference and retired to Northumbria, saying that he proposed
to be crowned without Cadwallo's permission. This news was
repeated to Cadwallo and he sent word back to Edwin to say that
he would cut the latter's head off underneath the crown, if Edwin
had the presumption to put one on inside the kingdom of Britain.

[xii.4]   War broke out between the two of them. Their men harassed
each other in a long series of forays, and then finally the two met face
to face on the farther side of the Humber. A battle was fought in
which Cadwallo lost many thousands of men and was himself
put to flight. He marched at great speed through Albany and then
crossed to the island of Ireland.

As soon as Edwin was sure of his victory, he led his army through
the provinces of Britain, burning the cities and inflicting great
misery on the townsfolk and the farmers.

While Edwin was giving full vent to his cruelty, Cadwallo
tried time and time again to return to his homeland in a fleet of
ships. He never succeeded, for, no matter which port he chose to
land at, Edwin marched to meet him with a huge army and prevented him from coming ashore. There had come to Edwin a
certain highly skilled magician from Spain, a man called Pellitus,
who was extremely knowledgeable about the flight of birds and
the courses of the stars. This Pellitus kept giving Edwin fore-
warning of all the misfortunes which were about to befall him.
In this way Edwin was warned of Cadwallo's return. He marched
to meet him, sank his ships, drowned his soldiers and closed every
port to him.

Cadwallo did not know what to do. Almost despairing of ever
being able to return, he made up his mind to visit Salomon, the
King of the Armorican Britons, so that he could ask his help and
receive some suggestion as to how he could return to his own
country. As Cadwallo was sailing towards Brittany, a fierce gale
suddenly sprang up. This scattered his companions' ships, so that
in a short time no two remained in sight of each other. Such terror
seized the helmsman of the King's ship that he dropped the rudder
and let the ship drift wherever fortune carried it. All night long
it was tossed up and down between the high seas as the waves vied
with each other, veering now this way, now that, to the deadly
peril of the Britons. The following morning as day dawned they
landed on an island called Guernsey and went ashore with the
greatest difficulty.

Cadwallo was so filled with grief and anger at the loss of his
comrades that he refused to take any food, lying ill instead in his
bunk. At first light on the fourth day a great yearning seized him
for some game to eat. His nephew Brian was summoned and
Cadwallo told him what he longed for. Brian took his bow and
quiver and started off across the island. If only fate would bring
some wild beast in his way, then he would take some of it to the
King for food. He wandered all over the island without discovering

what he was looking for. He was greatly concerned at not being able to gratify his master's wish. He was afraid that Cadwallo's illness might end in death, if he was not able to satisfy the King's yearning. He therefore tried a new device. He opened up his own thigh and cut off a slice of the flesh. He made a spit, cooked the meat, and took it to the King, pretending that it was venison. The King accepted that it was game. He ate some of it and so restored his strength, wondering that he had never tasted such sweet-flavoured meat before. When his appetite was satisfied, he became more cheerful and brisk, and within three days he was quite well again.

Then the wind they wanted began to blow. They made ready their ship's gear, hoisted the sail, and set out on their journey across the sea, landing eventually near the town of Kidaleta. When they came into the presence of King Salomon, they were kindlily received, as became such important people. As soon as he discovered why they had come, he made a speech in which he promised them help.

[xii.5]   'It grieves us[1] very much, young nobles,' said Salomon, 'that the land of your fathers should have been captured by this barbarous people and that you yourselves should have been expelled so ignominiously. All the same, seeing that other men succeed in protecting their own land, it seems extraordinary that your race should have lost such a fertile island and should find it impossible to resist the Angles, when our own folk think so little of them. When the people of this Britain of mine lived together with your subjects in your Britain, they held dominion over all the provincial kingdoms; and there was no race anywhere, except the Romans, who were able to conquer the island. As for the Romans, it is true that they held the island in subjection at a certain period, but then their leaders were dismissed and destroyed, and they departed and were driven away in shame. Once the Britons came to this region, under the command of Maximianus and Conanus, those who re-

1. The text here reads 'vobis, populum nostrum, populi nostri', which I have changed to 'us, your race, your people'.

mained behind never again had the good fortune to hold the kingship for any lengthy period. Although many princes have kept up
the earlier dignity of their forefathers, a series of weaker men succeeded them as their heirs, and these lost the island once and for all
when the enemy attacked. This is why I am so distressed at the
feeble behaviour of your people, for we come from the same stock
and we bear the name of Britons just as the men of your kingdom
do, and yet we manage to protect our fatherland, which you see
around you, when it is attacked by any of our neighbours.'

When Salomon had finished saying this and had added a number [xii.6]
of other similar remarks, Cadwallo, who felt slightly ashamed,
made his reply. 'We are indeed grateful to you, King, you who are
descended from a race of kings, when you promise to help me to
recover my own kingdom. However, when you said that it was
extraordinary that my people could not maintain the proud
position of their ancestors once the Britons had migrated to these
lands, I myself really find nothing to be surprised at. The nobler
members of the whole community followed the leaders whom
you have mentioned, and only the baser sort remained behind
and took over the lands of those who had gone. When these last
had started to raise themselves to noble rank, they gave themselves
airs beyond anything that their predecessors' position had ever
warranted. They were made proud by the very vastness of their
wealth. They began to indulge in sexual excesses such as had never
been heard of among other peoples. As the historian Gildas tells
us,[1] they not only indulged in this vice but in all the others which
are the lot of human nature, especially in the vice which over-
throws the very essence of all morality, the dislike of truth and
those who stand for truth, the love of lying and those who fabri-
cate lies, the preferring of evil to good, the reverence of viciousness
in the place of virtue, the accepting of Satan instead of the Angel of
Light. Kings were anointed, not in God's name, but because they

1. Here Geoffrey acknowledges his debt to Gildas. This passage is an
adaptation of §21 of the De excidio Britanniae.

were more bloodthirsty than their fellows. Soon afterwards they were murdered out of hand by the very men who had anointed them, not because of some charge properly levelled, but because others even more ferocious were preferred in their stead. If any one of their number seemed to come a pace nearer to moderation or truth, then the hatred and the violence of the whole nation were turned against him, as though he were guilty of betraying Britain.

'In the end all things seemed to weigh equal in the balance, whether they pleased God or displeased Him: that is, when the things hateful to Him did not simply turn the balance. They managed all their affairs in a way which was harmful to the common weal, as if no remedy whatsoever were offered to them by the true Physician of all men. Not only laymen, but the Lord's own flock, and His shepherds too, behaved in this same way, with no distinction between them. It is therefore hardly surprising that such degenerates, hated by God for the sins which I have described, should have lost their homeland which they had befouled in this way. God decided to take vengeance on them by suffering a foreign people to come and drive them away from the lands of their forefathers. Nevertheless, if God would only permit it, it would now be a noble deed to restore this people to its former dignity, so that the insult could not be levelled at our race that we, too, were feeble rulers and ones who made no effort in our time against all this.

'We had the same ancestor, you and I, and this encourages me to ask your help. For Malgo, that mighty King of Britain who reigned fourth after Arthur, begat two sons, one of them called Ennianus and the other Run. Ennianus begat Belin, Belin begat Iago, Iago begat Cadvan, and Cadvan was my father. After his brother's death, Run was exiled by a Saxon invasion. He came to this land and he gave his daughter to Duke Hoel, son of Hoel the Great who in Arthur's company conquered many countries. To him was born Alan, and from Alan came Hoel, your own father, who, while he lived, was no small terror to all Gaul.'

In the meantime, while Cadwallo was spending the winter with [*xii.7*]
Salomon, they plotted together that Brian should cross over to
Britain and find some way or other of killing King Edwin's
magician, to prevent him from warning the King of Cadwallo's
coming, as he had been doing so regularly.

Brian landed at Southampton and disguised himself as a beggar
by putting on the clothes of some poor wretch. He forged an iron
rod for himself, with a point at the end. With this he intended to
kill the magician, if only he should chance to meet him. Then he
set out for York, where Edwin was living at that time.

Once Brian had entered the city, he joined the throng of beggars
who were waiting for alms outside the King's door. As he was
walking up and down, his own sister came out of the hall, holding
a basin in her hand, for she was fetching water for the Queen.
Edwin had carried this girl off from the city of Worcester, when he
was raging through the lands held by the Britons, after Cadwallo's
flight. As she passed in front of Brian, he immediately recognized her.
He called to her in a low voice, bursting into tears as he did so. The
girl turned her face as he spoke, not being sure who he was. As she
came nearer she recognized her brother and almost fainted away,
for she was terrified that he would be recognized by some mis-
chance and so be seized by the enemy. They dispensed with kisses
and words of endearment for the time being, while she explained
to her brother as briefly as she could the lay-out of the court, just
as if she were speaking of something else, and then pointed out the
magician whom her brother was looking for, for at that very
moment by some coincidence he was walking about among the
beggars, while alms were being distributed to them.

As soon as Brian had made a note of the man's appearance, he
told his sister to steal secretly out of the Queen's apartments the
very next night and so come to join him outside the town near a
certain old church, where he would await her coming in the crypts
under the building.

Brian then went off to mingle with the crowd of beggars,

moving towards the spot where Pellitus was marshalling them. As soon as he had a chance of dealing Pellitus a blow, he did not waste a moment. He lifted up the pilgrim's staff which I have described above, and stabbed Pellitus in the chest with a blow which killed him on the spot. He immediately dropped his rod, slipped away through the crowd without anyone's suspecting him, and by God's grace made his way to the hiding-place which I have described. When night fell, his sister tried to escape by every way she could think of, but she was not successful. Edwin, who was terrified by the death of Pellitus, had posted guards all round his court to pry into every hidden corner, and these guards blocked every exit against her.

As soon as Brian discovered this, he left York and went to Exeter. There he summoned the Britons to meet him and told them what he had done. Next he sent messengers off to Cadwallo. Then he garrisoned the city of Exeter and announced to all the leaders of the Britons that they must take steps to see to the defences of their castles and cities, and then settle down patiently to await Cadwallo's coming, for in a short time, with Salomon to support him, he would arrive to organize their defence. This soon became known up and down the whole island. Peanda the King of the Mercians then marched on Exeter with a vast horde of Saxons and proceeded to besiege Brian there.

[xii.8]   While this was going on Cadwallo made a landing with ten thousand soldiers who had been put under his command by Salomon. He marched immediately to the siege which his captain, about whom I have told you, was withstanding. As he came within sight of the town, he divided his troops into four squadrons, and then lost no time in attacking his enemies. When the battle began, King Peanda was immediately captured and his army annihilated. When Peanda saw that he had no other means of safety, he surrendered to Cadwallo, gave hostages, and promised to attack the Saxons at Cadwallo's side.

With Peanda beaten, Cadwallo assembled his nobles who had been dispersed so long, and marched against Edwin in the direction of Northumbria, ravaging the country as he went. This was reported to Edwin. He made a treaty with the petty kinglets of the Angles, marched out to meet Cadwallo in a field called Hedfield,[1] and there joined battle with the Britons. The fighting was quickly over. Edwin was killed and so were almost all the people he had under command, and his son Offrid, together with Godbold, King of the Orkneys, who had come to help them.

Once he had won this victory, Cadwallo marched through all [xii.9] the provinces held by the Angles, and wrought great havoc on the Saxons. He was so determined to wipe out the entire race of Angles who were in the lands of Britain that he refused to spare the womenfolk or even their little ones of tender age. He inflicted hideous tortures on all whom he found. Next he fought a battle against Offric (who had succeeded Edwin), killing him and his two nephews who were to have reigned after him, together with Eadan, the King of the Scots, who had come to their assistance.

With all these killed, Oswald succeeded to the kingship of [xii.10] Northumbria. Cadwallo attacked him in his turn, once he had dealt with the others, and chased him from district to district until he came to the Wall which the Emperor Severus had built years before between Britain and Scotland. Then he sent Peanda the King of the Mercians, and the greater part of Peanda's army, to that spot, with orders to join battle with Oswald.

One night, when Oswald was besieged by this Peanda in a place called Hevenfield, that is, the Field of Heaven, he set up Christ's Cross there and told his troops to shout out the following words at the top of their voices: 'Let us all kneel down and pray together to the one true and all-powerful God, so that He may deliver us from the arrogant army of the British King and of his wicked commander Peanda. I know full well that we have undertaken this righteous war for the safety of our own people.' They

1. *Hedfield.* This battle, with the date 12 October 633, and the doings of Edwin, Cadwallo, Peanda and Oswald, are described at considerable length by Bede in his *Ecclesiastical History*, Bk II, ch. 20, etc.

all did as he had ordered. At first light they marched forth against the enemy and were rewarded for their faith by winning a victory.

When this was announced to Cadwallo, he blazed out in bitter anger. He assembled his own army and went in pursuit of the holy King Oswald. A battle was fought in a place called Burne and there Peanda attacked Oswald and killed him.

[xii.11]   Once Oswald was killed, and many of his men with him, his brother Oswi succeeded him in the kingship of the Northumbrians. Oswi gave many gifts of gold and silver to Cadwallo – who was now in command of all Britain – and did homage to him. In this way he gained peace.

Soon after this, Oswi's son Alfrid, and Oidwald, the son of Oswi's brother, led a revolt against him. However, they were not strong enough to resist him and they fled to Peanda, King of the Mercians. They implored Peanda to collect an army and to cross the Humber with them in an attempt to deprive King Oswi of his throne. Peanda was afraid to break the peace which King Cadwallo had established throughout the kingdom of Britain. He therefore put off launching an attacking expedition without Cadwallo's permission until such moment as he could persuade the King to march in person against King Oswi, or alternatively to grant permission to Peanda himself to fight against that King.

At a certain Whitsuntide court, when King Cadwallo was celebrating the feast in London by wearing the crown of Britain, and all the British leaders and all the kings of the Angles were present except only Oswi, Peanda therefore went up to the King and asked him why Oswi alone had absented himself, seeing that all the other Saxon princes were there. Cadwallo told Peanda that Oswi was absent because he was ill. Peanda said in reply that Oswi had sent to Germany for some Saxons so that he could take vengeance on them both for his brother Oswald's death. He added, moreover, that it was Oswi who had broken the peace of the kingdom, for it was he and he alone who had started the war between them, when he had attacked his own son Alfrid, and Oidwald, the son of his brother, and driven them out of their own homeland. Peanda therefore asked permission either to kill Oswi or to expel him from his kingdom.

The King could not make up his mind about this. He called for [xii.12] his advisers and ordered them to state what they thought should be done in such circumstances. They each gave their advice. Among the rest, Margadud, King of the Demetae, spoke. 'My lord,' he said, 'seeing that you have always intended to drive the entire race of Angles out of the land of Britain, why are you now changing your mind and permitting these men to remain in peace among us? At least you should give your approval when they want to fight among themselves and knock each other about, so that in the end they may be exterminated from our country. There can be no question of keeping faith with one whose every action is a treacherous attempt to catch in the snares which he has laid the man to whom he himself owes loyalty. From the moment when they first came to our homeland, these Saxons have never stopped their treachery and they have constantly betrayed our people. Why then should we keep faith with them? Give Peanda permission to attack this Oswi, about whom he has been telling us. Let there be civil war between the two of them, so that one can kill the other. In this way our island will be free of them.'

Cadwallo was influenced by this speech and by what the others [xii.13] said. He gave Peanda permission to fight with Oswi. Peanda then collected together a huge army and crossed the Humber. He launched a bitter attack against King Oswi and devastated the various districts of his country. Oswi, who was reduced in the end by sheer necessity, promised Peanda innumerable royal decorations and more presents than anyone could ever imagine, if only he would stop destroying his country, put an end to the invasion, and go back home. Peanda refused pointblank to yield to Oswi's entreaties. King Oswi then put his trust in God's help and joined battle with Peanda on the bank of the River Wunued, although he himself had a smaller army. Peanda and thirty of his leaders were killed and Oswi won a victory.

Once Peanda had met his end, his son Wulfred succeeded him in the kingship: this with Cadwallo's approval. Wulfred made an alliance with two leaders of the Mercians called Eba and Edbert, and then declared war once more on Oswi. In the end, however, Cadwallo ordered Wulfred to make peace with Oswi.

Finally, after forty-eight years, Cadwallo, this most noble and most powerful King of the Britons, become infirm with old age and illness, departed this life on the fifteenth day after the Kalends of December. The Britons embalmed his body with balsam and aromatic herbs and placed it inside a bronze statue which, with extraordinary skill, they had cast to the exact measure of his stature. They mounted this statue, fully armed, on a bronze horse of striking beauty, and erected it on top of the West Gate of London, in memory of the victory of which I have told you and as a source of terror to the Saxons. Underneath they built a church in honour of St Martin, and there divine services are celebrated for Cadwallo himself and for others who die in the faith.

[xii.14]   Cadwallader, the son of Cadwallo, succeeded his father in the government of the realm. This was the youth whom Bede called Cliedvalla. At first he ruled the kingdom bravely and peacefully; but, twelve years after he had inherited the crown, he fell ill and civil war broke out among the Britons. Cadwallader's mother had been the sister of Peanda, but only on her father's side, for she had had a different mother, a woman born from a noble family of the Gewissei. The famous King Cadwallo had taken her to his bed later in life, after the treaty which he had made with her brother, and by her he had become the father of Cadwallader.

[xii.15]   When Cadwallader fell ill, as I had begun to tell you, the Britons started to quarrel among themselves and to destroy the economy of their homeland by an appalling civil war. There then followed a second disaster: for a grievous and long-remembered famine afflicted the besotted population, and the countryside no longer produced any food at all for human sustenance, always excepting what the huntsman's skill could provide. A pestilent and deadly plague followed this famine and killed off such a vast number of the population that the living could not bury them.

The few wretches left alive gathered themselves into bands and emigrated to countries across the sea. Standing beneath the corded sails, they raised their voices in lamentation. 'Thou hast given us, O God,' they shouted, 'like sheep for meat, and hast scattered us among the Heathen.'

King Cadwallader himself, sailing off to Brittany with his miserable fleet, made his own contribution to this lamentation. 'Woe unto us sinners,' he cried, 'for our monstrous crimes, with which we never stopped offending God, as long as we had the time for repentance. The vengeance of His might lies heavily upon us, even to the point of uprooting us from our native soil – we whom the Romans, long ago, the Scots, the Picts and the Saxons, in their cunning treachery, were unable to exterminate. The fact that we have so often rescued our fatherland from these people now avails us nothing, for it is not God's will that we should rule there for all time. When He, the true Judge, saw that we had no intention of putting an end to our crimes, and that all the same no one could drive our people out of the kingdom, He made up His mind to punish us for our folly. He has visited His wrath upon us, and as a result of this we have emigrated from our homeland in vast crowds. Come back, you Romans! Return, Scots and Picts! And you too, Ambrones and Saxons! The door to Britain now lies wide open before you. The island which you could never capture stands empty now through the wrath of God. It is not your valour which is forcing us to leave but the power of the Supreme King, whom we have never ceased to provoke.'

Cadwallader went on lamenting in this way until the time came [*xii.16*] to land on the shore of Brittany. When he appeared with all his company before King Alan, the nephew of Salomon, he was received by him with all honour.

For eleven years Britain remained deserted by all its inhabitants, except for a few whom death had spared in certain parts of Wales. Even the Britons had come to hate their island; and it had no attraction for the Saxons, at this time, for they, too, kept dying there one after the other. However, once the deathly plague had ceased its ravages, those few Saxons who remained alive continued their age-old custom and sent a message to their fellow-country-men in Germany to tell them that the island had been abandoned by its native population and would fall into their hands without any difficulty at all, if only they would journey over to occupy it. As soon as this news reached them, the odious race gathered a vast horde of its men and women together. They landed in parts of Northumbria and occupied the waste lands from Albany to Cornwall. There was no local inhabitant left alive to stop them, except for a few little pockets of Britons who had stayed behind, living precariously in Wales, in the remote recesses of the woods. From that time on the power of the Britons came to an end in the islands, and the Angles began to reign.

[xii.17]   Some little time passed. The British people gathered its strength once more and Cadwallader began again to turn his mind to his own kingdom, which by now was purged from the plague about which I have told you. He asked Alan to help him to return to the position of power which he formerly held. The King granted him his wish. However, just as Cadwallader was preparing his fleet, an Angelic Voice spoke to him in a peal of thunder and told him to stop. God did not wish the Britons to rule in Britain any more, until the moment should come which Merlin had prophesied to Arthur.[1] The Voice ordered Cadwallader to go to Rome and visit

1. The text of Camb. Univ. Libr. MS. 1706 reads '*quod Merlinus Arturo prophetaverat*', and so, apparently, do the Berne and Harlech MSS. A curious feature of this statement is, of course, that Merlin never met Arthur. Apart from the final reference back, the last mention of Merlin is on p. 207, where he has just transmuted himself into a man called Britaelis and is about to arrange the scurrilous seduction of Ygerna and the conception of Arthur. Arthur's first appearance is just two pages and nine months later. The writer

Pope Sergius. There he should do penance and he would be numbered among the blessed. What is more, the Voice added that, as a
reward for its faithfulness, the British people would occupy the
island again at some time in the future, once the appointed moment
should come. This, however, could not be before the relics which
once belonged to the Britons had been taken over again and they
had transported them from Rome to Britain. Only when they had
on show again the relics of all their other saints, which had been
hidden away because of the pagan invasion, would they reoccupy
their lost kingdom.

When this message reached the ears of this God-fearing prince,
he went immediately to Alan and told the King what had been
revealed to him.

Alan thereupon took a number of books, such as the one about [xii.18]
the Auguries of the Eagle which had prophesied at Shaftesbury and
those on the oracular Sayings of the Sybil and of Merlin. He began
to read everything in these books, to see if the revelation made to
Cadwallader agreed with the written oracles. When he found that
they all did agree, he suggested to Cadwallader that he should obey
God's order, by postponing his plan for Britain and accepting the
advice which the Angel had given him. Alan encouraged Cadwallader to send his son Yvor and his nephew Yni to the island to rule
over what remained of the Britons, lest the folk descended from
this ancient race should lose their freedom because of the barbarian
invasions. Cadwallader then renounced worldly preoccupations
for the sake of God and His everlasting Kingdom. He journeyed to
Rome and was confirmed by Pope Sergius. He was then attacked
by a sudden illness and in the six hundred and eighty-ninth year

---

of Jesus College, Oxford, MS. LXI takes the point. In translation this reads:
'until the time should come foretold by Merddin Emrys before Gwrtheyrn'.
This is a clear reference to a passage in the 'Prophecies of Merlin': 'The
mountains of Armorica shall erupt and Armorica itself shall be crowned with
Brutus' diadem. Kambria shall be filled with joy and the Cornish oaks shall
flourish. The island shall be called by the name of Brutus and the title given
to it by the foreigners shall be done away with.'

after our Lord's Incarnation, on the twelfth day of the Kalends of May, he was released from the corruption of the flesh and so entered the hall of the Kingdom of Heaven.

[xii.19]   Yvor and Yni collected some ships together. They raised all the men they could and made a landing on the island. For seventy-nine years they harassed the English people with their savage attacks, but little good did it do them. Indeed, the plague about which I have told you, the famine and their own inveterate habit of civil discord had caused this proud people to degenerate so much that they were no longer able to keep their foes at bay. As the foreign element around them became more and more powerful, they were given the name of Welsh instead of Britons: this word deriving either from their leader Gualo, or from their Queen Galaes, or else from their being so barbarous.

The Saxons, on the other hand, behaved more wisely. They kept peace and concord among themselves, they cultivated the fields, and they re-built the cities and castles. They threw off completely the dominion of the Britons and under their leader Adelstan, who was the first among them to be crowned King, they ruled over the whole of Loegria[1].

1. The Berne MS. of the *Historia* and the Harlech MS. have an *explicit* which does not appear in Camb. Univ. Libr. MS. 1706: 'The Welsh, once they had degenerated from the noble state enjoyed by the Britons, never afterwards recovered the overlordship of the island. On the contrary, they went on quarrelling with the Saxons and among themselves and remained in a perpetual state of either civil or external warfare. The task of describing their kings, who succeeded from that moment onwards in Wales, I leave to my contemporary Caradoc of Llancarfan. The kings of the Saxons I leave to William of Malmesbury and Henry of Huntingdon. I recommend these last to say nothing at all about the kings of the Britons, seeing that they do not have in their possession the book in the British language which Walter, Archdeacon of Oxford, brought from Wales. It is this book which I have been at such pains to translate into Latin in this way, for it was composed with great accuracy about the doings of these princes and in their honour' (my translation). *Tatlock*, p. 5, discusses these three historians and Geoffrey's relationships with them.

Time Chart

THE *Historia Regum Britanniae* covers a period of nearly two thousand years, for it extends from the fall of Troy to the death of Cadwallader. Accustomed as he is to precise dates, the modern reader will wonder occasionally just where he is in time. In what year did Bladud have his flying-accident? When exactly did Leir die? When did Utherpendragon see the great star? It is not possible to answer these questions. Geoffrey gives only three dates: the death of Lucius occurred in A.D. 156, the abdication of Arthur in A.D. 542 and the death of Cadwallader in A.D. 689 He has, however, a curious system of synchronisms, borrowed perhaps from Bede's *Chronicon*, Isidore of Seville and Nennius, by which he is at pains to reassure his readers and add verisimilitude to his story. 'At that time the priest Eli was ruling in Judea and the Ark of the Covenant was captured by the Philistines . . .' (i.18). Some of these synchronisms leave us more confused than if we had not read them. In the following time chart I have set out on the left-hand side of the page the more useful of the synchronisms, adding traditional dates; and on the right-hand side I print a list of the Kings, with their length of reign as recorded by Geoffrey, keeping them in step with the synchronisms.

Time Chart

Geoffrey's Synchronisms *with approximate dates*	The Kings of Britain
c. 1240 B.C. Troy VIIa destroyed by the Greeks after a long siege [*i.3*]	Aeneas escapes from Troy, with his son Ascanius, and eventually becomes King of Italy. On the death of Aeneas, Ascanius becomes King of Italy. He is the father of Silvius; and Silvius has a son called Brutus. This Brutus, who is thus the great-grandson of Aeneas, leads the subject Trojans out of Greece and westwards through the Mediterranean, joins with Corineus and comes eventually to Britain.
1115–1075 Eli's judgeship [*i.18*]	*Brutus*, first King of Britain (reigns 23 years). *Locrinus* (10 years).
1075–1035 Samuel's judgeship [*ii.6*]	*Gwendolen* (15 years). *Maddan* (40 years).
1050–1011 King Saul reigns in Judea [*ii.6*]	*Mempricius* (20 years).
1011–971 King David reigns in Judea [*ii.7*]	*Ebraucus* (39 years).
971–931 King Solomon reigns in Judea [*ii.9*] . .	*Brutus Greenshield* (12 years). *Leil* (25 years).
874+ Elijah prophesies the drought, under King Ahab [*ii.10*]	*Rud Hud Hudibras* (39 years). *Bladud* (20 years).
753 Traditional date of the founding of Rome by Romulus and Remus [*ii.15*]	*Leir* (60 years). *Queen Cordelia* (5+ years).

Geoffrey's Synchronisms *with approximate dates*	The Kings of Britain

740–701 B.C.

Isaiah prophesies [*ii.15*] ....   *Cunedagius* (2 + 33 years).
    Rivallo, Gurgustius, Sisillius I,
    Kimarcus, Gorboduc, Ferrex and
    Porrex, the five unnamed Kings,
    Dunvallo Molmutius (40 years).

390

Sack of Rome [*iii.9*] ....   *Belinus* and *Brennius.*
    Gurguit Barbtruc, Guithelin, Queen
    Marcia, Sisillius II, Kinarius, Danius,
    Morvidus, Gorbonianus, Archgallo,
    Elidurus, Ingenius (7 years), *Peredurus,*
    an unnamed King, *Marganus,*
    Enniaunus (6 years), *Idvallo, Runo,*
    Gerennus, Catellus, Millus, Porrex II,
    Cherin, Fulgenius, Edadus, Andragius,
    Urianus, Eliud, Cledaucus, Clotenus,
    Gurgintius, Merianus, Bledudo, Cap,
    Oenus, Sisillius III, Beldgabred,
    Archmail, Eldol, Redon, Redechius,
    Samuil, Penessil, Pir, Capoir,
    Digueillus, Heli (40 years), *Lud.*

55–54

Julius Caesar invades Britain [*iv.1–10*]   *Cassivelaunus.*

44+

Augustus is in power [*iv.ii*] ....   *Tenvantius, Cymbeline* (10+ years).

8–7

Birth of Christ [*iv.11*] ....

A.D. 43

Claudius comes to Britain [*iv.12–15*]   *Guiderius, Arvirargus.*
St Peter is in Antioch, then Rome;
St Mark is in Egypt [*iv.15*]..........

Vespasian comes to Britain [*iv.16*] ..   *Marius, Coilus.*

175–89

Pope Eleutherius sends Faganus and   *Lucius,* who dies in A.D. 156 [*v.1*].
Duvianus to Britain [*iv.19*] ....

Geoffrey's Synchronisms *with approximate dates*	The Kings of Britain

A.D. 208–11
Severus comes to Britain, builds his Wall and dies in York [*v.2*] ....

Geta, Bassianus, sons of Severus.

303+
Persecution of the Christians by Diocletian [*v.5*] ....

Asclepiodotus (10 years).

296–306
Constantius I is in Britain, dying eventually in York [*v.6*]. ....

Coel, Constantius (11 years).

306–37
Constantine the Great is Emperor [*v.6*] ....

Constantine I, Octavius, Trahern, Maximianus.
Gracianus, Constantine II, Constans.

450–55
Hengist and Horsa come to Britain [*vi.10*] ....

Vortigern, Vortimer.
Aurelius Ambrosius.
Utherpendragon.

542

Arthur, who, seriously wounded in the battle of Camblam, hands the crown and throne to *Constantine III* (4 years) in the year 542 [*xi.2*].

597
Augustine, sent by Pope Gregory I, lands in Britain [*xi.12*] ....

Aurelius Conanus (3 years).
Vortiporius, Malgo, Keredic.

Three unnamed tyrants.
Cadvan, Cadwallo (48 years).

689

Cadwallader, who dies in 689 [*xii.18*].

Index

WHAT follows is at once an index, and an *index raisonné*, of my translation of Geoffrey's *Historia*. Every proper name and place-name mentioned in the text is listed in this index; and all the major events and most of the minor ones which occur are given in succinct form under the names of the characters concerned in them. No such complete index of the *Historia* has been printed before. After the entry of many of the place-names, I include, as relevant, the exact Latin reading of Camb. Univ. Libr. MS. 1706, the text I am following; the translation of the Welsh version in Jesus College, Oxford, MS. LXI, taken from Acton Griscom; the suggestions of Aaron Thompson, J. A. Giles and Sebastian Evans; and, above all, detailed cross-references to J. S. P. Tatlock's admirable book.

Index

A

division, and rages through the Roman army, 255; he hacks off the heads of Sertorius of Libya, and Politetes of Bithynia, 255; he wins the battle of Saussy, 256

Arthur winters in Gaul, 257; he subdues the cities of the Allobroges, 257; he is about to set out for Rome when he hears of Mordred's treachery, 257; abandons his attack on Rome, 258; returns to Britain, 258; lands at Richborough, 258; beats Mordred a first time at Richborough, 258–9; beats Mordred a second time at Winchester, 259; pursues Mordred to Cornwall, 259; catches him on the River Camblam, 259; the battle of Camblam, 260–61; Mordred is killed, 261; Arthur is mortally wounded, *letaliter vulneratus est*, 261; carried off to the Isle of Avalon, 261; this in the year 542 A.D., 261; 270; 274

The Angelic Voice announces to Cadwallader that the time has not yet come for the realization of the prophecy made by Merlin to Arthur of Britain's salvation and rejuvenation (i.e. the prophecy made by Merlin to Vortigern *about* Arthur, on p. 175), 282

Arvaius, Mount, where the giant Retho lived, 240; = Snowdon, Eryri, the same as Mount Aravia and Mount Erith, *q.v.*; (cp. *Tatlock*, p. 64)

Arvirargus, second son of Cymbeline, King of Britain, 119; when his brother Guiderius, King of Britain, is killed by Lelius Hamo at the battle of Porchester by a trick, Arvirargus takes command of the Britons' army and defeats Lelius Hamo and Claudius, 120; while Arvirargus is busy killing Lelius Hamo at Southampton, Claudius re-forms his troops and captures Porchester, 120; Arvirargus retreats to Winchester and is besieged there by Claudius, 120; he accepts Claudius' offer of peace and the hand of his daughter in exchange for tribute, 121; Arvirargus and Claudius together subdue the Orkneys, 121; Genvissa, the daughter of Claudius, arrives, and Arvirargus is married to her, 121; to commemorate his love for her, he founds Kaerglou, or Gloucester, which he names after her, 121; is left by Claudius to rule over Britain, 121; refuses to pay further tribute to the Roman Senate, 122; prevents Vespasian from landing at Richborough, 122; when Vespasian sails to Totnes and besieges Exeter, Arvirargus raises the siege, 122; Genvissa makes peace between Arvirargus and Vespasian, 122; together they attack Ireland, 122; Vespasian returns to Rome, 122; the fame of Arvirargus spreads throughout Europe, 122; when he dies he is buried in Gloucester, 123

Asaph, prophet in Israel, at the time when Ebraucus was King of Loegria, 79

Ascanius, leaves Troy with his father Aeneas, 54; replaces Aeneas as King of Italy, 54; founds the town of Alba, on the banks of the Tiber, 54; has a son called Silvius, 54; consults his soothsayers about the sex and destiny of his unborn grandchild, 54; son of Aeneas and grandfather of Brutus, 107

Aschil, King of Denmark, 227; is at the plenary court held by Arthur in

Kings of all Britain, 89; Cassivelaunus is expressly described as King *totius insulae*, 106

The island awaits Caesar's attack, 108; Caesar's first invasion is repelled and he flees from Britain, 108–10; the same thing happens to Caesar's second invasion, two years later, 112–13; Caesar finally forces Cassivelaunus and Britain to submit to paying tribute, 115–16

Britain becomes Christian under King Lucius, 125; is ravaged by the adventurer, Carausius, who forces himself into the kingship, 128; the island is crushed by the religious persecutions of Diocletian led by Maximianus Herculius, 130–31

Britain is deprived of much of its population by King Maximianus, when he first captures Brittany and gives it to Conanus Meridiadocus as a kingdom, and then captures Gaul and Germany and makes them his own empire, 139–41; in its denuded state is attacked by Wanius, King King of the Huns, and Melga, King of the Picts, 143; they ravage the island, 143; they are driven off to Ireland by Gracianus the freedman, 143; when Gracianus is assassinated, they return with Scots, Norwegians and Danes, 144; the Romans send help to Britain, 144–5; the Romans finally evacuate Britain, 145–7; utter devastation of Britain after the Romans have left, 147–8

The first coming of the Saxons to Britain, 155; Pelagian heresy in Britain 160; more and more Saxons come, 161; Britain is ravaged by Hengist and the Saxons after the massacre of Salisbury, 166; freed from the Saxons by Aurelius Ambrosius, 190–94; overrun again by Octa and Eosa, until Utherpendragon kills them at St Albans, 209–11

At the beginning of Arthur's reign, Colgrin and the Saxons overrun Britain from the Humber to Caithness, 212; under Arthur the Britons and Britain become the leading power in Europe, 214–25; by the victory of Saussy, Britain becomes the leading nation of the world, 246–57

Britain is ravaged by Gormund, King of the Africans, 263–4; the Archbishops flee with their holy relics to Wales, 265; the priests flee to Brittany, 265; under Cadvan and Ethelfrid, and then under Cadwallo and Edwin, north of the Humber is ruled by a Saxon, and south by a Briton, 268–70; Edwin quarrels with Cadwallo, beats him and ravages southern Britain, 270; Britain has a last heyday under Cadwallo, who reigns for forty-eight years and subdues all hostile peoples in the island, 276–80

Under Cadwallader, son of Cadwallo, civil war, famine and plague come to Britain, 280; God turns his face against the people of Britain, 281; Cadwallader emigrates to Brittany, 281; the island remains deserted for eleven years, 282; the Angelic Voice forbids Cadwallader to return, 282; Yvor and Yni look after the last Britons in Wales, 284; the Saxons rule the island at last, although Merlin has prophesied that the Britons will one day return to their land, 284

Britain, Little, another name for Brittany, Armorica, Letavia, 149

he is born, 55; when fifteen, kills his father Silvius with an arrow, by
accident, when they are out hunting, 55; as a result he is expelled from
Italy, 55; arrives in Greece, 55; makes contact with the Trojans, who
are enslaved by Pandrasus, King of the Greeks, 55; becomes well-known
in Greece as a military leader, 55; the Trojans flock to him, 55; he is
helped by Assaracus, a nobly-born Greek, whose mother was a Trojan,
56; becomes the acknowledged leader of the enslaved Trojans, 56;
fortifies the castles of Assaracus, 56; sends a challenging letter to King
Pandrasus, 56; sallies forth from the castle of Sparatinum and attacks
Pandrasus, slaughtering his army on the River Akalon, 57; destroys the
army of Antigonus, brother of Pandrasus, and captures Antigonus, with
his comrade Anacletus, 58; forces Anacletus to betray the Greeks, who
are besieging Sparatinum, 59-60; relieves Sparatinum and wins a third
victory over the Greeks, capturing Pandrasus, 60-62; debates with his
men how best to use this victory, 62-63; on the advice of Membritius,
one of the Trojan leaders, demands from the captive Pandrasus the hand
of his daughter Ignoge, ships, supplies, gold and silver, and permission
to lead the Trojans in an exodus from Greece, 63; Brutus marries
Ignoge, much against her will, and the Trojans sail away from Greece, 64
After sailing for two nights and one day, Brutus and his Trojans land on
the deserted island of Leogetia, 64; they discover a temple of Diana in
an abandoned city on the island, 64; Brutus visits the temple and is told
by the goddess, in a dream, that he will found a second Troy in an
island in the sea, beyond the setting sun, 65; leaves Leogetia and sails
to Africa, 66; passes the Altars of the Philistines and the Salt-pan Lake,
66; sails between Russicada and the mountains of Zarec, 66; he and the
Trojans are attacked by pirates, 66; passes the River Malve, 66; he and
the Trojans land in Mauretania for supplies, 66; off the Pillars of Hercules,
his ships are attacked by Sirens, 66

Brutus discovers, beyond the Pillars of Hercules, a second group of Trojans
which had escaped from Troy with Antenor, and is now led by Corineus,
66; the two parties combine and sail on to Aquitaine, 66; wins the battle
against Goffar the Pict, the King of the Aquitanians, largely through the
prowess of Corineus, 66-68; sacks and loots Aquitaine, 69; founds the
city of Tours, as an open camp in the first instance, 69; fights King
Goffar a second time, outside Tours, 69-71; with the help of Corineus,
he is again victorious, but decides to leave Aquitaine, as he can expect
no reinforcements, 71; he withdraws to his ships and sails to Totnes in
Britain, 71

Brutus is attacked by an army of giants, including Gogmagog, while
celebrating a religious festival in Totnes, 72; he decides to build his
capital on the banks of the Thames, 73; he names it Troia Nova, soon
to be corrupted to Trinovantum, 73-4; he presents the Britons with a
new code of laws, 74; he has three sons, Locrinus, Kamber and Albanactus by his wife Ignoge, 75; he dies and is buried in Trinovantum, 75.

106; he gives the town of Trinovantum and the Duchy of Kent to Androgeus, 106; he gives the Duchy of Cornwall to Tenvantius, 106; receives demanding letter from Caesar and sends proud reply, 107–8; awaits the attack of Caesar, 108; comes to the town of Dorobellum, as he marches to meet Caesar, 108; attacks Caesar immediately, while he is still putting up his tents, 109; defeats Caesar and forces him to retire in disorder to Gaul, 109–10; is thought by the Gauls to be about to follow across the Channel in pursuit of Caesar, 110–11; he prepares for Caesar's second invasion, 111; among other things, he plants the Thames below the water-line with iron-shod stakes, 111; Caesar arrives and his ships are gutted, 112; Cassivelaunus attacks the remainder and forces Caesar to retire in disorder once more across the Channel, 112; to celebrate the repelling of Caesar's two invasions, Cassivelaunus arranges a festival at Trinovantum, 113; at this festival Cuelinus, nephew of Androgeus, kills Hirelgdas, nephew of Cassivelaunus, 113; the King demands that Androgeus should surrender Cuelinus, 113; Androgeus refuses, 113–14; Cassivelaunus starts to ravage Kent, the Duchy of Androgeus, 114; Androgeus writes to Caesar and prepares to betray Cassivelaunus, 114–15; Cassivelaunus besieges Trinovantum, 115–16; he comes upon Caesar in a valley near Durobernia, after Caesar's third landing at Richborough, 116; Androgeus betrays the King at the battle of Durobernia and Cassivelaunus is forced to flee to a hill-top, 116; Cassivelaunus is starved out by Caesar, 117; he submits and pays tribute, 117–18; dies and is buried in York, 118

Cassivelaunus, killed on Arthur's side at Camblam, 261

Castle of Venus, the, 176

Castrum Corrigie, Latin name of Hengist's fortress = Kaercarrei, or Thanceastre, 159 (*Giles*, Thong Castle, in Lincolnshire; = Caistor? ; cp. *Tatlock*, p. 24)

Catellus, son of Gerennus, King of Britain, 105; becomes King himself on the death of his father, 105

Cathleus map Kathel, at Arthur's plenary court in the City of the Legions, 227

Cenomania, district ruled over by Borellus, 228 (*Thompson*, the country of Maine in France, *Giles*, copies; *Evans*, Maine; cp. *Tatlock*, p. 97)

Cenomanni, Gallic tribe which supports Arthur against Rome, 235; 246

Channel, the, crossed by Maximianus and Conanus Meridiadocus, 139

Chartres, 228; 235; 241; 242; 247 (cp. *Tatlock*, p. 97)

Chein, the nineteenth daughter of Ebraucus, King of Loegria, 79

Cheldric, a Saxon, 213; is to bring reinforcements from Germany to Colgrin and Baldulf, 213; Cheldric lands in Albany with six hundred ship-loads of Saxons, 214; escapes from Arthur at the battle of Bath, 218; killed by Cador on the Isle of Thanet, 218

Chelric, Saxon leader, in league with Mordred against Arthur, 258; is promised Kent and Britain from the Humber to the Scottish border,

H

N

W

MORE ABOUT PENGUINS, PELICANS AND PUFFINS

For further information about books available from Penguins please write to Dept EP, Penguin Books Ltd, Harmondsworth, Middlesex UB7 0DA.

In the U.S.A.: For a complete list of books available from Penguins in the United States write to Dept DG, Penguin Books, 299 Murray Hill Parkway, East Rutherford, New Jersey 07073.

In Canada: For a complete list of books available from Penguins in Canada write to Penguin Books Canada Limited, 2801 John Street, Markham, Ontario L3R 1B4.

In Australia: For a complete list of books available from Penguins in Australia write to the Marketing Department, Penguin Books Australia Ltd, P.O. Box 257, Ringwood, Victoria 3134.

In New Zealand: For a complete list of books available from Penguins in New Zealand write to the Marketing Department, Penguin Books (N.Z.) Ltd, Private Bag, Takapuna, Auckland 9.

In India: For a complete list of books available from Penguins in India write to Penguin Overseas Ltd, 706 Eros Apartments, 56 Nehru Place, New Delhi 110019.

PENGUIN CLASSICS

Bede

A HISTORY OF THE ENGLISH
CHURCH AND PEOPLE

Translated by Leo Sherley-Price

This wonderfully alive tapestry of Saxon England and Celtic
Britain written in A.D. 731 still has the power to transport us
back to the forests, fens, and mountains, and to the problems which men faced during these crucially formative
years when this land had still to be wrought into one
entity. Leo Sherley-Price has well succeeded in his aim of
producing an accurate and readable version of Bede's work
in modern English and, as he remarks in his introduction,
'we realize even more clearly that the past is not dead and
done with, but a force to be reckoned with, silently mould-
ing the present and the future'.

THE GREAT ICELANDIC SAGAS

NJAL'S SAGA

Translated by Magnus Magnusson and Hermann Pálsson

This magnificent saga, written by an unknown author in the late thirteenth century, describes a fifty-year blood feud from its violent beginnings to its tragic end.

HRAFNKEL'S SAGA AND OTHER STORIES

Translated by Hermann Pálsson

All seven stories in this volume date again from the thirteenth century, and exemplify the outstanding qualities of realistic fiction in medieval Iceland.

THE VINLAND SAGAS:
THE NORSE DISCOVERY OF AMERICA

Translated by Magnus Magnusson and Hermann Pálsson

These two medieval Icelandic sagas tell of one of the most fascinating stories in the history of exploration – the discovery of America by Bjarni Herjolfsson and Leif the Lucky, five centuries before Columbus.

LAXDAELA SAGA

Translated by Magnus Magnusson and Hermann Pálsson

This saga, composed by an unknown author c. 1245, has always stirred the European imagination profoundly. Romantic in style, in taste and in theme, it culminates in a beautifully-described triangle of love.

PENGUIN CLASSICS

THE SONG OF ROLAND

Translated by Dorothy L. Sayers

The Song of Roland, as Dorothy Sayers remarks in the introduction to this excellent translation, is 'the earliest, the most famous, and the greatest of those Old French epics which are called Songs of Deeds'. Writing around the end of the eleventh century, and recalling an actual disaster in 778, the anonymous poet describes in detail the betrayal and slaughter by Saracens of the rearguard of Charlemagne's army under Roland at Roncevaux and Charlemagne's bitter revenge. Nowhere in literature is the medieval code of chivalry more perfectly expressed than in this masterly and exciting poem.

PENGUIN CLASSICS

THE MABINOGION
Translated by Jeffrey Gantz

'On the bank of the river he saw a tall tree: from roots to crown one half was aflame and the other green with leaves'

Nothing illustrates the strange nature of these Welsh stories better than this vertically halved tree. The combination of fact and fantasy, of myth, history and folklore in *The Mabinogion* conjures up a magical enchanted world, which is nonetheless firmly rooted in the forests, hills and valleys of ancient Wales. The eleven stories were composed orally over a span of centuries, before being written down in the thirteenth century; they represent, in their virtuosity and panache, one of the high points of the Welsh imagination.

PENGUIN CLASSICS

GERALD OF WALES
The Journey Through Wales/The Description of Wales

Translated by Lewis Thorpe

Gerald of Wales, a grandson of Gerald of Windsor and the Princess Nest, was born in about 1145 at Manorbier, Pembrokeshire. He was one of the most dynamic and colourful churchmen of the twelfth century and knew many of the most powerful figures of his day.

The Journey describes, in almost diary form, the mission to Wales, undertaken in 1188 by Baldwin, Archbishop of Canterbury, with Gerald as his companion. His approach was encyclopedic: as well as providing us with an accurate and quite comprehensive history of events in twelfth-century Wales, the book is crammed with lively accounts of of local miracles, natural prodigies, folklore of all sorts and scenic descriptions of great beauty.

In *The Description* Gerald offers us a detailed and fascinating picture of the day-to-day existence of ordinary Welshmen – their methods of agriculture, what they ate and wore and how they could fight and resist the English.

CLASSICS IN TRANSLATION
IN PENGUINS

☐ *Remembrance of Things Past* **Marcel Proust**
☐ Volume One: *Swann's Way, Within a Budding Grove* £7.95
☐ Volume Two: *The Guermantes Way, Cities of the Plain* £7.95
☐ Volume Three: *The Captive, The Fugitive, Time Regained* £7.95

Terence Kilmartin's acclaimed revised version of C. K. Scott Moncrieff's original translation, published in paperback for the first time.

☐ *The Canterbury Tales* **Geoffrey Chaucer** £2.95

'Every age is a Canterbury Pilgrimage . . . nor can a child be born who is not one of these characters of Chaucer' – William Blake

☐ *Gargantua & Pantagruel* **Rabelais** £3.95

The fantastic adventures of two giants through which Rabelais (1495–1553) caricatured his life and times in a masterpiece of exuberance and glorious exaggeration.

☐ *The Brothers Karamazov* **Fyodor Dostoevsky** £4.95

A detective story on many levels, profoundly involving the question of the existence of God, Dostoevsky's great drama of parricide and fraternal jealousy triumphantly fulfilled his aim: 'to find the man in man . . . [to] depict all the depths of the human soul.'

☐ *Fables of Aesop* £1.95

This translation recovers all the old magic of fables in which, too often, the fox steps forward as the cynical hero and a lamb is an ass to lie down with a lion.

☐ *The Three Theban Plays* **Sophocles** £2.95

A new translation, by Robert Fagles, of *Antigone, Oedipus the King* and *Oedipus at Colonus*, plays all based on the legend of the royal house of Thebes.

CLASSICS IN TRANSLATION
IN PENGUINS

☐ *The Treasure of the City of Ladies*
Christine de Pisan   £2.95

This practical survival handbook for women (whether royal courtiers
or prostitutes) paints a vivid picture of their lives and preoccupations
in France, *c.* 1405. First English translation.

☐ *La Regenta* **Leopoldo Alas**   £10.95

This first English translation of this Spanish masterpiece has been
acclaimed as 'a major literary event' – *Observer*. 'Among the select
band of "world novels" . . . outstandingly well translated' – John
Bayley in the *Listener*

☐ *Metamorphoses* **Ovid**   £2.95

The whole of Western literature has found inspiration in Ovid's
poem, a golden treasury of myths and legends that are linked by the
theme of transformation.

☐ *Darkness at Noon* **Arthur Koestler**   £2.50

'Koestler approaches the problem of ends and means, of love and
truth and social organization, through the thoughts of an Old Bolshe-
vik, Rubashov, as he awaits death in a G.P.U. prison' – *New States-
man*

☐ *War and Peace* **Leo Tolstoy**   £4.95

'A complete picture of human life;' wrote one critic, 'a complete
picture of the Russia of that day; a complete picture of everything in
which people place their happiness and greatness, their grief and
humiliation.'

☐ *The Divine Comedy: 1 Hell* **Dante**   £2.25

A new translation by Mark Musa, in which the poet is conducted by
the spirit of Virgil down through the twenty-four closely described
circles of hell.

CLASSICS IN TRANSLATION
IN PENGUINS

☐ *The Magic Mountain* **Thomas Mann** £4.95

Set in a sanatorium high in the Swiss Alps, this is modern German literature's most spectacular exploration of love and death, and the relationships between them.

☐ *The Good Soldier Švejk* **Jaroslav Hašek** £4.95

The first complete English translation, with illustrations by Josef Lada. 'Hašek was a humorist of the highest calibre . . . A later age will perhaps put him on a level with Cervantes and Rabelais' – Max Brod

These books should be available at all good bookshops or newsagents, but if you live in the UK or the Republic of Ireland and have difficulty in getting to a bookshop, they can be ordered by post. Please indicate the titles required and fill in the form below.

NAME _____ BLOCK CAPITALS

ADDRESS _____

_____

_____

Enclose a cheque or postal order payable to The Penguin Bookshop to cover the total price of books ordered, plus 50p for postage. Readers in the Republic of Ireland should send £IR equivalent to the sterling prices, plus 67p for postage. Send to: The Penguin Bookshop, 54/56 Bridlesmith Gate, Nottingham, NG1 2GP.

You can also order by phoning (0602) 599295, and quoting your Barclaycard or Access number.

Every effort is made to ensure the accuracy of the price and availability of books at the time of going to press, but it is sometimes necessary to increase prices and in these circumstances retail prices may be shown on the covers of books which may differ from the prices shown in this list or elsewhere. This list is not an offer to supply any book.

This order service is only available to residents in the UK and the Republic of Ireland.

● ● ●